ROGUE
INTENSITIES

ABOUT THE AUTHOR

Angela Rockel was born in Aotearoa New Zealand and has lived all her adult life in rural Tasmania. She is interested in finding language for a conversation in landscape, community, history and family, towards a politics of the imagination.

ROGUE
INTENSITIES

ANGELA ROCKEL

UWAP
UWA PUBLISHING

First published in 2019 by
UWA Publishing
Crawley, Western Australia 6009
www.uwap.uwa.edu.au

UWAP is an imprint of UWA Publishing,
a division of The University of Western Australia.

THE UNIVERSITY OF
WESTERN
AUSTRALIA

ISBN: 978-1-76080-099-4

NATIONAL
LIBRARY
OF AUSTRALIA
A catalogue record for this
book is available from the
National Library of Australia

Cover design by Upside Creative
Cover image by Angela Rockel
Typeset by Lasertype
Printed by Lightning Source

This project is supported by the Copyright Agency Cultural Fund

COPYRIGHTAGENCY
CULTURAL FUND

uwapublishing

Before all else, I want to acknowledge the Melukerdee People of the South East Nation, traditional owners on and from and about whose land this book was written.

Thanks, always, to Terry for bringing me here.

And thanks to Kathleen Mary Fallon for nagging.

Contents

CONTENTS

Year 5

Riddle

There's a memory I carry as a series of sensations, wordless, all through my childhood:

I'm looking at something that fills my visual field. It's a surface, squarish, textured and undulating, patterned with lines. Around its edge it separates into projections – I discover that I can move the thing, turn it and find another side, a different texture.

Eventually words attach themselves to this experience – *surface, line, projections, move* – but it's twenty years or more before I put them together – *an adult hand, my infant hand reaching to hold a finger.*

Another memory – this one with words in it:

Bright colours, their soft edges on a flat field that can be moved, turned to show more. A yellow animal, a blue animal and words connect them. My sister knows the words, the same each time. I lean against her, feel her voice in the bones of my face and chest.

In time I learn *book* and *page* and *read*, and that sitting, being held, being told, looking at words and pictures is part of *story*. But being read to brings both comfort and danger – stories are full of violence, misunderstanding, betrayal. Malevolence and damage ride in on the bodily conviction of a voice. Rustem and Sohrab, father and son, manipulated, unknowing, fight in the dust between the camps of their opposing armies. Grendel and his mother erupt from their den beneath the lake. Relentless, my sister reads on as the Happy Prince gives away even his eyes.

I want to read for myself, to find out whether or not stories will be more intelligible if I have control of the book. Impatiently I pursue the skill, though words and their fixed meanings don't match my world and leave me feeling mysteriously askew; my moon and sun travel backwards in these stories' skies. Stories are interlocking collections of fixities that move inexorably to their conclusions; they are artefacts, found items, inscrutable, finished. Stories are, as words seem to be, closed.

Then, when I am about seven, my mother gives me a prayer book filled with the wild laments and praise-songs of the Old Testament:

My dwelling is plucked up and removed from me like a shepherd's tent; like a weaver I have rolled up my life; he cuts me off from the loom.

Deep is calling on deep in the roar of waters; your torrents and all your waves swept over me.

Poetry shows me that fixity can be turned, unfolded; these voices speak a response, have their say about the stories they are

2

caught in. I begin to recognise that while language has created the world view into which I am born – where experience is prescribed from outside by a monstrously capricious *He* – it also offers possibilities of resistance and change.

Divinities and the cultures they ratify are modes of (un)consciousness at play in language. Consciousness widens with attempts in language to encompass styles of thought that are adequate to experience. Rainer Maria Rilke describes this as a process of *stretching* by which the gods work things out, take counsel: *der Gott beraten sein* – from *rat*, read, riddle ('As once the wingèd energy of delight').[2]

But it's a risky thing, to offer advice to a culture or a god, to seek a way to work with those inhuman voltages. Exhilarated as I was by the opening-out achieved by poetry, as a reading child I didn't yet understand that the attempt to confront and reorganise received consciousness is costly, undertaken out of necessity. Anne Carson speaks about this cost in an essay on the poet Stesichoros. She says:

> Born about 650 BC on the north coast of Sicily in a city called Himera, he lived among refugees...A refugee population is hungry for language and aware that anything can happen...
>
> What is an adjective? Nouns name the world. Verbs activate the names. Adjectives...are in charge of attaching everything in the world to its place in particularity. They are the latches of being...In the world of the Homeric epic, being is stable and particularity is set in tradition...Into the still surface of this code Stesichoros was born. [He] began to undo the latches... All the substances of the world went floating up...To Helen of Troy...was attached an adjectival tradition of whoredom already old by the time Homer used it. When Stesichoros

3

unlatched her epithet from Helen there flowed out such a light
as may have blinded him for a moment…[3]

Temporarily or permanently, writing can be disabling.
Escaping 'the still surface of the code', the writer must tolerate
exile and bewilderment within what theorists Gilles Deleuze
and Félix Guattari call a 'foreign language within language':

> The writer uses words, but by creating a syntax that makes
> them pass into sensation that makes the standard language
> stammer, tremble, cry, or even sing: this is the style, the 'tone,'
> the language of sensations, or the foreign language within
> language that summons forth a people to come.[4]

But first this 'foreign language' summons a *self* to come. As
a young woman I wrote to make a song in the bleak standard
English that was my inheritance as a mid-twentieth century
New Zealander; I knew that this was possible because of the
work of Janet Frame and others who wrote a particularity of
place unlatched from its epithets in a syntax that stammered
and sang. But in learning to do this for myself, I had to meet
and come to terms with the existence of a non-standard cast of
internal characters or modes who could make this local music,
with whom I had till then been unfamiliar. I had to endure
understanding that I didn't know myself, and I was panicked at
times by what I learned.

The process of writing brings change, both freeing and
frightening; it sends me out to practise a riddling conversation
with the world that steps towards me each day, each night.
Sensations – 'rogue intensities' as Kathleen Stewart calls them –
bring me into a new relation, through thought and narrative

and song, with 'all the lived, yet unassimilated, impacts of things, all the fragments of experience' that would otherwise be 'left hanging',[5] in the absence of this habit of attunement, of paying attention through writing. This journal is part of that conversation, here in Tasmania with its history of cruelties and dispossessions, resistances and recoveries, in which things continue to unlatch from what I know about them and, looming close, emerge in all their strangeness. I touch, I turn things over, I wonder about them. I answer.

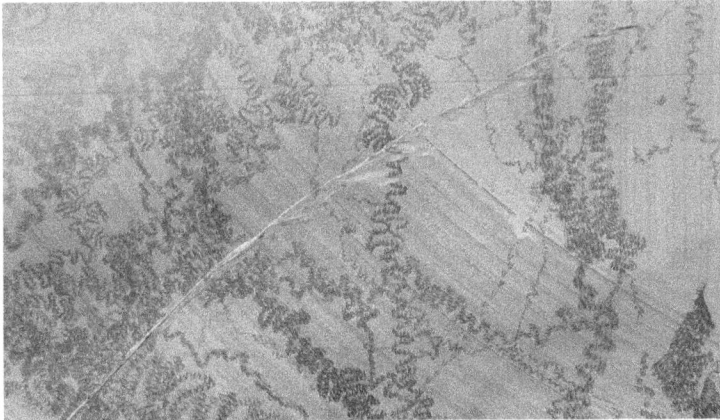

Year 1

Fire

Defenceless, illumined,
when the house burns to its foundations,
what I notice is how small it was.

As a girl in the early 1930s, my mother-in-law lived through wildfires that burned across Tasmania. Her family home, just down the road from where I live, was among those lost; for days afterwards, she couldn't see or speak. The huge fires of February 1967 missed this place but burned on either side. Not long after I moved to Tasmania, a builder said to me: *This is fire country – houses stand until they burn.* In November 1981 the old wooden farmhouse we lived in did burn down, though not in a bushfire: a spark from the chimney caught in an eddy of the sea breeze blowing up the valley and landed in hay stacked in a lean-to. It taught me about the speed at which fire can work – the whole building alight in minutes and burning fiercely enough to melt glass and collapse the aluminium kettle over the front of the stove like a Dali clock. If you survive it, wildfire is an unforgettable meeting with the contingency of things – here, then gone – and with unexpected balloonings and shrinkings of the mental and emotional space occupied by what remains and what is lost.

If you haven't lived through intense fire weather, it's hard to imagine the strength of the wind, the furnace-heat, the way smoke reduces visibility so that you can't tell if the fire front is metres or kilometres away, the speed at which flames can leap ahead of themselves through the detonating forest canopy. Looking into the green and blue and gold distances in the days that come before it, *If you didn't know, you wouldn't know*, as an old friend used to say. Fire has changed the way I see the landscape; we all hold our breath at this time of year, when eucalypts begin to exhale a blue shimmer of volatile oils that will explode in the spark from a dropped match, the lens of a broken bottle, the heat of a car exhaust, a lightning strike. Sclerophyll forests like these are communities of disturbance – they can't regenerate without it and fire's their disturbance of choice, the perfect tool to crack a hard seed-case and settle the germ in a bed of fertile ash.

In the first weeks of the new year, forests and farming districts and towns burned to the north and east of here, and on the mainland it seemed that all the eastern seaboard was alight. These fires that devastate whole landscapes come in a perfect storm of high temperature, low humidity, strong wind and heavy fuel load, especially after good rains when growing eucalypts shed bark and pile it up around themselves in bonfire heaps. On the mainland, the interval between these storms is decreasing. Here in eastern Tasmania, climate modelling offers a mixed prognosis. Bad luck – many more days of high temperatures in summer; good luck – more rain; bad luck – this rain will arrive as downpours that will increase erosion. The currently high-rainfall west coast of the island will receive much less summer rain and that could be the end of fire-sensitive wet sclerophyll forest and rainforest and an extension of range for dry sclerophyll communities. Realisation is dawning that current fire-management practices aren't working. Indigenous methods, disrupted and disregarded here and on many parts of the mainland since colonisation, will need to be employed once more, both to decrease the risk of catastrophic wildfire and to safeguard and increase remaining biodiversity.

From my desk I look out into the canopy of a quince tree. Its leaves have been damaged by pear slugs and the skeletonised patches have scorched russet in the heatwave that preceded and accompanied the fires. Through and over and around the quince grow the long branches of a young English oak, distorted by nightly use as a possum runway and food source. The trees are part of a deciduous thicket we began to plant thirty years ago – plum, linden, chestnut, apple, pear, medlar and hazel, with bird-sown hawthorn and elder seedlings coming up here and there – fenced from the cattle and sheltered by a macrocarpa windbreak. Most are food plants, it's true, but all satisfy a longing for the shade and light of a broadleaf forest. So far, this from-elsewhere idea of a garden, an encampment of heart and mind and body, is surviving quite well. Nothing has died in the heat, though green leaves on the north-westerly side of the linden and red chestnut baked brown in the hot wind and the foliage of the elder has paled and drooped. And in the hazel bushes, all through the glaring days, like an emblem of survival, a silvereye sat panting on her nest, a marvellous airy hammock of moss and cattle hair and rootlets and strands of orange plastic baling twine suspended below the leaves and twigs of an outer limb.

We've been lucky, so far. It's cool again now and the windbreak is loud in a westerly wind that lifts high and cold from the mountains across the river; the leaves of the quince and oak move a little in the breeze that gets through the

windbreak's shelter. Parrots – green rosellas – sidle foot-over-foot along the branches of an apple, stealing unripe fruit for the pips, leaving the ground littered with chunks of bitten and discarded pulp. A long skein of cloud winds across from a cyclone in the Indian Ocean – the monsoon has begun at last, and for the moment, here in the south, its damp air shields us from heat blasting down out of the mainland desert. It's not rain-bearing cloud, though, and with weeks to go before the days shorten and the ground begins to cool, it's a provisional reprieve. A lick of burning air could still flick down from the red centre and take us out. It may be that even here on the edge of change, catastrophe will come to make us reimagine how to be in this landscape. But I guess every life is a series of camps in fire country where all our ideas about the world burn down again and again or we burn ourselves, trying to save them. In our need for shelter, we have the habit of rebuilding, till death when the walls can stay down.

FEBRUARY

Owl

Round eye out of feather and fur, their tracks are all over me –
map and compass bearings, my belly the night sky

Our farm sits on the ridge of a kind of peninsula or promontory
that runs roughly north–south, bounded by a river to the west
and to the east by a bay that's part of a complex of waterways
sheltered by islands that shadow the coastline. After invasion
and colonisation, the eastern slopes of the ridge were mostly
cleared and farmed, while the steeper western slopes, although
logged last century and extensively burned in 1967, are now
largely reforested. In the drier places, eucalypts grow – mainly
stringybark and blue gum – and the cypress-like native cherry
that's parasitic on their roots; on the southern slopes of gullies
and where the soil is better, silver wattle, pomaderris, daisy tree,
white gum. An understorey of varnished wattle, pea flowers,
prickly coprosma, shrubby helichrysum and goodenia, with
bracken and blackberry and grasses in the more open places. In
October and November the intense blue haze of love creeper
appears from nowhere, with yellow hibbertia, pink heath, and
purple, green, white and blue ground orchids.

In the 1960s, for a nominal price, an uncle gave my husband
a block of this regrowth forest, just along the ridge to the

south of the farm. Stony and steep, it was judged to be nearly worthless (the uncle had bought it for a bag of potatoes). In the days before chainsaws, a local contractor worked over it with an axe, cutting the smaller timber for furnace wood to sell to fruit-processing factories in the area. After the 1967 fires burned through it, my husband and his father sowed grass seed in the ashes of the less steep parts, up near the road. At that time they were dairy farming, and as the block has a permanent spring, in winter, when the cows were not in milk, T used to walk them along the road and turn them in to graze the rough pasture. Since he stopped dairying in the 1970s after his father died, the block has been left to grow as forest once more.

Now that the bushes and young trees of the understorey aren't chewed or trampled by cattle, there's cover for all sorts of creatures. There is food and nesting for thornbills and wrens and ringtail possums and pademelons – the little local wallabies that have grazed fine lawns and kept open spaces where some grass has persisted. There are insect grubs and other invertebrates for bandicoots; bull ants and jack jumpers for echidnas; plenty of food and cover for root-eaters and fungi-eaters like potoroo and bettong, and for rats and mice, local and introduced. Nest-holes in mature trees for parrots and owls and cockatoos and bats and brushtail possums. Birds – insect-eaters and honeyeaters – forage their specialised feeding strata from ground level to the top of the canopy. And the predators that follow all these creatures are there too – antechinus and quoll and devils and feral cats and raptors.

This time last year we went for a walk there, where neither of us had been for many years. I don't know what prompted me to suggest it – I usually walk alone, on the road or in bush closer to the house – except that I was restless and heartsore and full of dread at news from Aotearoa New Zealand that my friend M was sick. The day was fine and still, with the first feel of autumn in clear, cool air. We pushed through waist-high undergrowth. Wallabies crashed away in the bracken; a snake moved off its sun-warmed patch of flattened grass; a yellow-throated honeyeater called loudly somewhere close by – *pick-em-up, pick-em-up* – and the warm, astringent resin smell of varnish wattle was close around.

After about twenty minutes we came out onto a dry ridge that overlooks a steep gully. To our left was a big native cherry, perhaps five or six metres tall. There's something about these trees that draws the eye – a kind of backlit darkness, yellow-green against the grey-green and red-green of the growth around it. As we looked, there was a movement in among the branches and a slantwise lattice of sunlight and shadow resolved to barring on the plane of a wing. Then out of the dense shade of the foliage a face turned to us. Dark eyes in a chestnut disc circled by a brown-black line, like a Wandjina cloud spirit blown here from the Kimberley, a face looking into us from another world. It was a masked owl. Half a metre tall with a wingspan of nearly a metre and a half; biggest of all the barn owls – big enough to take possum and wallaby. I'd seen one only a couple of times before, at intervals of years, hunting around the windbreaks close to the house.

She (the dark disc told it) watched us over her right shoulder. I held my breath at the delight of it, the wondrous luck. And then she turned to face us, and we saw why she was in plain view in daylight. Blood streaked the left side of her chest and the feathers on her shoulder were dishevelled; she kept lifting her left foot as if it bothered her. We stepped closer and she turned again as if to fly but fell flailing, hard onto the hard

ground. When we reached her we saw the damage: from the wrist where the flight feathers should spread, her left wing was gone. I remembered a friend saying, when he heard that there'd been a murder in a park he loved and went to for refuge and solace, *I felt as if it had happened inside me.*

She leaned back and clashed her beak at us when we approached, showing her talons. Her feet were huge, the size of my hand, and hand-like with their padded grips. She was strong, the wound was fresh, the wing-stump still bleeding. Ah, what to do. What prospect for a wild owl that can't fly? Should we kill her? Leave her? She seemed to want her life.

We wrapped her in a shirt and took her home. Half an hour from here is a place where a local man has established a refuge for injured raptors, caring for them and releasing all those that have a chance of survival. I phoned him and we drove there with the owl. I had a sick apprehension that I was merely passing on the job of killing her. He unwrapped her and looked stoically at the wound, holding her firmly by the legs and talking to her as he handled the damaged wing. He thought she'd been hit by a car while hunting insects in the headlights; it happens all the time, he said. He didn't know how she'd go – we'd just have to wait. With the help of his young son he transferred her to a dark box in a quiet place where she could rest and we went home.

All night her face was in my mind, fierce. She can't survive, I thought; unable to fly, unable even to reach a perch, she won't want to live. I should have killed her. I couldn't kill her. And we had walked straight to her in 50 hectares of bush unvisited for years. Foggy rain fell through the darkness and in the morning, light came up blue through mist with the sound of black cockatoos in the pine hedge, their creaking speech, their wild wailing, cracking cones and throwing them down.

It's a very young self who is summoned by the wounded owl, looking as if for the first time into the face of damage and death, understanding that some hurts are irreversible and must be accommodated, somehow. Feeling the dread of that knowledge, bone-deep and throwing out links across all space and time to other damages suffered and inflicted, intended and unintended, to persons both human and non-human, and to communities and cultures.

The next day there was an email from C at the refuge – a few hours after we left, the owl took food and let him dress the wound. *If she survives*, he said, *she can share an aviary with another female masked owl, who can't be released because she's blind in one eye and can't hunt. Day 5: The owl is one of the most amazing birds*

I have dealt with. I moved her into the aviary after 4 days and she went straight to the mid-height perches (tho I had placed lower ones for her). The next day she was on the highest perch. She has great courage, strength, spirit. She has met the other owl and the 2 sit together.

Now it's one year on. The owl is healthy and moves around a lot, jumping big distances from perch to perch and from perch to ground. The aviary has a pool, trees, cover. Owls love water and C says she's often down by the pool when he comes to do his rounds in the mornings. She interacts with the two others now in the aviary with her, a male and a female. There's also a wild male who visits; there's thought of making a hole in the netting so that he could come and go. C hopes there will be a mating – it has happened successfully in other places and the young birds seem to do well when released. Something from the wreckage. A life; new lives.

When I was young I would have found intolerable the owl's adjustment to being confined, to being unable to fly. I had a great need to see damage resolved, healed, made good, and assumed that I knew what healing was, what good was. I would have had an idea of what being an owl must be. Now it seems to me that the owl wants to live and she's accepting the life that's possible. The ongoing negotiation of the grown-up self – how to tolerate limitless uncertainty about what one must have or be.

As seemed somehow presaged by the meeting with the owl, in July M died, a few days after his sixty-fourth birthday, following a return of the cancer he had first experienced twenty years earlier. In my adolescence, the friend who described his response to the murder in the park also said, speaking about his father's last illness, *He struggled bravely to stay alive.* I was shocked – my friend knew about suffering yet praised the desire to live, right there in the midst of it. More than anyone else, M was the one who showed me how that contradiction could be lived. He loved his life and drank it to the last drop, the bitter with the sweet, enduring his own pain and grief and also ours. He lived from the clear heart of an understanding that it's all worth it, accepting loss as one of the faces of love.

The family story about our surname is that it means owl, and that the clan chose or were chosen by it somewhere in the forests of northern Europe, up near the Baltic Sea – the name is a piece of onomatopoeia like *morepork, boobook, ruru*. Humans love to identify with nodes in the fractal soul of things as it buds up, buds down to infinity, its parts at once discrete and unified, continuing. Universes come and go. The cosmos has these ideas – star fields with their planets, planets with their

landscapes dreaming up stringybarks and truffles and bettongs and owls and humans.

Early in the morning a few weeks ago I heard a racketing of honeyeaters and blackbirds and thornbills and wrens in the hedge. It wasn't the hawk call or the snake call but the one they make when they've found a ringtail possum outside its nest or a young boobook caught in daylight, before it can find dense cover. I went out and found the birds, beaks aligned like filings to a magnet, calling and pointing to a place about six metres up in one of the macrocarpas. And as I stood and watched, out of the background twigs and chiaroscuro emerged the form of a masked owl – my death, my life regarding me, calm, alert, wild.

Room

Ground waits, counting the slow sun slower

I'm sitting in my workspace. It's a room about six metres square, the upper level of a building dug into the slope of a hill. Access is from the outside via laddered steps and decking – there's no direct way between the levels to the room below. We built this place in the 1980s after our old farmhouse burned down, and we lived in it while we worked on the new house. At that time I was milking two cows and so, in addition to somewhere to sleep and cook and wash, we needed somewhere to do the milking and keep the cream separator and store cheeses. A place for a workbench and tools too.

When we were collecting materials for the building, we heard that a wooden church was being demolished on the way to Hobart; we bought the wall studs and hauled them away as the wreckers took them down. The builders of the church had put a 1905 sixpence under one of the plates to mark the year it was built – the year my father was born. The timbers were long enough to allow us to build a place with two levels – living space above and milking stalls and storage below. The old fever hospital in Hobart was also being demolished (there had been no polio outbreaks since the early 1960s) and we bought weatherboards as they were stripped from the long, verandahed ward buildings. Floorboards and the massive bearers to which they had been nailed came from the nearby town, where the dark, use-smoothed, cavernous space of the original post office and store was being collapsed to make way for a public library and a newsagency. T carted sand in our old ute from a nearby quarry for the concrete foundations and downstairs floor, and we searched salvage yards for doors and windows and iron for the roof.

For extra uprights and rafters, T felled a big stringybark eucalypt, still sound all the way through, growing on a dry slope across from the house. He walked around and around it, looking from all sides, before he made the notch that would drop it without tangling in nearby trees, in a place where he'd be able to get to it to drag it out. When he stepped away from the final cut the tree came down groaning, a kingdom falling, and struck the earth with a sound like the end of the world. I looked differently at things made from wood after that. The local sawmiller cut it for us and said when we went to collect it: *That there's good, hard-grown timber. You can put that up green and it won't move. Hard as God's forehead.* And so it was. We did rack it out to dry, but it didn't shrink and never looked like warping.

Needing to build quickly, we didn't insulate the wall and roof cavities and soon they became a tenement, just as a hollow tree would do – creatures recognise living spaces. When we put out the lights at night I would hear the *frrpfrrp* flitter of tiny forest bats hunting moths and mosquitoes in the dark air of the room. Rats and mice scuttered. Brushtail possums clog-danced on the iron. Downstairs a ringtail possum made its home in the wall, swallows glued their mud houses to the rafters, and over the years, starlings and a shrike-thrush and grey robins have taken turns to add straw to a nest in one of the corners. Spiders and insects of all kinds claimed their various niches; bees soon discovered an old pipe inlet in one of the weatherboards and moved into the wall cavity. For a while, one and one and one, worker bees would find their way into the upstairs room and congregate, baffled, against the windows as they tried to get out, until I found the tiny knothole through which they were coming from their hive in the wall, and blocked it with clay. Since then we've been good neighbours. Their soft growling accompanies me day and night; sometimes I hear the little, hoarse contralto of a young queen calling as she hatches and the answering agitation of the swarm, as workers and drones prepare to pour out with her for the mating flight. If I tap on their wall they roar in operatic chorus but otherwise ignore me, except when one butts against the outside of the glass, disturbed by the light if I work at night and forget to close the curtain.

We lived here for several years as we made mudbricks for the new house, collected various materials and completed other projects. The building began to be called the barn because I milked the cows downstairs and because we planned to use the upstairs space for a hayshed when we moved out. We never stored hay here but the name stuck – it's still the barn. Once the new house was habitable, this upper room became a spare bedroom and then my workspace, every surface piled with files and documents, hot in summer and cold in winter, a place where I add and remove many layers of clothing according to season. The room has shelves around the walls, a pot-bellied stove in the middle, various storage chests and cabinets and drawers, a desk where my computer and printer sit, a bed, a sofa, a table and chairs, a refrigerator. Outside on the decking there's a small

rainwater tank and a dish of water for the birds that come and go all day through the garden. Downstairs is a chaos of tools, the now-unused cream separator, welding equipment, an air compressor, surplus building materials, old suitcases, bee gear for the hives in the garden.

Autumn has begun and the room is full of the smell of ripening honey. The stringybarks are in flower and everything is sprinkled with a frazz of fallen stamens; the bees in the wall are working to bring nectar in while the blossom lasts and before the temperature drops and they can't move around. They're filling cells in the comb they've built, fanning water from the newly collected mix of nectar and enzymes to concentrate it so that it won't ferment. When it reaches the right consistency they'll seal the mouth of each full cell with a cap of wax, but until then the rich scent pours out.

As the days shorten towards the equinox, fog materialises over the surface of the river on still nights and hangs around the hills in the mornings as it lifts. Sea mist rolls across the tops in the afternoons, but these past months have been dry, dry; eaten-down, dusty pastures make golden interstices in dark forest, the ground parched and waiting. One after another, huge high-pressure systems have rolled across from the west to sit over the island, holding off rain that has flooded northern New South Wales and Queensland for months. With each one comes an immense quiet like the stillness after an outbreath. In that space, sounds carry – birdcalls, a conversation half a kilometre away, the whirr of insect wings. The blue expanse of the daytime sky seems limitless, a present moment formed by the rising breath of all things; the night sky comes close and opens, miraculous, into deep time as each star sends its radiance to touch my eye.

Not everything survives this clarity. Rainwater tanks and farm dams empty; gardens fail and rock faces reappear where the saplings that took root there die off; certain fantasies of unceasing verdancy and unimpeded agency exhaust themselves. Grandiosity withers, understanding that the light that's in us, which we send out helplessly and which continues long after we're gone, comes from all that we're made of – everything we bring or receive at the beginning, structures handed on, ineluctable constraints that shape us; everything we take for ourselves and the damage we inflict and incur in the taking; everything that comes to us unasked, welcome and unwelcome – all of it gathered together in that room, the selving-place.

And at last, as the hemisphere tilts away from the sun, a storm swings up from the Southern Ocean to clip the island. The first showers roll off the surface, scouring earth from garden beds and gravel from the road, but then moisture begins to soak in. Overnight new growth appears – a prickle of green in the paddocks, red tips on the eucalypts; forest truffles form and field mushrooms push up from threads of the underground universe on which everything depends, vast networks of exchange quietly elaborated under bushland and pasture all through the dry.

I'm sitting in my workspace and rain has come.

Táin Bó Fráich

Wind's coming down in gobbets
that wrinkle the skin of the world like milk,
like a beast's hide gathering, nervous at a touch

It's windy, a bellowing gale that doesn't let up but has degrees of wildness, with gusts coming uphill through the treetops in a tumult like an approaching stampede. It reminds me of the first years I was here, in the early 1980s, when this noise seemed to go on for weeks at a time every spring and autumn, and the sensation was like being bawled at, day and night. Since then, the band of wild weather that used to characterise the roaring forties has moved several degrees south as the climate shifts, and we don't get such a constant battering now. But it does blow hard just the same.

This place faces straight into wind that rushes unhindered across a river valley from mountains to the west, gathering speed on the uphill slopes on this eastern side. The farm is a long strip of land that runs down towards the water – one of many properties in the district whose boundaries reflect the post-invasion carve-up of land in the nineteenth century, into ticket-of-leave grants to convicts who had served their time. In the late 1850s, newly married and in their twenties, T's great-grandparents came to one of these parcels of land. They were both from County Tipperary – he was transported to Van Diemen's Land in 1853 for sheep stealing; she arrived as an indentured servant.

They lived on what is now part of the farm next to ours, to the north, where they built a hut of timber slabs on a little step in the hillside. The first time I walked near the spot, before I knew its story, the place announced itself with a blast of joy that came out of the air and hit me in the chest, so hard it nearly knocked me down: *Despite everything*, it said, *someone has been happy here.* Just up the slope above the hut was a permanent spring; they planted a couple of acres of apple orchard around the source, enclosed by a hawthorn hedge. T's grandfather was the third of their six children; he stayed on the farm after he married.

T's father and his thirteen siblings grew up in a later house that succeeded the slab hut and was built inside the hawthorn hedge, close to the spring. When they talked about the place, the aunts and uncles said: *People came from miles around for that water.* That used to puzzle me – *why* did they come? There was rainfall enough to keep stock and grow gardens and orchards, and people dug ponds and reservoirs along winter creeks, so it wasn't a desert oasis. And then I realised two things. First, the spring would have been in the network of water sources looked after by the Melukerdee people as they moved around their country. Family stories describe visits that I had assumed were purely social in nature; now I wonder if they might also have been ceremonial. Second, there was a solitary hawthorn at the head of the spring, and the remains of a wooden enclosure around it. I think the Irish great-grandparents planted the tree (or protected a seedling) and made the enclosure to mark the place as they would have marked a holy well in Ireland. Bereft of their home landscape and its local powers and presences, they were beginning to map a new topography of meaning for themselves. The spring, life-giver, was already acknowledged as sacred, and the convict whitethorn was their way of marking it so – an opening between worlds and an embodiment of the current that pours through things, with strips of cloth tied to the tree to let the wind carry their prayers. I wonder if they made the rounds of the well as they would have in Ireland, those first transportees, and if they kept the left-to-right direction of the sun's movement there, or dared to follow what must have been for them its uncanny *widdershins* path in this hemisphere, right to left.

Grieving and disoriented though all those who came must have been, the water continued to flow like a promise of healing.

The slab hut and the later house and the orchard are long gone. The hawthorn hedge is still there but the tree at the spring was cut down years ago and the water dammed. Even so the enclosed space still feels alive of itself, benign, and a new hawthorn sprout has appeared beside the source – whether from the old rootstock or a seedling I can't tell – a thorny, determined little shoot half a metre high.

So it's windy, and when T comes to say that a tree has come down on the boundary fence and the cattle have got in next door, I'm not surprised after we make the trek down across the steep slope, to find them on the flat where the slab hut once stood – that field of happiness – chewing cud with their tails to the wind. The neighbours' bull is with them (so that's why they're out – they've gone looking for him) and when we start to move the herd back towards the gap in the fence, he heads uphill, deeper into his own territory, and they follow. They're excited by the unfamiliar ground, by being with the bull, by the windy day, and as we move out onto the exposed slope the wind picks up further. They lift their heads and lean eagerly into the climb; we run with them, breathless and buffeted, gusts loud in our ears as we zigzag up the hill, following grooved tracks that cross and recross and turn back on themselves, and as we scramble higher the whole of the valley and the mountains beyond come into view, wide and silver-grey and open to the gale. Shafts of light finger through blowing cloud to bring into momentary clarity distant peaks, forested slopes, houses and farms, the surface of the river. And swerving across the wind, a young wedge-tailed eagle stoops close and hangs for a long moment, wings steady, pale shawl-feathers shifting as it turns its head this way and that to take in the curious sight of humans and a herd of cattle running erratic circuits around and around a hilltop paddock.

31

For my fortieth birthday, T and my friends helped me to build a labyrinth in the garden, its eleven circuits like those set into cathedral pavements in medieval Europe. Though undoubtedly haunted by earlier labyrinths' uses as ways of experiencing consciousness and of approaching monstrous forces such as those embodied by the Minotaur, these cathedral patterns framed the quest as a pilgrimage, to be walked by those unable to make a physical journey far afield. Dark lines paved into the church floor marked the walls of the labyrinth and the walker passed between them. Ours follows the pattern laid down in Chartres Cathedral, which has a six-lobed centre that has been described as gesturing towards *six crises of consciousness* – the mineral and vegetal and animal and human and angelic and unknown realms.

T used the tractor and blade to level a circle about 12 metres across, and within it we put down old carpet and covered it with a thick layer of sawdust, then marked the circuits using a stringline pegged to the centre. The paths are delineated by stones, some gathered from around the farm and others brought by friends; the entranceway and centre are paved with old house bricks. Working anticlockwise as the sun moves here, in the mineral lobe I put pebbles I'd gathered over the years from local beaches, and from Kaitorete Spit south of Christchurch and Hamurana Springs near Rotorua in Aotearoa New Zealand. In the lobe of the plants I put a linden tree because I love its shade and perfume and because it's one of the trees of life in European folklore. In the animal lobe I put a pot with fish in it, knowing that other creatures would also come to drink and bathe there. In the human lobe I dug a hole for a box (Tupperware inherited from my mother-in-law) and in it put an ocarina for music, hawthorn heart tonic for the healing arts, and various implements for drawing and writing – all covered with a copper lid made from a piece of an old hot-water cylinder. The lobe of the angels has a fireplace; the sixth lobe is empty. In the middle, touching and touched by all the lobes, I put sand, and smooth beach glass to play and make patterns with, and a cast-off cow's horn pushed into the sand as a vase and water scoop. At the turns of the paths I made small gardens planted in the colours of the spectrum with red at the outer edge, working inwards to violet.

All that was many years ago and since then the space has had ideas of its own. The spectrum of plantings has rearranged itself as things self-seed or die out. A pomaderris seedling took root among the pebbles of the mineral sector and has grown as high as the linden; lizards and frogs (and once a little snake) come and go under the copper lid in the human sector; the aloe I planted to guard the entrance has grown enormously and blocks the way so that I have to cut it back from time to time.

Half a world away, pecked into glacier-smoothed rock in the Camonica Valley north-east of Milan, are labyrinths with eyes. They were made by a Celtic people and predate the Cretan labyrinth on which the medieval cathedral patterns were based. In a reversal of the Cretan and medieval images, the lines of the Camonica labyrinths are drawn so as to mark the path itself rather than the delineating walls, and the eyes at the centre form two foundational points from which the lines of the pattern are drawn. That is, they're not the eyes of something *in* the labyrinth, *they're the eyes of the labyrinth itself.* As Aidan Meehan says in his book *Celtic Design: Maze Patterns*: 'We are in no danger of meeting the Cretan Minotaur *en route* to the centre of the Celtic maze.'[6] Though this *is* a cattle story, it's of a very different kind.

Meehan argues that the Camonica labyrinths are connected with the collection of Irish tales known as the Ulster cycle, in which the heroes Fráech and Conall Cernach travel from Ireland to the Alps, searching for Fráech's wife and children, and for his cows (given to him by his mother, one of the Sídé and sister of the river goddess Boand), which are his wealth.[7] The cows have been stolen away and hidden within the fortress-coils of a great serpent; this labyrinth is not a path leading to an entity – it *is* an entity. Despite its reputed ferocity, when the heroes approach, the snake does not attack but leaps to wrap itself around Conall's waist, thus releasing its captives; this done, Conall uncoils it from around him and lets it go, 'and neither has done harm to the other'.

We built our labyrinth at a time when it seemed to me that the riches of my lucky life had been stolen away, made inaccessible. A period of satisfying productivity as a writer had ended quite suddenly when all energy for the work vanished.

I could still write, but like walking a dry watercourse, joy was gone – the work no longer helped me to make sense of my life. I dreamed of a mountainous pilgrim road that followed a river until the water disappeared underground.

I hoped that making and walking my garden-labyrinth might teach me how to think about what was happening, and it did – by way of jokes and tricks and indirections. Walking the pattern shakes up ideas about what progress feels like; it turns you around and around like a hostage or an initiate or a child at a party so that you don't know whether you're going forward or backwards. It takes you straight in towards the centre when you begin walking it, so that you think you've made it! – then throws you to the outermost edge and makes you work your way back, slowly.

Once you've stepped onto its path you can never see the whole of it – in fact, the further in you go, the less you can see, until at the centre, whichever way you turn, half of the pattern is out of sight behind you. And it's useless to try to encompass it from outside/above because its meaning resides in being *in* it. If you walk it with another or others, your paths approach one another and swing apart, go in opposite directions before coming abruptly face to face, or move in companionable parallel until one doubles back.

I don't know what determines the pattern of a life or why it sometimes takes those turns – inward, downward – that feel like sinkholes, *cliffs of fall* as Gerard Manley Hopkins describes them,[8] which wrench hopes off course and abduct the feeling of *weal*-th, wholeness, wellbeing. There are disasters of many kinds that might bring about such a dropping-away, and there are forces – cultural, familial and perhaps otherworldly – that steal life and wall it up; there are necessities that take life

35

elsewhere, out of sight, the way cattle go out away to pasture or to the bull or to give birth or die, or to find their calf that's slipped under the fence. Whatever the cause, part of me went underground like the river in my dream, and for fifteen years, while the life of the daylight world with its loves and deaths and work and study continued, I was also following that muscled stream through the dark, hauling along, hand over hand, as its coils wound around me. There I learned the strange textures of a place where familiar structures fall apart and even (especially) a sense of self dissolves.

The aunts and uncles never claimed any special powers for the spring in its hawthorn enclosure, except *It's very good water and it runs all through the dry*. And I suppose that's it, really – the Melukerdee knew it, and the convicts who moved onto their country learned it. Starved and shamed and brutalised, the great-grandparents found this source welling here as if waiting for them, as if the stream of life saw them and knew them, all that time while they thought themselves shut away from goodness, its eyes of mercy were all through them as it took them along in the bright world and then down, in, under. And one day like them (again, now, always) I too find that the way leads up and here I am, alive on the hillside below the spring in the blustery riches of an autumn day, with the water winding away and the cattle around me.

Metamorphoses

Under the bay, faults ray out –
something presses up,
dense enough to skew a compass.

There's a lizard living in the scanner that sits on my desk. It strolls out from the depths of the machine onto the expanse of the paper tray, as onto a patio; it looks around, cocks its head to see me better with its golden, round-pupilled eye, blinking steadily. It's a small, gold-brown, slightly iridescent garden skink with a pale rose underbelly – *Carinascincus metallicus*, metallic cool-skink – common here and one of several cold-adapted species found in Tasmania, which give birth to live young, are able to raise their body temperature 14 or 15 degrees Celsius above their surroundings and have the capacity to go into a kind of hibernation in winter.

The skink appeared one day in summer – I heard a scritching inside the scanner's plastic casing and its head and forelimbs emerged from the memory card slot. It looked around, then turned itself and went back in, showing a curving side and length of tail. Later it came right out, unworried by my presence as it investigated the entrances and exits of its new home – the card slots, the various approaches to the paper tray. Having settled in, it began, over the next days and weeks, to explore its territory more fully. It walked to the edge of the desk and peered over into the abyss; it patrolled the perimeter, looking up to catch my eye from time to time as I loomed overhead at the keyboard. If I reached towards it, it licked the air before touching my finger with the tip of its little black tongue, and accepted pieces of strawberry (an offer based on the passion for this fruit shown by the big blue-tongue skinks that live in the garden).

Strawberries it can take or leave, but when a blowfly blunders against the window, the skink is galvanised. It rushes from its lair and leaps to the sill to stare at its prey, which is quite a lot bigger than its head – although that's no obstacle given a jaw that can unhinge like a snake's. I think, though, that despite this tail-lashing, big-game-hunting posturing it must live mainly on silverfish, since it spends most of its time stalking among the document-sheaves and clinking about in the depths of the paperclip basket. It's curious, experimental, and does something that looks very much like play.

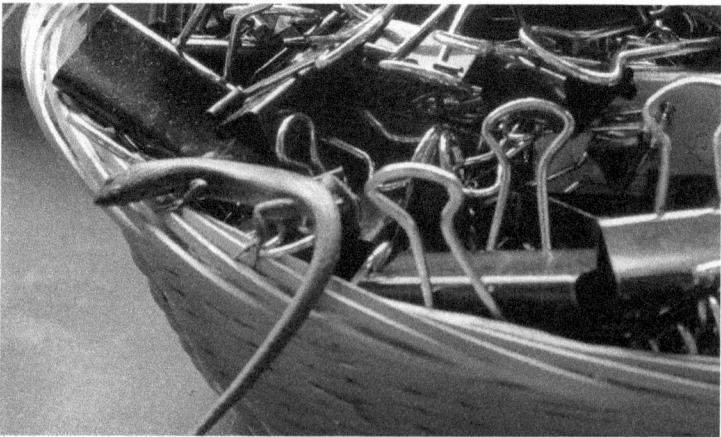

I grew up in a culture that imposed a fixed hierarchy of being, with humans at the top – our consciousness was the only real consciousness; we alone had souls. According to most churches, animals had neither consciousness nor soul – not the black cat who birthed her kittens in the shed and spoke to them with her eyes and her body and her calls; not the racehorses in the paddock behind our house who kicked up their heels in the wind; not the greenblack tui who hung upside down to drink nectar in the yellow shade of the kowhai tree; certainly not the tree itself or the ground that stretched away down beneath, with its seams of fire, seams of water. Intellectually, it was the heyday of the triune brain theory developed by American neuroscientist Paul MacLean in the 1960s.[9] According to this schema, human neuroanatomy is structured (and human behaviour is therefore determined) by a kind of evolutionary archaeology of competing needs and drives: there's a 'primitive' brain-base inherited from reptile ancestors which is hardwired for aggression and territoriality; over this is laid the nurturing emotionality of the protomammalian limbic system; on top is a neocortical veneer peculiar to modern mammals, which prepares the way for 'higher' functions of language and abstract thought.

Current studies in comparative anatomy and behaviour, however, suggest that it's much more mixed up than that. It seems that the first mammals and the first dinosaurs appeared at the same time, around 225 million years ago, and the precursors for neocortical structures were there from the start in both.[10] The structure of modern bird and reptile brains is much less 'primitive' than was thought. Birds and some reptiles and fishes nurture their young; cognitive and language-like abilities show up in non-mammals. And although there's comfort in a tidy formula, I'm happy to relinquish it in favour of the tensions of complexity.

The first cold days have come and the skink is much less active. During the hot weather it was out and about all day; I put out a little dish of water for it and when the level got too low, it would pace and stare into the dish until I refilled it, though I knew it could get outside to the windowsill that was soaked with dew each morning. Now days go by without a sighting. Will it disappear for the winter? I know so little about the creatures living their lives around me.

For instance, how long might this population of skinks have lived among the rock piles and leaf litter on this hillside? Certainly through the last ice age, which peaked about 18,000 years ago – glaciation was limited in Tasmania and the cold was modified by surrounding oceans. Skink species survived in Aotearoa New Zealand under similar conditions. How long before that, then? Skink-like reptiles appeared in the mid-Jurassic around 140 million years ago, along with the first flowering plants and their coevolving panoply of insects. Ninety million years ago, these plants and their attendants reached the cool-temperate supercontinent of Gondwana, of which the Tasmanian landmass was then a part (connected to what is now Antarctica, along with mainland Australia, South America, Africa, Madagascar, India, New Zealand, Papua New Guinea and New Caledonia). Sixty-five million years ago, the extinction of the dinosaurs opened the way for a flourishing of insect- and fruit-eaters, and recognisably modern reptiles, birds and mammals appeared. When Tasmania finally began to cast off from Antarctica 45 million years ago, lizards in the *Eugongylus* group to which the snow-skinks belong were almost certainly on board for the northward journey.

Amazing to think of these life forms shaping in geological time, adding their bones to the bones of the world as continents formed and re-formed, drifted and sank and re-emerged, carried along by the slow tides of the rocks. The geology of this area is complex.[11] We sit on a ridge a couple of hundred metres above sea level; under my feet as I walk the paddocks is a 300 million-year-old matrix more than twice that depth, comprising glacial sediment from the Carboniferous period overlaid by mudstone full of fossil shellfish, fan corals, snails, laid down in a shallow, ice-covered ocean; under all that, volcanic domes of Jurassic dolerite that pushed up 175 million years ago. And forcing its way through and between all these layers is more magma, formed from molten crust 97 million years ago in the Cretaceous period, during the rifting and breakup of

Gondwana. None of the Cretaceous magma reached the surface then, but it's visible in places now, where the sediments above it have weathered away. It formed enormous sills and pillars of porphyry and brought with it superheated, silica-saturated water that steamed the rocks around it, and forced its way into veinlets and fractures in the sediment, dissolving pebbles and fossil-casts and replacing them with quartz containing gold, silver, zinc, lead and arsenic that had been carried up in the magma.

On these long-cooled rocks, generation on generation for millions of years, snow-skinks have lain in the sunlight, flattening and turning themselves like tiny solar panels, learning to add their own metabolic heat to what comes from our star; to keep their young inside their warm bodies and feed them there, threaded to a placenta till they're ready to be born; to shut themselves down in the cold; to make use of new habitats and foods. This is, after all, a place of reversals and convergences and metamorphoses, where what's oldest may be what's on the surface; where what's new can arrive from miles down, deep under with a cargo of treasure and poison that transforms everything around it. Where what's little and ancient and disregarded can turn to gold.

Char

We crawled down into the dark and we waited

When I was a child I loved to take charcoal from the fireplace and grind it to a paste with water to make ink whose deep opacity fascinated me – I would hold the jar to the sun, tilting it to find the thin meniscus at the very edge of the liquid through which some light could find its way. It was the world of darkness in small; I could come nearer to it, hold it in my hand, touch its surface and watch the end of my finger disappear into its mystery. And I could find images there; I used it to write and draw and paint lines and washes in velvet-black and soft grey, with a brush made from a chewed twig and a pen cut from a kelp gull feather brought back from the beach. It was satisfying to find the materials I needed close at hand. Sometimes I added the purple juice of phytolacca berries that grew in a weedy corner of the garden, and which we children called *deadly nightshade*, though of course it is not.

Downhill from here, the inky water of the river, stained purple-brown-black by buttongrass tannin from the high country, reminds me of those experiments in depth and darkness. In places on the west coast of the island where rainfall is very high (as on the west coast of the South Island in Aotearoa

New Zealand), huge volumes of fresh water, tannin-dark, pour off the land and create an opaque layer on top of the salt water of the sea, limiting available light – and so the deep comes nearer. Feathery sea pens, corals, sponges that usually live very far down move up to reefs and outcrops just metres below the surface.

I'm thinking about all this because, now that it's cold enough to light the fire each evening, T has begun to collect the silky-brittle logs of char that are left in the morning ashes after the stove has been shut down overnight. He'll crush them and soak them in seaweed tea before adding them to the garden beds. Charcoal is porous – each piece becomes a little outpost like a sunken wreck that hosts a world of life, supporting bacteria and fungi that sweeten and fertilise the soil. And if the char is made in a fire that's not too hot, it retains oils and tars – an aromatic chemistry of persistence that allows it to last and last in the ground, doing its work without breaking down.

All over the world, rich black earth can be found where people have settled and stayed; where they've lit their cooking fires and dug the charcoal into their gardens with the kitchen scraps and broken pots, with the liquor from their ferments and pickles and brews thrown in to bring it to life. It's there in the dark earth under the streets of Roman London; it's there in the *terra preta* of pre-Columbian Amazon settlements abandoned hundreds, sometimes thousands of years ago, quietly regenerating itself in collusion with earthworms, while the leached soils around it slurry and bake in the tropical wet.

In the southern hemisphere, it's only a little while till the shortest day. The sun grinds in its black bowl – shining chunks, our planets and moons. Almost a year since M died, seven years since J died – my companions, going ahead into the dark – one breath then gone, sounding. Night rises and I step in – sometimes it's all I have of them, this ink that swallows the world.

There's a heap piled in the paddock ready for the solstice fire – bonfire, *bone fire*, the year's accumulation of everything that's unassimilable, waiting to be burned airy and dark, ready to go back under. Each year the flames unfurl their hands and the cold lump of the heart hisses and wails in the embers where everything speaks and sings in its own voice and that is the song. The bonfire's a chance to hunker down together; we watch the sparks go up and let the smoke catch in our hair and clothes, breathe it in, let it wash around us. Against all evidence of the immensity of cold and dark at our backs, we turn our faces to this spot of warmth and light we've made to signal our hope that, truly, after this night, once again our part of the Earth begins to lean towards the sun.

Humans everywhere have their ceremonies to mark the turns of the year – the time when Gugurmin, dark emu in the Milky Way, shows that it's time to collect eggs; when offerings are due at Matariki, after harvest when the Pleiades rise at midwinter; at the birth of the sun, when winter solstice fires are lit from a splinter of last season's wood, to make the black, the coals and dust, the body of ink, unknowable, from which the next thing can come. This year, in a strange and wonderful reversal, I am celebrating inside out – while at home they add the last pieces to the bonfire heap and feel around on the top shelf of the pantry for the fireworks box, I am a world away in the long days of Europe, where the fires are soon to be lit for midsummer and the char and ashes ploughed into fallow ground or scattered among the growing crops; I've leapfrogged to the place where renewal has already started. Wind has shaken the leaf buds open; branches plough their furrows, leave their tracks on the air; the lindens are in blossom and the young chestnut lifts its candelabra to the sun.

After winter, something can happen; the ground rises in steam like a dark loaf – lives come up, trumpets and bells from underground, out of this fabric that we have a hand in creating and to which we return, ourselves and all that we make and do, for better and for worse, out of our own necessities. This journal, for instance, these pages of char.

Foreigner

stones, stories that broke your back
and were your treasure too,
abandoned on that track

There's a small, dark otter-shape moving quietly across the surface of the dam. It rolls neatly under and reappears moments and metres away at the end of a trail of bubbles – platypus! I've never seen one here on the hilltop before, although I've watched them play in the turbulence of creeks and at the edges of twilit dams roundabout. It's a young one, perhaps, chased out to find its own territory. From summer on the other side of the world I came back to winter with its low, sharp sun and then days of soft, fine easterly rain that soaked the ground so that roadside drains filled and seasonal creeks and springs began to run and the dam overflowed – the platypus must have followed the running water to this place.

Now it has moved in under the upturned canoe, coming and going via the prow, which is submerged since the water level rose. Usually secretive, active in darkness or at twilight, this one has openly cruised back and forth for days. Returning from far afield, nothing could make me understand more clearly where I am than the familiar strangeness of this creature – billed, furred, lizard-gaited, it lays eggs and makes milk for young that are born with teeth, which are lost before they leave the nesting burrow. Its bill has electrical sensors to detect the muscle contractions of its small invertebrate and crustacean prey in the muddy dark where it hunts.

I hope there's enough food for it here. The dam holds a sizeable body of water – it was dug in the 1960s to irrigate acres of orchard at a time when apples were exported to Britain. Later, as the last ties of empire began to dissolve, that market collapsed and all through the district, fruiting trees were bulldozed. But the dams remain and sometimes the old orchard rows are visible as lines of stump-hole depressions in late afternoon or morning light.

So here I am, then. *Pilgrim*, I went to hear and see and touch and taste for myself, *peregrine, foreigner*, going *per ager, across the field*. I took my foreignness to the foreign place of my maternal ancestors in Ireland, who had left a country scoured and ruined by the mid-nineteenth-century famine. My maternal grandmother's family were farmers outside Bantry before her parents moved to town and her father became a publican. After he died aged thirty-one, she emigrated to Aotearoa New Zealand with her mother and three younger siblings in 1884 when she was fourteen, following two older sisters who had made the journey earlier. I saw their little house on the edge of the town in Bantry. She married my grandfather in Aotearoa New Zealand after he and all but one of his six siblings also emigrated from West Cork.

My maternal grandfather's family house is in a townland outside Schull. Small rooms, thick walls whose stones persisted while, nearby, the turf and thatch dwellings of a village of 200 melted away or were torn down, when the landscape emptied itself of millions through starvation and epidemic disease after the potatoes failed for several years in the 1840s. Wonder crop from the new world, potatoes had allowed the Irish to survive and even thrive, in terms of population at least, though pushed to the poorest ground in a regime of plantations populated by English farmers brought in by the landlords.

The eldest great-uncle stayed on when my grandfather and the rest of the family emigrated. I met a woman who had lived all of her long life nearby and who grew up with his children. She spoke with love of my great-uncle's kindness and of how she and her brother had been made welcome when her parents were sick or had to travel away for work. We spent the day together – she took me to the family house, beautifully restored by its present owner; she did her best to respond to my questions, looking into my face to see if I'd understood what she was trying to tell me. *That house, it was the first stone house around here. See that hillside? That was called by their name – it's 100 acres. In the old days they used to keep horses, grand horses, you know.* Seeing my blankness, eventually she looked away and said quietly, *Back in those times, they were the landlord's agents.*

I stumbled through to the end of our meeting. *It was too much,* she said as I took my leave. *Too much for one day – walk away! Walk away now, girleen! That family was good to me!* Pieces of information snicked into place – the British name; my grandfather's curious ineptitude as a farmer though he was very good with horses; his own father's deathbed conversion to Catholicism.

With knowledge like stones in my shoes I went limping, and everywhere I went, stones and the marks on stones caught my attention; their solidity stopped me floating away. I saw boulders dug out of glacial till, dressed and fitted together as intricate puzzles whose solution was shelter, defence, exclusion; I followed field walls of limestone and slate and sandstone, pieces gathered out of the bog, whose style announced the work of families and districts and epochs.

Inconspicuous and half-overgrown by flowering dock in the middle of a field beside a farmhouse in Ventry was a standing stone, marked with a Greek cross, equal-armed inside a broken circle like an omega symbol, its ends curled up into spirals. The farmer's wife told me: *That's Leac na Ré – the Stone of the Age of the Crescent Moon – see its curve there? It marks the grave of Conmael, son of Dáire Donn, king of the world. With his father he tried to take this place for his own and was killed in battle here.* It wasn't the narrative I was expecting (a Christian cross, a monastic site perhaps). But the stories here are older and play themselves over and over in empires and their collapse; in battles fought and won, fought and lost again with the death and rebirth of the sun, the Son, the age.

On roads skirting ancient fields, going west with the light I came to Cnoc Bréanainn, where Brendan looked out to a string of islands vanishing into sea-haze and launched his little boat to follow the sun. In my complacency I had thought pilgrimage would be safe, an eyewitness adventure that would build on what I already knew – that we were virtuous escapees; hadn't we sailed from famine and injustice to Aotearoa New Zealand, isles of the blessed? Now I had to let myself be shaken apart – here be monsters. Neither fish nor flesh nor fowl, I was set against myself, invader and invaded, the old wars still present in me.

Back home, sleepless in the company of this unease, which adds itself to the knowledge that here in Tasmania I am on unceded ground, I walk the moonlit gravel of the unsealed road that makes a dogleg along the farm boundary where early last century, neighbours refused to allow a straighter way through their land. I go out the gate and turn left, up to a junction where a road drops steeply down to the river. The air is cold and bright, and long shadows fall across the paddocks. When I come back, the platypus is a series of dark intervals – head, back, broad tail – in the band of light on the water of the dam. It rolls and dives, weightless, between worlds, between forms, *pilgrim*.

Black cockatoos

how their calls, supple as black rope, shine,
thrown out on swells to drift

The days are getting longer. Overnight along the track to the house, elder twigs have sprouted clusters of leaves and here and there a flower head in miniature, its umbel of blossoms still green but complete with tiny buds. Wattles brighten like lamps coming on, and frogs have begun their rattling songs around the edge of the dam, so loud it hurts my ears. A brown bandicoot digs the rain-softened ground of the yard each night in search of worms, her belly round with newly furred young that grow like golden buds from the nipples inside her pouch.

It's snowing in the mountains. A flock of black cockatoos has come down to work over dead trees in sheltered gullies on this side of the river, stripping bark and cracking rotted branches to find borer grubs. They visit the garden around the house most days, checking out the acacias for dead wood and the banksias and pines for seeds, filling the air with their creaking conversation: *Are you there? Here. There? Here. There? Here. Here.* They look at me sidelong, massive pincer-beaks and yellow cheek-patches in profile, crests lifting and subsiding. When they move on, they launch themselves along undulating paths mapped by their wailing cries, pivoting slantwise on one drooping wingtip then the other, out over the valley.

Plovers are nesting near the gate into the school paddock (named for the one-roomed schoolhouse and teacher's residence over the road where T's parents learned to read and write); four eggs are bedded on hay tucked into a cow's footprint. The sitting parent runs quietly from the nest, head low, when I come near. Something – *quollratdogdevilcurrawong* – took the eggs of the pair that settled on the worked ground of a vegetable bed below the dam.

I'm filled with a heaviness that comes at this time most years when, just as everything surges up towards the returning sun, the weather gets colder. New life is vulnerable; creatures are

hungry and death is in the wind. Sleet blows stinging and the cattle lie with their backs to it on whatever dry ground they can find. The air is damp and bitingly cold. To go out or even to sit inside and work, I need to put on thick layers of clothing that make me feel hindered, muffled; water leaks though the seams of my boots in the wet grass; mud clots their soles on the miry track. Everything seems effortful and my mind leaps ahead to all the effort to come – difficulties to be encountered, losses yet to be endured. Powerful, the impulse to narrate the world in advance. To call myself back I need to come to my senses again and again, momently, to my bodily life where this ache around the heart can take its place among other sensations. Then the world steps forward and I am in it.

My flesh and bones and blood, my turn of mind is shaped by processes tangled away back in darkness behind me where the ancestors sit or lie in their attitudes of anguish and repose. Luck or imagination sometimes lets me glimpse a pattern there – the crimp of famine or the habit of shame, implacable in body and soul along generations, even through the lustre of good years. Deliberate amnesia or mere distance in time and place may mean that the language of events is lost but their emotions roil on in silence and are felt as cravings, aversions, anxieties that flesh themselves out in religious or cultural obsession or grandiose or fearful fantasy. My agency, the tiny part of living that belongs to me alone, resides almost entirely in becoming less reactive and more curious. And my exercise of this capacity can also alter what I pass along – it's not much but it's all I've got.

In a cave system at Niaux in the south of France, nearly a kilometre into the darkness I saw delicate charcoal outlines of bison, ibex, horses, drawn 13,000 years ago at the end of the last ice age. Most of the images are in a semicircular gallery,

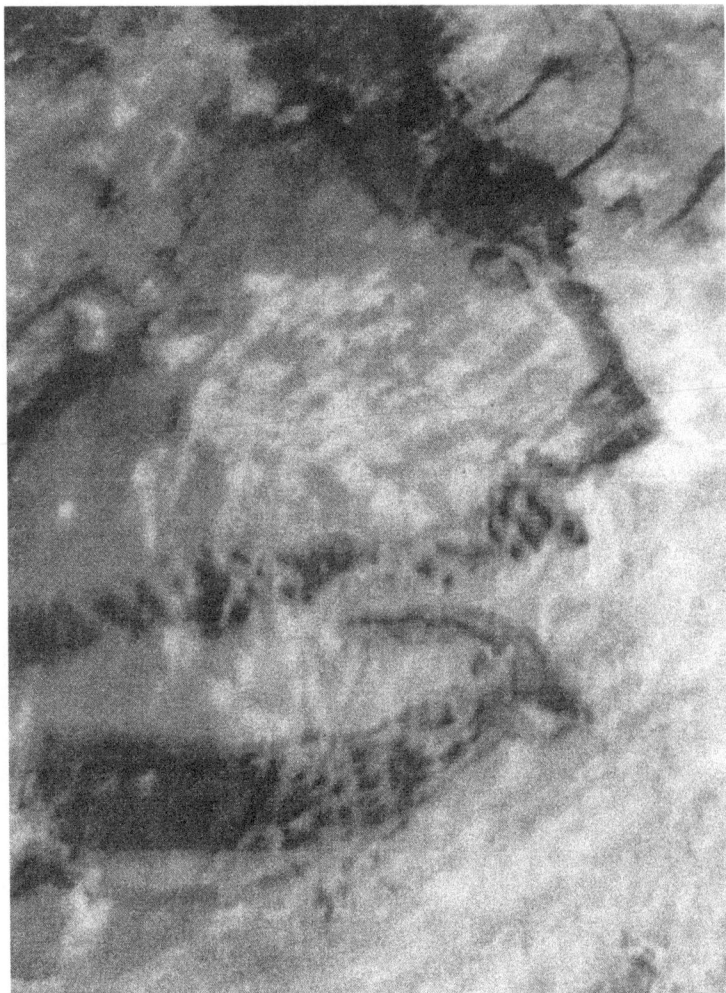

a natural amphitheatre whose high, vaulted roof catches and projects sung and spoken notes far into the dark. The animals are drawn as individuals and in relation to one another – they look like characters, *persons*.

The artists' DNA is ours, give or take minute variations – they are us with differing technologies. This understanding and the material traces they left is all that's knowable about them, which leaves me free to wonder. Here's a story I tell myself about the drawings: The people went to that place far from daylight as if on a journey to origins, to ancestors so deep they speak from the body – the animals who gave the skills needed for survival. *This one taught us how to plough through snow and endure and how to live as a group, how to look after our young; this one made us agile and cunning, able to leap away and look back, laughing; this one taught us courage and play and speed.*

Some of the drawings have arrowlike lines scratched on their flanks, though (as the archaeologist who was our guide pointed out) the people who made the drawings did not use bows and the shafts are too short for spears. In that storying-place, chosen for its acoustic as well as its visual possibilities, maybe those lines describe voices, songs thrown towards the gift-givers.

I can hear the black cockatoos, *mangana*, down out of sight in the wattles and seedling pines that grow on the steep, easterly slope where the old raspberry bed used to be in the days when small-fruit money paid for local families' shoes and clothes and schoolbooks. Warm in their glossy feathers, the cockatoos grip the branches with strong feet and talk among themselves. See this image from the cave of my skull, hear my call sent towards these teachers who show me how to come down out of the cold; how to find food in difficult and unlikely places; how to follow my voice out into the current of things.

Caduceus

The river brims, spills over the road
as the tide lifts. I look in
and the river looks back, clear as an eye.
There's life in it.

Spinning, tilted, Earth comes to a place in its orbit where the southern hemisphere leans towards the sun. More light reaches us; air near the equator warms and rises, flows south and sinks as it cools, then travels along the surface through the mid-latitudes before it rises again over the Southern Ocean and continues on towards the pole. There it sinks to the surface and begins to flow north once more, rising and falling in the reverse of its southward pattern. Our weather systems are driven by these interconnected equatorial, mid-latitude and polar cells of rising and falling air, their currents looping under and over one another like the entwined serpents of the caduceus.

The surface of the Earth at the equator – the globe's maximum circumference – spins at more than 1,600 kilometres per hour and the warm air that rises from it moves fast, but at lower latitudes where the cooling air mass reaches the ground, the Earth's circumference is smaller and its speed of rotation is slower by hundreds of kilometres per hour. Where the fast-moving air hits the slower moving surface, the difference is felt as gale-force winds known as the roaring forties. In recent years, higher ocean temperatures have increased the size of the equatorial cell – the rising air is hotter and takes longer to sink so that it touches down with its gales further south.

At this time of year though, as the sun moves away from the equator, bringing the locus of rising air with it in our direction, there's still a sense of something passing over, scouring. Even though we're not at the heart of the tempest, there's more energy in the system now, and cold winds from deep over the Southern Ocean are drawn up to pour across the island from the west, squall after squall.

In the intervals, everything warms and loosens. Willow catkins plump and show gold at the roots of their silver fur then put out hairy stamens; a smoke of pollen goes up from the pines with each swing of the air; bees collect fat beads of the orange and yellow dust to feed the brood to come, packing it into comb emptied of honey over winter. Nesting goes on everywhere – blackbirds make cups of dried grass and moss and line them with mud; New Holland honeyeaters weave strips of tea-tree bark and gather velvety banksia tips for lining; pardalotes search for holes in the mudbrick walls of the house or refurbish last year's burrows in clay banks along the road.

Lizards are coming out of hibernation. The skink that lives in the scanner on my desk reappeared today; I hurried to fill its water dish and it came to drink, dipping its round black tongue. The rocks around the garden are alive with little ones, many of them missing their tails. Perhaps they've escaped the shrike-thrush that hunts and calls urgently across its territory or the family of currawongs that works over the garden or the kookaburras that have recently extended their range here after being introduced to the north of the state from the mainland. Any of these will make a grab for a lizard but sometimes all

they get is the wriggling tail, which detaches itself along pre-existing lines of weakness where muscles contract to prevent blood loss – a costly but successful diversionary tactic. The tail regrows within weeks – a darker colour and glossier, made of cartilage and muscle without bone, not as finely pointed as the original but almost as long. It does its job, enabling the animal to balance properly as it runs.

Now the snow comes again and water streams down off buttongrass moorland; the river runs full and dark as the tide comes in against it with the wind at its back. Out at Sandrock, the platform of yellow-and-pink stone is going under, there where we sent our New Year rafts out to sea and lit fires to cook oysters and mussels; where we squatted with our toes hooked over the rock lip to watch seahorses browse and where H cut her hand on the sharp oyster shells; where the dog swam up and down the bay, hopeful, ecstatic, in the wake of disdainful swans; where porpoises came to startle us with their sudden breath.

When I first arrived here in the late 1970s, Sandrock would submerge in a spring tide now and then – we would go to look at the shining levels and marvel at the water's unusual reach. Then the rock began to flood more often, and recently the cracked and eroded rectangular pans and loaves of sandstone are covered over often enough to have grown a fur of algae. Purple marks left on the pavement by campfires are now lit by spark-swarms of phosphorescent plankton, single-celled *Noctiluca* that flash blue-green with every disturbance of the night. Silver shoals of garfish needle along the current; a spotted stingray beats across the surface of the ledge.

A drought broke in 2009; so much water poured from the catchments of the mainland coastal ranges into the island continent's inland basin in 2010 and 2011 that global sea levels paused and even dropped for a few months. Now the rise continues, 10 millimetres per year.[12] It's amazing to think that we are witnessing something not seen since the end of the last ice age – the ocean rising appreciably in a single lifetime. Indigenous Dreaming stories from around the coast of Australia describe features of the landscape and events that took place on land now flooded and far out to sea.

I'm thinking (still, again) about the stories that emerged around me in Ireland, glimpses into a past that has been covered over and out of reach for generations of my family. I'm thinking about how the self-protective tide of distance and forgetting that followed trauma, shame and helplessness also drowned memories of happiness: *See that stone up there on the hillside? That's where we children played – your cousins and me – it's*

Finn MacCool's fingerbone! That's his seat across the bay. He looked over and saw something and he broke off his finger and threw it and there it is. We played on that old stone – it's as big as a house! I'm thinking about how to approach and reclaim a connection with some of what's been lost – the grief and also the sounds of play breathing through like light from those stony hills.

Here in Tasmania, Indigenous peoples have addressed this question through a project that combines creativity and scholarship. In it they have drawn on remembered elements of pre-invasion languages and used historical and linguistic research to revive, teach and learn *palawa kani*, now spoken increasingly within their communities.

Somewhere the life that goes under continues. Individually, collectively, in the realm of the caduceus, wand of the trickster who steals with one hand and gives back with the other, our stories sink and rise and turn back on themselves. Presiding over transitional states, god of travellers, traders and interpreters, of verbal trickery, puns and wordplay, of liars and poets, Hermes smuggles inside information across the borders of the past, puts words in my mouth. He takes my history from me and in its place confers the terrible lightness of being – freedom to make it up for myself as I go along. Though broken and discarded in the grip of necessity, changed but functional, my tale can regrow.

OCTOBER

Steam

Lie down. Let memory grow like a thorn-tree from your chest,
its shade the ground where breath and speech can come
to scatterlings from all the worlds.

Some days are warm now but still the ground is damp and it's
safe to light a fire outside. I've been using the firebath – an old
cast-iron tub with chipped and pitted enamel that did paddock
duty as a cattle trough for years. We set it into the bank behind
the house with room for a fire underneath to heat the water,
and made a chimney from an old milk can whose bottom had
rusted out, and a platform of ceramic tiles in the bottom of the
bath so as not to have to sit directly on its heated floor.

I fill the bath with water from the dam and light the fire with
fragrant macrocarpa branches from a windbreak tree cut down
to let in winter sunlight. Smoke breathes all around as I step in.
Earth, wood, flame, metal, water. Astounding good fortune,
these moments of quiet, suspended in sunlight with moving air
on my face and arms. Honeyeaters forage in the blackwoods
nearby, wrens work over the grass beside me and swallows
practise their aerial calligraphy. Seams and currents of perfume
from the lucerne hedge and the flowering pittosporum; stink
of crushed pearlwort and cabbage stalks from the garden beds.

Away down below me the fire at the planet's core heats water too. Seawater dragged down with the ocean floor as it slides under continental plates at subduction zones mixes with molten rocks of the mantle, 100 kilometres deep. Where a volcanic plume pushes up, the water rises with it as steam, superheated, intensely compressed. If it doesn't reach the surface the water may be trapped in hardening domes and sills of lava or forced into underground cracks and seams, depositing its supersaturated metals and minerals. If the plume does reach the surface, the superheated steam, no longer compressed, expands violently, firing multi-tonne lava bombs into the air like corks and turning the liquid rock to foam.

The metal of the bath did not come from ore deposited by supersaturated steam but was extracted, like the enamel that coats it, from sediments laid down in ancient oceans. Iron is abundant as an element but is often bound to minerals such as silicates, forming compounds from which the metal is difficult to extract. In the aeons before the appearance of life, iron slowly weathered from these compounds and was dissolved in the mineral soup of the seas, along with the silica it was bonded to. About 2,500 million years ago, the first oxygen-producing organisms appeared, and when oxygen began to dissolve in the seawater it bound to the iron there; iron oxide in the form of haematite and magnetite precipitated out and fell to the sea floor. Huge deposits of these rusty ores built up over millions of years, alternating in a seasonal pattern with layers of silica-rich chert, and this sedimentary rock is the source of most iron that is smelted today.

In Taoist terms, the elements are not imagined as states of matter so much as processes or active principles or seasonal phases of a (cool-temperate) climate, with transitional 'earth'

65

interphases: *wood, spring, growth / earth, flowering / fire, summer, maturing / earth, ripening / metal, autumn, harvest / earth, dormancy / water, winter, death / earth, sap-rise* – and then a season of growth once more. In the cycle of generation, wood feeds fire; fire creates the ash that builds earth; earth yields metal ore; metal salts enrich water; water nourishes woody growth. There are non-generative, controlling or destructive cycles too: tree-roots disrupt earth; earth dams water; water antagonises fire; fire melts metal; metal cuts wood.

Destruction, nourishment, generation, control. Here, metal of the invaders brought destruction – guns and axes against flesh and wood – and also a means of resistance, changing hands, and of survival through long winters after the endings of worlds.

Still haunted by my own family history, I'm reading Patrick Hickey's *Famine in West Cork*, which deals with the years 1800–52, the interval that prepared the way for catastrophe as well as the period of *an Gorta Mór* – the Great Hunger.[13] Hickey describes the start of the century as a time of prosperity for landlords and tenant farmers who could export grain and fish and beef and butter at high prices to feed the armies of the Napoleonic Wars. The landless poor increased in numbers, their food supply guaranteed by the potato crop and money for rent coming in from steady employment in the workforce of the landed classes. When the fighting ended after the Battle of Waterloo in 1815, prices crashed and farmers could no longer afford to pay labourers, but rents and taxes remained high. Famine was never far away – in the hard winters of 1816 and 1822 and the cholera epidemic of 1832, many thousands died of the diseases that shadow malnutrition. Then for two years in a row from 1845, a strange blight rotted most of the potato crop and death by frank starvation, fever and dysentery was assured for between one and two million, in the presence of a British free-trade policy that refused interference in market prices for food. I find myself scanning descriptions of those years, seeking my people among the desperate crowds – those who died of starvation-induced heart failure in make-work road gangs (*if any man will not work, neither let him eat*) and those who were their overseers; those guarding the government food stores and those breaking in; those who tore off roofs to evict dying tenants and those whose bodies rotted with the shells of their houses.

By January of 1847, mortality rates in Ireland had so shocked even hardline free-trade advocates in the British government that parliament passed the Temporary Relief Act, allowing food to be distributed free or at prices the poor could afford – effective only until the September harvest. Though hunger-related diseases continued to kill thousands each year well into the 1850s and social devastation was complete in many places, the respite provided by the Relief Act, along with a lessening in the virulence of the blight, eased the grip of famine.

That was a time of hunger throughout Europe. Poor farmers everywhere had become dependent on the abundance provided by potatoes and were devastated when the new blight blasted their crops. The Napoleonic Wars left all sides destitute, stripping the countryside of supplies and inflating prices. Millions poured out, as those who could 'pay for the steam' took ship for America and Canada and Australia and Aotearoa New Zealand, in seaworthy vessels and in coffin ships, just as today they scatter from the war zones of North Africa and the Middle East.

Spring deepens. Up here on the ridge, growth begins a couple of weeks later than it does at sea level, even though we have fewer frosts than in the valleys because the cold air pours down, away from us. Waves of blossom pass over the fruit trees, followed by a flush of leaves. The almond-scented flowers of the cherry plums and damsons, greengages and prunes are finished now and so are the apricots and the fishy-smelling pears. Quinces and cherries and apples are in bloom but buds are still forming on the little medlar that was broken in half by the wind last year. Elders and hawthorns brighten to white. New leaves open on the English oaks, leaf sprouts lengthen on the walnuts. The chestnuts and the young hornbeam unfold their green concertinas to the light; leaf buds on the birches and lindens are beginning to move.

With the welcome swallows, into this flourishing landscape have come cuckoo-shrikes, shining cuckoos, grey fantails; pallid cuckoos repeat their maddening scales; swamp harriers quarter the paddocks in search of plover chicks and beat over the rushes at the edge of the dam for ducklings. Everywhere a frenzy of pairing and nesting: a bronzewing pigeon broadcasts its muffled *oom-oom-oom* from the litter of dried seed-pods under the wattles; yellow wattlebirds hurl endearment-curses at each other as they chase among the flowering branches; from a eucalypt a pardalote calls, tiny and startlingly loud like a gumnut with a megaphone – *Seeyou! Seeyou! Seeyou! Seeyou!* A blue wren doggedly fights its reflection in the side mirror of my car until I put a paper bag over the glass. Honeyeaters and grey robins and thornbills have already raised their first nestlings ahead of the cuckoos.

Like my mother's people who fled Ireland, my father's Scottish and English and German great-grandparents – *blacksmith, weaver, carpenter, soldier* – were among the nineteenth-century migrants who left Europe, displaced and displacing. Spat out like lava, each human wave burns, cools, weathers to earth and ore, part of a new community, a new life. Here we are. Each moment interleaves generation and destruction, *laminae* hammered out – forge-tool, sword and ploughshare. Finished in the water tub that stands always nearby.

Awakened

Thoughts like birds
in a hedgerow I did not plant...
these leaves, this cloud of wings,
our cries that make a shape

A shining cuckoo flew into the windowpane and broke its neck. The bird was one of a pair that had been chasing headlong through the garden; I was outside behind the house but I knew the sound as soon as I heard it. This not-seeing-the-window-glass doesn't often happen now – most birds seem to have mapped the place and its mysteries (and I leave the windows uncleaned much of the time), although some remain puzzled and infuriated by their reflections. But now and then a new arrival like the cuckoo is caught unawares.

When I was a child in the North Island of Aotearoa New Zealand, my father once brought home a fan-tailed cuckoo that had been killed in the same way. We lived next door to his workplace at a hydroelectric substation and the bird flew against a window of the transformer repair room. Like the shining cuckoo, there was no mark of injury beyond the lolling head. Full of fascination and grief I touched the astonishing satin of its feathers. This was in the 1960s, and the combined effects of deforestation and DDT meant that already there were not many land bird species beyond those introduced from Europe and

Asia – sparrows, blackbirds, starlings, finches, mynas. Among those endemic to New Zealand, we sometimes saw or heard a tui or a korimako – nectar-eaters that had been able to adapt to garden environments – and swamp birds such as pukeko still lived in the remaining wetlands; an occasional harrier hovered overhead. The others were elusive or vanishingly rare. I was amazed to see the cuckoo, a visitor from the lost world of my father's childhood, before land clearing for farming had reached its limit.

On 17 January 1770, while the *Endeavour* was anchored in Totaranui/Queen Charlotte Sound at the northern tip of the South Island, Joseph Banks made a now-famous journal entry:[14]

I was awakened by the singing of the birds ashore, from whence we are distant not a quarter of a mile. Their numbers were certainly very

71

great...and made, perhaps, the most melodious wild music I have ever heard, almost imitating small bells, but with the most tunable silver sound imaginable...they begin to sing about one or two in the morning, and continue till sunrise...

The previous day's entry (16 January) contains the following account:

After dinner we went in the boat towards a cove about two miles from the ship...where we found a small family of Indians...employed, when we came ashore, in dressing their provisions, which were a dog, at that time buried in their oven. Nearby were many provision baskets. Looking carelessly upon one of these, we by accident observed two bones pretty cleanly picked, which, as appeared upon examination, were undoubtedly human bones...[with] marks of their having been dressed on the fire; the meat was not entirely picked off them, and on the gristly ends...were evident marks of teeth...On asking the people what bones they were, they answered: 'The bones of a man.' – 'And have you eaten the flesh?' – 'Yes.'...'Whom, then, do you eat?' – 'Those who are killed in war.' – 'And who was the man whose bones these are?' – 'Five days ago a boat of our enemies came into this bay, and of them we killed seven, of whom the owner of these bones was one.'

Within days of making landfall three months earlier, the crew of the *Endeavour* had shot and killed Maori who threatened them as they came ashore. And so Europeans added themselves to the cycle of enmity. Maori–European tensions continued to rise as more and more land was alienated, culminating in the Land Wars of the 1860s and 1870s.

My maternal grandparents' families emigrated from Ireland in the 1870s and 1880s, leaving behind the ruined social and economic framework that was a legacy of the Great Hunger. After my grandparents married in 1893 they moved inland to farm, in the then-remote Pohangina Valley in the Manawatu district of the North Island. There's a photograph of them outside their house, built by my grandmother's brother, with a hillside of shattered stumps behind them.

When my grandfather was away – road-building to earn extra money or drinking in the nearest town – my grandmother was frightened to stay alone in the house with the children. She took them outside to sleep whenever she could, onto the newly cleared ground. As a child I was puzzled by this story and scornful about what I perceived as my grandmother's timidity, such was the silence into which our past was swallowed. I didn't connect her fear with the Land Wars so recently fought, though I grew up in an area that had been fiercely contested, and where, in 1864, a force of 230 Ngai te Rangi fought off 1,700 British soldiers who, in addition to their muskets, were backed up by seventeen artillery pieces – a level of bombardment not to be seen again until World War I, such was the fear engendered by the fighting strength of Maori.

If I was ever taught this history, I remained insensible to it. The past was shut off in amnesic silence that had its origins not only in immediate colonial experience; along with whatever anxieties they brought with them regarding Maori, immigrants from Ireland like my grandparents would also have carried famine stories – never to be passed on directly – relating to the human capacity for ruthlessness when survival is at stake, such as the rumours and second-hand reports of cannibalism from those years. Just as haunting must have been experiences of choosing one's own life over the life of others or choosing whom to support and whom to abandon. Gnawed bones are

ANGELA ROCKEL

our inheritance; we may countenance horrors in order to keep ourselves and those who are close to us alive in times of crisis, or when, as throughout the colonies of empire, we are caught in some cultural-historical machine that asks to be fed living flesh. Here in Australia, numb aversion also continues for all these reasons.

Full moon. Rain has cleared a haze of smoke blown south from fires that began a month ago – so early! – in New South Wales; light, like visible quiet, floods the landscape. The quolls that live in the ceiling go out over the iron and down our roof-access plank to the ground on their nocturnal business; hours go by. Then as the moon descends towards the western horizon, into the silence come the first birdcalls – blue wrens stir in the grevilleas planted round the house, wattlebirds clear their throats, cuckoos start up and a blackbird sweetly defines its territory from the tip of one of the macrocarpas in the windbreak.

We hit the unthinkable and fling away, stunned – there are capacities that never recover; we learn bluster and avoidance. Some trauma is heritable, transmissible, acquired as modes of speech and silence. After an age of destruction, a distancing numbness takes hold; speaking and listening and thinking become difficult or impossible, and the past is reduced to a record of events situated *elsewhere*, unconnected.

With luck and attention, some healing can also be learned and passed on, returned to the world from the inexhaustible well. We wake in the night, our broken hearts composed once more as new thoughts come like birdsong out of the dark.

Souls

All week the night sky shakes like firelight

Summer solstice. The blue gums are flowering and suddenly my workspace fills with the smell of honey as the swarm in the wall ferries in astringent, toffee-coloured nectar to the comb. A strange season, still rainy, still lush after a wet, dark spring. I'm grateful for the cool of it, watching mainland temperatures rise into the red zone day after day. Everything flourishes – rose petals scatter, fruit swells and the green of deciduous trees deepens to full shade. Eucalypts shed their outer bark; split by rainfed growth, it piles up around them, the makings of a bonfire. The days are long now and far into the evening the sky stays bright. Venus hangs sharp in the west while the east darkens and each night a little boobook owl calls but no one answers yet.

The same warmth that created a typhoon in the Philippines brings cyclones spooling across the Torres Strait – continent-wide bands of moisture stream southwards over the mainland to be sucked into the westerly flow that crosses Tasmania. Cloaking mist draws in from the east as anticlockwise weather systems pass over and curl back onshore from the Tasman

Sea. Cloud descends to ground level, looms purple in banks and shoulders that appear and disappear in the depths of the valley, then out of the cloud comes thunder and all is unified in steady, soft, continuous rain. When the cloud lifts, the sky clears to stinging heat that quickly burns pale skin. Ultraviolet radiation is in the extreme range now, as the hole that forms in the ozone layer over Antarctica in spring disperses and widens to take in these latitudes – our protective screen is very thin. Ice clouds form in the polar stratosphere during months of winter darkness; as soon as returning sun hits them, these crystals make a perfect substrate for a solar-driven reaction in which chlorine breaks up ozone molecules. The hole keeps its position over the pole for about two months, peaking in October, before dispersing as an area of thinned ozone coverage that extends northward as temperatures begin to rise and new reserves of air are drawn into the polar vortex.[15] It's bad timing – spring growth is exposed when it is most tender.

My mind is on the southern skies for another reason too – I've just signed up for a Meteorological Bureau aurora alert that will let me know when there's been a solar flare and/or when geomagnetic activity has increased to a certain level. I've had my first email letting me know that geomagnetic activity has risen above the normal range, but the night sky has mostly been cloudy, and even when it clears I've been unable to see any brightening that can compete with the moon.

We're in a good spot to see the aurora – 43 degrees south and away from the lights of the town. It's easy to miss it, though – it can come and go unnoticed unless I happen to step outside in the night at the right time. It's a strange sensation to discover, after the event, that the sky has been hung with flickering curtains of light while I slept. And strange to think of the Earth on its course, bathed and buffeted by the solar wind, a stream of plasma, stripped-down atomic components pouring out from the sun. When it meets the magnetic field generated by Earth's metallic core, it compresses the side of the magnetosphere nearest the sun and on the other side, blows it out into space in a cometlike tail that extends to a distance of more than a hundred times the planet's diameter. When charged particles of the plasma stream are caught in the polar magnetic fields they cause oxygen and nitrogen to fluoresce like the gas in a neon tube – bands and arcs of auroral light appear. If there's a storm on the sun and a flare comes our way, this light becomes more intense and widespread and can be seen at latitudes far from the pole.

As a child in the North Island walking at night with my mother, I once saw an aurora – a red glow on the horizon that might have been a diffuse and distant searchlight. Mysterious and exciting, I knew it was very unusual to see it so far north. But the first time I really saw those lights was soon after arriving in Tasmania – I think it was at about this time of year. Sometime before midnight, on my way to my room which was separate from the house, I closed the kitchen door behind me and walked outside to find half the night sky, from the southern horizon to the zenith, bannered with pulsing folds and ripples of light. I'd seen images of the aurora and this didn't look like any of them. It was like standing inside a wondering mind as thoughts and sensations passed through it.

I've always been stolidly literal-minded and sensate; I've never had an out-of-body experience. But I did feel then and have felt again whenever I've seen those lights that they image the working dream of the planet as it conjures us up, wondrous and shot through with nightmare, nourished and scorched by a

77

wind that blows from outside. They give me a sense that in our very materiality, all creatures are souls, appearing as we do from the matrix so briefly and disappearing into it once more like a shift of light. And in a kind of mirroring of this experience, some of us behave as if in truth our souls are outside us and the world speaks our inner life. My father, inarticulate about his own interiority, pointed, mostly wordlessly, to birds and insects, stones and stars and music and the texture of things in what I think of as a lifelong pattern of acknowledgement and identification.

Sometimes the world seems to return the gesture. The day after my father died, a male fantail accompanied me, not just catching insects stirred up by my few steps through its territory but staying with me all the way around a circuit of the park near my parents' house, flying up to look into my face again and again. (*I once saw a fantail's nest,* my father said, *in a low branch over a stream. I watched it every day. The male used to shuffle his mate aside to take his turn sitting. And he saw off birds twice his size if they wandered too close – I'd hear his beak snapping, chasing them out of sight, down along the creek.*) Again, years later, as I prepared to go to J's funeral, I heard a wild clamouring like geese calling and looked out to see a pair of paradise ducks land on the chimneypot of the house next door, where they sat and stared in at me before flying off. (*In another life,* J said, *I'd have been an ornithologist – I love them for themselves and for their names. I chose my house partly for the birds along the river and estuary.*) When M died, a thrush came to sing in the top of the pear tree, looking back at me with his bright eye. (*See this one?* M said, pointing to the bird's image among the photographs we'd put beside his bed. *I had to wait but it came close enough in the end!*)

If these things are only coincidence, I'm still consoled by them. The ones I love remain alive for me this way, in my mind and senses and thus in the mind of the world. I can hold them in my heart and also acknowledge that they are changed; no longer as I knew them but becoming something else, they go on.

Year 2

Damage

Anoche cuando dormía
soñé ¡bendita ilusión!
que una colmena tenía
dentro de mi corazón;
y las doradas abejas
iban fabricando en él,
con las amarguras viejas,
blanca cera y dulce miel

Antonio Machado[16]

Last night while I was sleeping
I dreamed, (blessed illusion),
that I had a beehive inside my heart;
and the golden bees were making
white wax and sweet honey
from my old bitterness.

The first hot days have come to the island, though not the heatwave that was forecast (and nothing like the endless-seeming sequence of days in the 40s endured by some mainland states). Such a contrast with this time last year, when parched country up and down the east shimmered and exploded in flame under hot winds. This year, week after week, cool, moist air has blown in off the Southern Ocean bringing rain. Fire-adapted plants in last year's burnt zones have put out shoots, some birds and animals have returned and people have begun to rebuild their houses, communities, livelihoods, or they've gone, discouraged, leaving another generation, another wave of newcomers to take their place.

Till now, it's been cold enough to wear layers of wool as I go out walking in the mornings. Buds still haven't opened on the December-flowering pohutukawa a friend from Aotearoa New Zealand gave me; the pumpkins aren't putting out runners yet and the cherries are late – backpackers who arrive each year to work the orchard along the ridge only began their daily trek from the youth hostel to the rows of trees a couple of weeks ago. Long watershoots have appeared on the banksias; leaf tips are sprouting on the eucalypts. Everything is still green; cattle loll about, glossy, contented, *fat as mud*, as people say here. Till now, hay has stood uncut in the paddocks, too wet to mow – with this first heat, suddenly there's a scramble to bale it while there's still goodness in it. And as all the new growth hardens and dries we begin to scan the sky anxiously for smoke.

The big blue-tongue lizard that spent last summer foraging for snails and strawberries and slaters in the polytunnel greenhouse has reappeared to take a berry from my hand. This morning I met what is probably her offspring beetling along beside the house, trying to get away from me, I thought, until I saw the young tiger snake tasting the air in the lizard's tracks. Bright-skinned, the snake's pattern of yellowish banding showed vivid against a brown background; later both pattern and ground will darken to a damask effect, visible only in certain lights, before the skin is shed and the markings become clear again for a time. It saw me and turned back – a few minutes later it was metres up, exploring the topmost twigs of a shrubby hakea. Birds are still nesting and frogs and skinks and mice have been plentiful in this season of rainy abundance – the snakes are doing well; they can swim and climb, they nose their way into rock piles and burrows.

In a good year, predator numbers increase with available food; all day I hear alarm calls from wrens and blackbirds and honeyeaters. Ravens patrol the airspace above their nesting trees, hurling themselves upwards with frantic cries to intercept and harry the pair of wedge-tailed eagles that hunt the valley slopes to feed this year's chick. A young falcon begs noisily as it hop-glides from tree to tree. The delicate-looking quolls that have made their dens in the ceiling are out all night feasting on pasture grubs and unlucky small animals. Probably related females, they thump, heavy-footed, back across the roof at intervals towards dawn to throw themselves into sleep – or so I read their sudden silence apart from an exchange of sneeze-like hisses if their paths cross on the way to their separate nests.

Bees are working a flush of white clover and blackberry and false dandelion, carrying nectar and pollen to the hives for themselves and the thousands of larvae hatched from eggs laid by the queen. When they run out of room to build new comb, they attach a big, bean-shaped cell to the edge of the brood and feed the larva ensconced there a supercharged diet, *royal jelly*, which turns it into a queen. Just before the new queen is due to hatch (if the beekeeper hasn't removed the cell), the old queen flies, taking half the workers with her, leaving the new queen to emerge and continue in her stead. The flown queen lands somewhere close – usually on a twig or branch of a nearby tree and all the others cluster round her; they'll stay for anything from hours to days while scouts go out to look for another

85

nest site – a tree hollow, a wall cavity. During this interval, if they've landed in an accessible spot, it's possible to shake or scoop the swarm into a container for transfer to a hive box.

The bees in the wall of my workspace swarmed while I was away at Christmas; T caught this and another swarm that flew out with their queen in the days that followed – but I had no spare boxes ready. The boxes I thought would be okay are in bad shape; wood rots in the muggy 32–35 degrees Celsius of the colony – not much less than human body heat. I caught a swarm one year that had settled on the ground, and after I picked up the humming mass, the flattened grass where they had been was warm, as if an animal had rested there.

Hastily assembled boxes are stacked in the living room – full-depth *supers* for brood and shallower *half-supers* and *ideals* for honey – along with the rectangular frames that sit inside them, strung with fine, banjo-twanging wire that supports sheets of hexagon-stamped foundation wax on which the bees build their comb. The white, protective beekeeper's overall with its black mask hangs from a chairback like an abandoned chrysalis. We've given the new swarms a freshly made brood box and an extra super each, and they're already drawing comb, ripening honey and hatching brood. The hives sit under the pine hedge at the vegetable garden, facing east, sheltered from the prevailing winds and hot afternoon sun.

These bees are descendants of a swarm given to T by a neighbour forty years ago, and they in turn are likely descended from bees kept by previous generations of T's family. His mother told me: *My father used keep bees in an apple box. In February-time, he'd cut out the comb and hang it up in a hessian bag to drip. I didn't like them bees buzzin. Oh I was frightened they'd get in my hair!*

The first European honeybees were brought to Australia in the 1820s. Asian bees have also become established in the warmer parts of the mainland. Here in Tasmania, bumblebees appeared about twenty years ago, thought to have been brought accidentally from Aotearoa New Zealand via a nest stowed away on a yacht; from that one source, they spread quickly throughout the island. There are hundreds of species of native bees in Australia, with which the introduced species compete for nectar and pollen.

The days of relatively uncomplicated beekeeping are almost certainly numbered here. *Varroa destructor* mites (like a *Harry Potter* nightmare) have wiped out honeybee colonies all over the world, since a mutation occurred in the 1960s that allowed the parasite to jump from its original host, a relatively resistant species of bee (*Apis cerana*), to the European honeybee (*Apis mellifera*), which had very little resistance. The mutation is thought to have happened in the Philippines, where introduced European bees were brought into close contact with local *Apis cerana* swarms. Australia and some countries in Central Africa are the only places where the mites have not yet spread to. It's only a matter of time before they find their way across the Timor Sea or the Torres Strait to Australia or are imported in beekeeping supplies. Indonesia and West Papua were affected early; Papua New Guinea has been affected since the 1980s and Aotearoa New Zealand since 2000.

Mites get into hives when affected bees are accidentally brought in by beekeepers or when they stray in from other swarms. A female mite hides herself under the surface of food put by worker bees in the bottom of a brood cell containing an egg. The mite stays submerged and puts up a tube to breathe through – in this way she can't be seen and removed by nest-cleaners. Worker bees close the cell; the bee egg hatches and the bee larva begins to eat the food left for it; this frees the mite who emerges to feed on the larva's body fluids and lay her eggs in the cell. When they hatch, the five or six young mites also feed on the larva; when it matures they emerge with it, ready to begin the cycle once more. Mite numbers increase exponentially and the swarm weakens and dies. Wild honeybee swarms disappear and apiarists who go down the chemical path in an attempt to stop infestation in their hives fight a war of attrition as mites become resistant to one product after another.

There's something horrifying to me about parasites – their furtive sapping of life and energy seems worse than frank predation, somehow. And parasites on *bees* – an acrid incursion from the underworld into sweet sunlight. But the game of parasite and host, predator and prey is never over. Already some honeybees have developed resistance, learning to detect reproductive-phase mites (by pheromone signature?) and remove them; beekeepers are speeding up this process by selective breeding.[17] In the interim, thousands of local species of bees all over the world get another go, free of competition from honeybees.

It's a touch-and-go foxtrot of damage, collapse, resistance, recovery, back and forth across balance points that allow all sides to go on, each forcing the other to learn new tricks. Stark oppositions become less clear; bands and braids of the pattern deepen to a damask sheen, *there, not-there, there, not-there*, as secret worlds come to light and creatures of sunlight learn subtlety. Under pressure, something breaks or emerges, something dies or flies out – perhaps it comes to the same thing; mined from inside, the work of transformation has to begin.

The turn

this long wait for rain at the door that swings
back and forth in the wind

At the start of the month I'm uneasy, all the parts of me
ragged in the looming blue of summer, oils going up from
the eucalypts, waiting. High pressure systems roll in, each one
formed when a lofted tower of tropical air cools as it rises and
so begins to fall, stripped of moisture – a clear, dense column
that presses down and blows the rain away; a lens hundreds of
kilometres wide that focuses sun. All across Victoria, fires burn.

There's been a forest fire on the other side of the valley; for
days, helicopters water-bombed its edges while smoke billowed
up over the ridge. Insect-small in the landscape, the aircraft
hovered over the river to scoop up their loads, then laboured,
rotors thudding, up the flank of the hill to reach the hidden
flames. Are the embers really quenched? A stump can smoulder
down into its roots and flare weeks later when the wind is right.

If the fire doesn't come today. If I can settle for a while
under the windbreak pines, those pillars of incense in whose
shelter the crackle of my disturbance subsides. Birdsong mends
the morning; a family of robins combs the barley grass under
the trees for insects and a flock of thornbills works the low

branches. Hatched from a nest high overhead, this year's brown falcon fledgling lands on a twig and calls to its parents; when it gets no answer it flies to feed, hunched, feathers ruffled, on a wallaby carcass in the paddock below. And bringing temporary respite, a breeze draws in off the sea and blows back the fringe of grass from the hot face of the hillside. I walk back down to the house, which is cave-like under its wide eaves, its heavy curtains drawn, and sit in the dim kitchen podding peas, soothed by the feel of their squeaky rosary under my thumbs. Summer fruits and vegetables are in – apricots and greengages glow, magnified, in jars of syrup; tomatoes boil down for sauce; cucumbers ferment in brine.

Separate from the house, my workspace is not so easy to keep cool. Uninsulated, it becomes stiflingly hot in the afternoons even with all the blinds and curtains closed. The desk-skink is

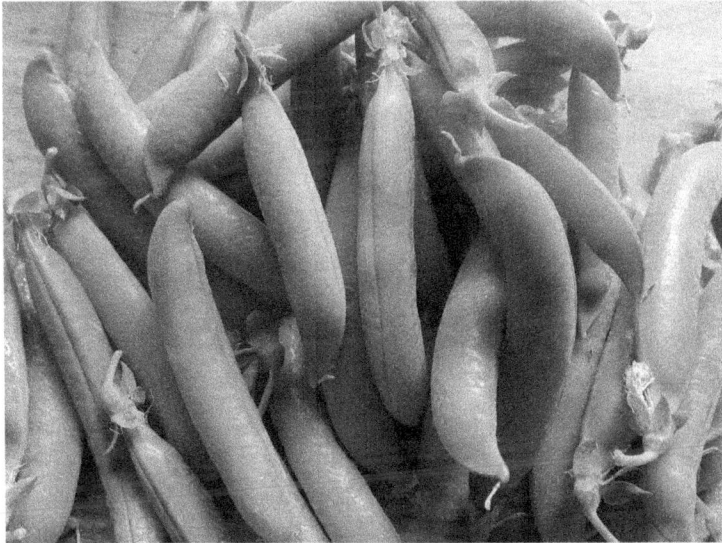

active all day and into the night; when I take the cloth from the keyboard and screen each morning, it skitters from the darkness at the back of the scanner's paper tray like an irate apartment-dweller coming to check out a street disturbance. Yesterday it climbed to the top of the pencil-heap and regarded me; I rested my open hand on the desk – the skink climbed down and scrambled to examine my fingers and lick the salt from my palm.

Heat continues to build and finally, as air sucks across the differential from high to low pressure, a fierce westerly front blasts through, announced by a clap of thunder and a spattering of horizontal rain. Thick branches of tall trees whip like saplings, and anything cracked or top-heavy breaks and falls. Green fruit litters the ground and two fat bronzewing pigeon chicks, stuck with wispy comb-overs of down, lie dead under the macrocarpa hedge, blown from their flimsy platform of twigs. Nests are dislodged everywhere but perhaps it's not such bad timing – many of them are empty, the young birds flown. Boats capsize or drag their moorings and smash ashore; roads are blocked and powerlines are cut by fallen trees, but the fire across the river doesn't reignite. The storm is over in a few hours.

And just like that, the season has turned. A few days after the storm, it rains properly – 30 millimetres, more than an inch in the old measurements – as a curl of cloud reaches south from a cyclone over the Northern Territory. Everything breathes out; my heart no longer punches in my chest. Wrens and honeyeaters bathe in droplets showering from foliage; they dive among the wet leaves as through the waters of a fountain. Morning fogs and days of cool sunlight follow; it seems we've survived another summer.

In the wet, early apples sweeten and plump – Gravensteins, Cox's Orange – the white pips darkening in their starry hearts. Flocks, *murmurations* of starlings sweep into the elder hedge and fill it with whistling, shortwave static as they feed on the ripe black fruit and stain the ground under the trees with purple shit. Scarlet robins chase in twos and threes, down from their summer haunts in the high country. With nesting over, some migratory birds are leaving already – most of the grey fantails have gone, and the cuckoos. Forest ravens gather in bleached pastures that have tinged overnight, it seems, with green, to dismantle dried cowpats in search of beetles and worms emerging from the softened ground.

With their young safely out of the nest, the ravens seem to have declared a watchful truce with the eagles, which have come to feed on roadkill carrion I picked up and heaved over the fence into the paddock, where creatures attracted to it – by night, by day – won't be hit themselves. *Carrion*, from *caro*, meaning flesh, cognate with *carnal* and *crone*, and also, I can't help hoping, with *carus*, meaning dear one, and *karis*, grace. *Full of the only grace we can know, the dear flesh comes to its end.* And this wallaby-or-possum flesh comes to a sky burial with the birds. There's no fledgling with the eagle pair – perhaps some mishap or malice has ended its life.

Now is the time to take honey, if I'm going to, before the days get too cool, while the bees can still replenish their stolen stores – but probably I won't. There's not much there this year; most of the summer was too wet and cold to allow the workers to forage, and when the heat came, what blossom there was quickly scorched and dried. And because I was away at a critical time, I didn't remove the queen cells to prevent successive swarmings, so the colonies have been weakened.

I learned a new word – the second or third swarm from a hive in a single season is called a *castling*, the same name that's used for a miscarried foetus.

Hunkered down in a season first cold-sodden, then parched, things ripen or exhaust themselves; sweetness can fail. Then the storm, engine of damage and renewal, crashes in to move the year along, leaving carrion and nectar in its wake. Now the stringybark eucalypts are budding, and here and there a branch comes into flower as stamens unfurl, filled with new moisture pushing up from the roots. Perhaps the bees will have a chance to catch up after all.

Donna donna

In the winds of the equinox, all our flags are ribbons

Until I was ten, we lived in the last house on our side of the main road out of town. On the other side of the road the houses continued but on our side it was us, then the racecourse, a sawmill, and after that, farms and remnant bushland. Where our house was, farmland had only recently been overrun by the town. There were paddocks behind us where tart-sweet, misshapen navel oranges, a local variety, could be found on half a dozen twisted and lichen-encrusted trees, the remains of an orchard. Around the corner, a block or so back from the main road, was an abattoir where trucks still brought their loads of cattle and sheep to the killing pens; sometimes the oily stink of rendered blood-and-bone drifted over the house. Just along from the abattoir, in a paddock donated by the owners of a subdivided farm, sat the little, early 1960s asbestos-sheet church where we went to Mass. The road there was still fronted in places by the remains of a fiercely thorny field hedge of sloes.

The church was built like a prefab classroom, with altar and crucifix taking the place of teacher's desk and blackboard, and stations of the cross around the walls instead of student artwork.

It was dedicated to St John Fisher, tutor of Henry VIII and chancellor of Cambridge University, beheaded for opposing the king. On the left near the altar was a statue of Mary and on the right, a statue of the saint, a worried-looking man in a red-brown gown and cap, clean-shaven, with a bluish five o'clock shadow painted onto his plaster cheeks and chin. A career academic who brought the scholar Erasmus to Cambridge as professor of divinity and Greek, he was an odd choice of patron for a working-class suburban church in twentieth-century Aotearoa New Zealand. But of course he was not chosen for his scholarship – rather, he was singled out for his loyalty in the face of the reforming revolution overturning Catholic society in sixteenth-century Europe. A reminder to members of the Catholic diaspora in the Antipodes to stay true.

Church authority went unchallenged, for the most part, while I was growing up – in fear and hope we had given over our minds and hearts and so we were easily bound. Abuses were carefully framed as matters of personal shame and failure – usually ours – and though we felt the injustices keenly, we were silent – or we spoke in symptoms. The institution itself was hedged about, never identified as a locus of corruption, and examples of heroic suffering in its defence, like that of John Fisher, were everywhere offered as guarantee of its worthiness. Now, another revolution is taking place as institutions undergo reform once more, called to account for their part in fostering and condoning abuse, and for blocking attempts to seek reparation.

The little church is long gone, but sloe and barberry and gorse still sprout, just as they do in Tasmania, brought in by nineteenth-century colonists along with other species, propagated over thousands of years for food and healing, comfort and protection, some of them fulfilling all these needs at once. Hawthorns were planted as hedging and their berries made a remedy for heart disease; seedlings were also used as rootstock for the earliest plantings of pome fruits. In the old orchard paddock near our house here, a huge butter pear sprouts a collar of thorn from its roots. Once grown, fruitwood could be cut back and regrafted over and over as old varieties fell out of favour and were replaced – sometimes at the base of an orchard limb, above the rootstock and below the current graft, you can still find a Five-crown apple or a Lalla or a Cleo, yellow and popping with juice.

Among introduced species, some, like blackberry and gorse, quickly spread calamitously here in Tasmania. Others have not grown so rampantly and can be found here and there on roadsides or around old house sites: gallica roses; pheasant's eye narcissus; *Gladiolus tristis*; sloe bushes with their tiny, black-skinned fruit covered in white bloom, and their descendants, the damson plums; mulberry; medlar; barberry; holly; hawthorn; elder. They compete with native species and can play havoc with ecosystems, but also provide food and habitat and create a protective environment for young forest trees, as can be seen after wildfires when blackberry thickets are quick to establish themselves and, in their protection, wattles shoot up; as the wattles mature they shade out the blackberries and in turn provide cover for eucalypts – which shade out and replace the short-lived wattles, until fire takes the eucalypts once more.

The days are shortening fast, already matched by night at the blustery equinox and now overtaken, as the southern hemisphere swings away from the sun. It's safe to light a fire outside and I'm making the most of the interval before it gets too cold to enjoy the firebath and cook in the outdoor oven, unused since spring – I lifted away its wooden door and found a mouse nest inside, a little heap of straw and shredded newspaper.

In the hedgerows, the damsons have finally sweetened and the sloes are ripe – the neighbours have picked their crop to make almond-astringent gin liqueur; hawthorn berries are red.

It has rained. Perhaps there will be mushrooms out of the still-warm ground. During the summer months, many kinds of fungi extend hairlike mycelial networks through the soil, ready with their miraculous hydraulics when moisture does come, pushing up fruiting bodies overnight or fattening secretly, underground. Some of the dozen or so inoculated truffle oaks we planted four years ago are beginning to develop a vegetation-free area of 'burn' around the root-run, indicating that, in preparation for fruiting this winter, mycorrhizal growth may have established itself. It's an ancient symbiotic agreement between many plants and the fungi that live on (and sometimes in) their roots. The plant gains extra absorptive capacity by using the fungal network as an extension of its root system and the fungus gains access to nutrients in the plant's sap.

And if truffles do appear, there's a new addition to the household who might – who knows? – be able to help us find them. She's a two-month-old pup, a soft-furred, smiling-mouthed, golden-coloured mongrel with a wrinkled face and button eyes. Adopted from a nearby animal sanctuary, she's already showing herself to be intelligent, quick to respond and keen to be part of the social order here. Maybe she will learn to sniff out truffles – although with so few trees, we will probably be able to do that for ourselves, searching on hands and knees for the buried fruits.

I was wrong about the eagles – they have raised a chick this year. Out on the hill, watching the adult pair slide northward upriver like beads on a windy abacus, I heard, off to the south, the soft, yelping, kelp-gull call of a third; a few moments later the youngster came into view. It hadn't, as I had feared, failed somehow in learning to fly or hunt; it hadn't been shot. Now it comes down alone to feed, with a flock of ravens in deafening attendance. But they don't attack, even when it's on the ground, vulnerable, and there are dozens of them.

A few nights ago I dreamt I began a journey, from a house between the abattoir and the church in that first neighbourhood at the edge of town. Thorny and fruitful, we sprout where we're set down and enter the endless, shifting play between slaughter and flight, terror and longing. Creating meaning, we cast our shadows without even trying, as language attaches itself and runs its roots through everything – neural pathways that grow a world of opposites. Between submission and revolt, we strengthen those in power with our sappy belief then watch them teeter as doubt matures. And each night the soul holds up these pieces of the world, shows the monstrous treasure whole, remembered and contained in a mortal truce. It offers a third way, and in that space between the rootstock and the graft above, forgotten fruit appears; what was formidable loosens its grip for a time.

Red

There is a road. It goes down into silence.
Syllables of my name roll underfoot,
the known ways smashed.

Days shorten and cool. The sun is lower in the sky – there's less light and what there is falls obliquely, travelling further through the atmosphere before it reaches the ground. In the process, the blue, high-energy end of the light spectrum used by plants for photosynthesis is filtered out. Without it, everything slows. Deciduous species stop producing chlorophyll; green gives way to other underlying pigments as sap no longer flows to and from leaves and the corky abscission layer at the base of each stem readies itself for rupture. Bright carotenes begin to glow yellow and orange; red anthocyanins appear as sugar levels rise; already, leaves on some of the grapevines are green-veined carmine and the little hornbeam behind the house is a cloud of yellow.

This spectral shift is mirrored in the skins and flesh of many fruits. The lovely purple-flowered, black-seeded *rocoto* chillies have ripened from green to black to red or clear orange on plants that live for a decade or more and grow about two metres tall. They fruit in all seasons but especially in autumn; the flesh is variably hot, depending on how much sun there's been, but the seeds are always fiery. Sauce tomatoes are ready too, by the bucketful. I bring them to the boil in a preserving pan to soften them, and when they're cool, run the fruit through my fingers to take out as many skins as I can, then strain out the seeds. It's a dreamy sort of job. Boiled down with a splash of olive oil, the pulp that's left is free of bitterness the seeds impart.

In the orchard, the nectarines and clingstone peaches are finished and most of the pears, and the quinces and mid-season apples are fragrant; European wasps swarm on fallen fruit. All summer the trees have used the energy of sunlight falling on their leaves to power the production of food in the form of starch. As seeds mature, starches break down to simpler sugars and plants bargain for mobility and a fertile start in the dung of creatures who accept the offer of ripened fruit.

Now towering pyrocumulus clouds go up from fires in logged-out forestry coupes. The wildfire season is over and, instead of water, helicopters drop incendiaries around the edges of each coupe; as they flare and catch, the combined updraft sucks their flames inwards. They're burning bulldozed understorey and windrowed rainforest species not usable as paper pulp – the trashed surplus hurls skyward in smoke and gas and a thundercloud of moisture that was sap and blood. The fur of green, the skin of surface life, patched and charred. In the ash-bed, eucalypt seed will be sown. Fire-adapted species can survive this disturbance and even thrive, putting out shoots from lignotubers or epicormic buds; rainforest species cannot – it kills the ancient Gondwanan conifers and the ferns and understorey trees such as leatherwood, bee-fodder for fragrant honey.[18]

Fire undoes the bonds created in living things and returns their simplified compounds to the world. Once kindled to flashpoint by friction, detonation, electrical spark, whether as

the bud of flame at the end of a struck match or the explosion of a bomb, fire is self-propagating, limited only by availability of heat, fuel and oxygen. The team at the Alamo weren't sure that the chain reaction begun in the first atomic blast wouldn't ignite Earth's entire atmosphere.[19]

It's been a month of bloody skies – vermilion sunlight filtered through smoke, and then a pair of eclipses. At mid-month, the full moon was reddened by Earth's shadow and now as I write two weeks later, somewhere above clouds the dark moon is about to bite the disc of the sun. Angled at about 5 degrees, twice a month the moon's orbit around Earth intersects Earth's path around the sun so that sun, moon and Earth are in the same plane. Once, sometimes twice a year, the intersection happens at full moon and there's a lunar eclipse as Earth intervenes between sun and moon; if it happens at new moon, there's a solar eclipse as the moon comes between Earth and the sun.

These ascending and descending points of intersection are known as the *north node* and *south node* of the moon, potent for many cultures, imaged as head and tail of a light-devouring principle. This year, the eclipse fell on the full moon after the vernal equinox, marker of spring festivals of death and rebirth throughout the northern hemisphere – moon of Passover and Easter and Nauruz and Holi; the eclipse enacted and underlined their theme of winter darkness and the return of light.

As a child I loved entering into the detailed attention of naming – *lunar node, anthocyanin, abscission layer, lignotuber, equinox* – each word a careful, delighted touch that connected me with the world and shored up a cosmology in which I wanted to believe. Though I now understand the given categories and divisions within and between things to be a human story, naming still feels like a kind of worship, calling up the gods of parts and processes in which sweetness gathers and withdraws, as living wood returns to black powder of charcoal and the slick of bare rock, as ash leaps once more to shape the branches of a seedling tree.

Deep in the furls of a pattern close and huge, we angle ourselves towards light; not knowing what it is, we take it in, use it for our own devices, piece together divinities from what the world provides. With energy of the unnameable we make language-webs; they keep us warm and we sustain ourselves. But light has pulses of its own outside control and sometimes we ourselves stand in its way. Then the blue-white glow dims to red and stories falter, partial, no longer adequate. Swallowed by the dragon in whose gut all certainty and comprehension is undone, bonds break and fragments scatter; wordless, we witness the death of whatever has given meaning. In that pause – an age, an hour, a winter, a generation – no language yet exists. Terror and freedom. Light returns; words begin to rise and gather.

Even now

A passion of longing holds and rattles the whole brief encampment

Parrots and currawongs are eating the not-quite-ripe fruit from my one tree of late-season apples. They're tart-sweet Sturmer pippins; when stored properly, rather than rotting or going floury, they keep right through the winter. Their dense, chewy flesh dehydrates slightly and the skin wrinkles; the juice becomes more concentrated. When I was little, we had apple trees at home but no Sturmers – my mother's favourites. She used to send me to buy them when our own apples were finished; I chose the wrinkled ones when I could find them.

I've tried to wrap the tree in netting but it does more harm than good. The net catches on next year's fruit buds; silvereyes and honeyeaters that come to eat already-damaged fruit become entangled; parrots find ways in and out through any chink; and currawongs get in under the edges. In the end I tire of my attempts to keep the birds away, like some tin-pot Jehovah by whose decree good and evil enter the world. They already have knowledge and, to this, cunning has been added, learning to evade my self-interest. I remove the net and pick the apples, taking the role of transgressor for myself. Even though the fruit is really not mature, it will ripen in the box.

Leaf-fall continues. Cold nights and clear days brought intense colours this year – brilliant avenues of orange and gold in the cherry orchards, the apple-rows yellow, liquidambars in the old gardens around Hobart deep cerise-purple. Then after a day and a night of gales, many trees were bare. The oak outside my window clings to its brown leaves as usual. Everywhere, next year's leaf buds are already forming, tightly sealed in their resinous sheaths. Flowers on the wintersweet are pale-yellow spheres about to open; even before the shortest day, the air nearby will be filled with their scent, bright and cool, like olfactory sunlight. Flower buds form on the wattles and eucalypts too, and new leaves lengthen their filaments from the tips of stringybark twigs.

It's not much of a season for field mushrooms, but the purple discs of forest species appear under the eucalypts. Scarlet *Amanita* emerge under the birches and pines; something eats them, perhaps bettongs, whose diet of fungi may render them immune to the poison and may also explain their jittery, spaced-out demeanour. On expanses of rock and bark, tiny worlds of moss and lichen plump and grow vivid after dewy nights.

The sun shines obliquely. Winter is coming; the shortest day is almost here. As leaves on deciduous trees drop, pools of shade lessen and shrub thickets are bare in places. A lone wallaby, sick with toxoplasmosis, sits unconcealed among the sticks and doesn't move when I pass by. The *Toxoplasma gondii* parasite breeds in the intestines of cats – its primary host – and is spread in their faeces. One of the most common causes of otherwise unexplained deaths in marsupials,[20] it can be picked up by most mammals. Affected animals show decreased awareness of danger. For example, rats are no longer wary of the smell of cats and even appear to seek them out – and so the parasite gets back to its host where it can reproduce. Infected humans also show decreased ability to recognise risky situations, and become more than two-and-a-half times more likely to be involved in traffic accidents.[21]

Parasite–host relationships in which the parasite messes with its host's neural functioning are common in the insect and arachnid and crustacean worlds. Only recently has it become apparent that the behaviours of a range of warm-blooded hosts are also manipulated by their parasites. It seems that a significant portion of the human population may in fact be in the grip of biochemical possession of this sort, with symptoms that range from the subtle to the gross.

Toxoplasmosis, along with malaria, is part of a group of single-celled parasites called the Apicomplexa. They're unusual in that, along with the genetic material contained within their nucleus and mitochondria, they have a third source, housed in structures called plastids, and this DNA is organised in the same way as that found in the photosynthesising chloroplasts of plants. Like the anciently engulfed bacteria that were retained as mitochondria in the cells of all complex organisms, plastids are also a relic – in this case of blue-green algae that were brought into symbiosis.[22]

Though these plastids no longer make chlorophyll and their function is unknown, we can assume that they have an important role. Perhaps they contain something comparable with what used to be called 'junk' or 'non-coding' DNA, once thought to be a kind of molecular bubble wrap surrounding the 'useful' DNA that contains the codes for protein production.

'Non-coding' DNA is now understood to determine the *how* of genetic expression. Working in tandem with the *what* of protein produced by coding DNA, it orchestrates the processes and timing of cellular growth, interaction with other cells, self-maintenance and death.

All eukaryotic (non-bacterial) cells contain remnants of other organisms – bacteria and algae incorporated as symbionts – which carry out essential functions. Current thinking is that almost all of today's eukaryotic life forms are descended from a handful of cells in which these originary engulfing events occurred.[23] Were bacteria taken in as food? Did they themselves enter in order to feed or find protection or a favourable environment? However it happened, both engulfer and engulfed persisted and something new came into being.

Categories dissolve in close-up – and close-up is all we have. We influence and are influenced, but what this means and even how it works is obscure. Swallower and swallowed may be neither destroying nor destroyed. To ignore risk may be suicidal in one set of circumstances and necessary in another, and at that moment, a parasite-induced pathology might be a means of survival.

Though we suffer and inflict change that may be catastrophic and lasting, still I incline with hope towards the intuition, recurring across time and across cultures, that cruelty is local but compassion informs the matrix, the deep tissue from which things come and to which they return. Unverifiable except in the experience itself, this intuition, which, as psychoanalyst and philosopher Michel de Certeau puts it, 'proliferates in proximity to a loss',[24] is nevertheless functional. Working with torture survivors, de Certeau found that those who remain unbroken are those who can invoke 'some other real'[25] beyond the regime of pain and coercion to which they are subjected.

Even in the midst of deathly abuses of power, when peace is blasted and refugees are fenced away from hoarded wealth, the paradise garden is all around, inalienable because everything is part of it. We're inside an agglomeration, arrived at who knows how, a universe-sized *Gestalt*, a gigantic impulse that enacts itself moment by moment with unguessable intent, and that learns, acquires faculties, transforms as it goes. It's branching even now.

Intervals

and the morning star rides the swell

The three eagles settle at night in a tree at the edge of the bush just downslope from the house, beside a small dam on whose wall young wattles grow, their delicate branches touching the water. Not a good idea to leave the trees there – they're short-lived and when they fall they could breach the dam – but they provide cover for small animals and birds that come to drink, and so we've let them grow.

Early each morning I hear the eagles' call-and-response cries that seem so much part of the way of speech. As daylight strengthens, they fly across to sit in a dead tree in the paddock, killed twenty years ago in a rainy winter when water stood for months around its roots. The young one throws back its head and calls softly, tentative, as if learning that sound is part of its repertoire.

Their breeding season begins now. The nest to which the adult pair returns year on year is across the river, I think, but they spend time here in looping, plummeting courtship flights that mark the place as part of their territory. It's a good spot, with tall trees on a slope from which they can launch

themselves into the prevailing westerlies and lift with one, two heavy wingbeats, high over the forests and farms and roads of their hunting and scavenging grounds.

Birds everywhere are feeding and preparing to nest, and all through the short days, the bush understorey is full of the spark-like, *tchip tchip* contact clicks of scarlet robins, the thready songs of overwintering fantails and silvereyes, flocks of thornbills buzzing. The honeyeater's alarm cry – *danger from the sky* – is a dotted line that marks the flat glide of a brown goshawk roused from its ambush among the leaves of a eucalypt. Around the garden, beginning before dawn and continuing until after dark, little wattlebirds and yellow wattlebirds, New Holland honeyeaters and spinebills and yellow-throated honeyeaters converse and fight and forage in the grevilleas and banksias that offer their beak-adapted, nectar-filled flowers all winter.

From their hiding places, creamy-brown tree frogs creak to announce rain and a blue heron steps slowly through the wet grass, stalking, eyes and beak held gyroscope-level, poised to stab. There's a pair of swans on the dam in the shining black of adult plumage, their white flight feathers folded away as they swim. They arrive like dark angels in a whistling disturbance of wings, and land feet-forward in a rush and bow-wash; their fluting-honking saxophone voices sound through the night. Though they court, necks entwined, they haven't nested, so far. They come and go for a few weeks most years, feeding on waterweed in the shallows, accompanied by a flotilla of ducks and grebes and coots that eat insects and crustaceans brought to the surface with the weed.

It has been a strange start to winter, warm enough for bees to be active, their summery sound loud in the damp stillness and low light. Another month of record high temperatures, as the East Australian Current continues to push south – 350 kilometres in the last fifty years – warming the seas along the east coast of Tasmania. Now species such as sea snakes and loggerhead turtles, box jellyfish and manta rays, normally found much further north, are starting to show up in these waters, and cold-dependent species are being displaced.[26]

At night the valleys of the river and its tributaries fill with fog as moist air rises from the water and condenses in the cooler air above. Here on the ridge we're clear of it and wake surrounded by its pale sea, the lowlands drowned and the heights transformed to a series of islands. At sunrise, light dazzles from the flood till it begins to rise and stream over the valley lip as from a cauldron; the landscape dissolves, disappears,

113

emerges glimpse by pearly glimpse, shining, drenched. Some days the fog lifts only high enough to form a low ceiling, grey and still, under which sounds carry – voices float across the river; dozer treads clank in a logging coupe 10 kilometres away. Washing hangs heavy on the line, still wet at the end of the day.

I've been running my hands over the ground beneath the truffle oaks, pushing my fingers into the dirt to see if I can stir up the garlicky-mushroom smell that would signal a ripe fruiting body – so far without success. Tasmanian growers say the truffles are late to appear everywhere this year because it's been so warm – but they should be ripening now if they're there at all. If not, for me the search is a pleasurable encounter with the rich scent of living earth – sweet and musky and full of savour. As a child I tried repeatedly to eat soil from my father's vegetable garden because it smelled so good, before

finally being convinced by its frightening bread-mould taste –
Don't eat that! – that it wasn't edible.

Venus is huge in the predawn sky, and the blue-white cluster
of the Pleiades, and late in the month the old moon, a worn
knife sharpened thin and thinner, vanishing. The longest night
has passed. For weeks on either side of the solstice, day length
changes very little, poised at the end of its pendulum-swing;
everything seems suspended, as in the quiet between breaths.

A week-long midwinter festival is held in Hobart,
50 kilometres to our north. As part of it, along the waterfront,
intense blue searchlights go up, which passers-by can direct at
will. The beams are visible from here – all night they scissor the
horizon, twitchy, frenetic. Towards the end of the festival, by
chance there is also a solar flare – a coronal mass ejection from
the surface of the sun – and when the plasma charge reaches
Earth, an aurora begins to glow; we watch slow columns
of white and green rise from the southern horizon, as if in
response to the lights in the north.

Solar flares add energy to Earth's system and often bring
wild weather. In the days after the aurora, the first storm of
winter passes through, so big that the worst of the winds
and cold wheel north and south of the island, which sits in
relative calm at the centre. Now snow falls in the mountains
and westerly winds bring fine rain in stinging droplets electric
with the memory of ice. Squalls push up hourly over the peaks
of the range to the west in the ripple effect of a mountain
wave pattern. Swells on the west coast build and the waverider
buoy anchored at Cape Sorell records wave heights of 14 and
15 metres. Every few years, 18 and 19 metre giants ride in
off the winter ocean, and the buoy is said to have broken its
mooring one year in a storm on a reading of 23 metres.

Storms are a terror, with their waves – seconds or years or
aeons long – of cold or heat or gamma radiation or armies
on crusade. Across time and distance they gather momentum,
overtake and swallow other surges, adding them to their own
sum of energy. In the intervals before and after, life proliferates.
The little song is sung, bright feathers prickle and shine as the
ground takes everything back and starts again.

Seed

Now you're climbing years compacted blue

The first snow has fallen – a few flakes that drifted down after rain and didn't settle. But the foothills of the mountains are white and the mountains themselves are invisible, wrapped in purple and grey. Wrens and silvereyes bathe in puddles and sit to preen; their bodies, the size and weight of a walnut, seem doubled in volume by ruffled feathers. Increased insulation from clean plumage after bathing must make the risk of catastrophic heat loss worthwhile.

Twenty kilometres west as the raven flies, this side of the first range, there's a memorial at a place where two prospectors died in a blizzard in the spring of 1897. I've been up there myself in horizontal sleet blown so hard I felt sure my face must be raw. As I look across and see squalls pass over, I know how vulnerable even the hardiest are, how close death is, always.

On 4 July in the winter of 1881, my paternal great-grandfather returned to his wife and children on the farm he had called Onepu, meaning *sand*, near the mouth of the Rangitikei River in the North Island of Aotearoa New Zealand, after more than a year in prison. He was born in Potsdam on 14 July 1844, the

illegitimate son of a Prussian army officer, and came as a child with his mother and stepfather to the German community in South Australia and subsequently to Aotearoa New Zealand. He worked as a shepherd for his stepfather, and later for his wife's family both before and after his marriage, and in part-payment, built up a flock of his own. A natural mechanic and engineer, he was also a road-building contractor for the local Highways Board. With these sources of income, he was able to take out a mortgage on a piece of farmland close to properties owned by several of my great-grandmother's siblings.

He began to be active in local politics and it was said of him that, *though sincere and well-intentioned, he was long-winded to the point of pomposity; seeking approval and the plaudits of his followers, he was fearless to the point of recklessness when espousing a cause.*[27]

In 1879, quoting from a popular poem by George Linnaeus
Banks, which must surely have come to haunt him later, he
wrote in his pocketbook:

I live...
For the cause that lacks assistance;
For the wrong that needs resistance;
For the future in the distance;
And the good that I can do.

In 1880 this self-image was put to the test. The country
was in economic crisis and contracting work for the Highways
Board had ceased. He had six children, the final mortgage
payment was due on the farm, and his stepfather was facing
bankruptcy after a series of legal disputes. To raise the money
he needed, my great-grandfather sold part of his flock but
was not paid. Taking matters into his own hands, he forged
a cheque on his debtor, was caught, and on 30 May 1880 was
given an eighteen-month sentence and sent north to prison in
Whanganui.

He served several months fewer than the full term. In November of 1880, he wrote home to say that he was to be *removed
to Taranaki*, having been *invited by the government* to oversee
construction of a coastal road there. This road was essentially
a military enterprise, intended to outflank local Maori who
continued to occupy land confiscated during the wars of the
1860s, and which the government was encouraging European
settlers to claim. The town of Parihaka was an important
centre in this dispute. Situated between Mount Taranaki and
the sea at the most westerly part of the North Island, it had
become the locus of a highly organised, non-violent resistance

119

movement under the leadership of Te Whiti o Rongomai
and Tohu Kakahi. In the 1870s its population grew to more
than 2,000, with stock and croplands sufficient to support
this number. As European settlers moved onto confiscated
land nearby and planted crops, Maori ploughed them up.
Ploughmen arrested and taken to prison were immediately
replaced by others who took up their work.

The new road was to be a route along which troops could
be moved to bring an end to the resistance. By the time the
roadworks reached Parihaka, so many of the men had been
arrested and imprisoned that women, children and the elderly
comprised most of the remaining population. On 5 November
1881, 1,600 soldiers sacked the town; Te Whiti and Tohu were
arrested and taken to prison. The troops raped and looted; they
demolished buildings and destroyed crops. Most townspeople
were expelled and those who remained were issued with
government passes restricting their movements.

My great-grandfather did not refuse the work that made
all this possible. Courage blasted, he took charge of the gang
that drove the road through the fenced gardens and crops and
livestock paddocks of Parihaka, and drove it through again as
Maori ploughed up the roadway and re-erected fences. His
nerveless comment was that *he felt himself to be outside the conflict
between the militia and the Maori whom he found to be quite friendly.*

Once the road had reached its objective he was allowed to
return home and was not required to serve the rest of his sentence.
He never again involved himself in any cause. He never again
owned land. The mortgage on Onepu was foreclosed the week
his sentence was handed down and quickly passed into the
hands of his wife's brother, after which the family was allowed
to stay on as guests. Such was the shame of this time that my

great-grandparents never spoke about it to their children, and the story is known only because of the investigative work of a cousin who has spent his life researching family history.

My father loved his grandfather and vividly remembered visits to the house with its books and instruments, including a telescope, and its productive garden where some things were also grown for pleasure and curiosity. He recalled being woken in the night as a four-year-old and, wrapped in a blanket, carried outside by the old man to see the Great Comet of January 1910, unexpected precursor to Halley's Comet, which was due to appear some months later. The tail of the Great Comet stretched across half the night sky and was bright enough to be visible in daylight, its dust and ice adding itself to the mix of our air while the Earth passed through its train. It must have reminded my great-grandfather of the comet, also visible in daylight, that appeared from September to December of 1882 after the sacking of Parihaka, and was read by the imprisoned Te Whiti as a sign of the imminent end of the world.

Soon enough the world did end for many, Pakeha and Maori alike, as a tenth of the country's young men went to fight in World War I. Almost half of this number were wounded and between 16,000 and 18,000 killed, from a total population of just over 1 million. Hatred of all things German gripped the country; some of my great-grandfather's children took refuge in anglicised names. He died in 1917 while carrying two full buckets in from milking, and was found collapsed in the doorway of the cow byre with one bucket spilled and the other still upright beside him.

The third stage of a Soyuz rocket burned up in the atmosphere over south-eastern Australia early this month – a slow-moving fireball visible from Tasmania to New South Wales and filmed by many, having delivered its satellite payload. Most satellites sit in the zone known as low Earth orbit between 160 and 2,000 kilometres above sea level. This is still within range of the atmosphere's upper reaches – its drag slows objects so that they drift lower and burn or fall. In years of high solar activity, the atmosphere expands and captures objects that might otherwise take hundreds or thousands of years to find their way back, if they ever do.

The mass of objects placed in low orbit by human activities continues to grow, as more satellites are launched and as existing objects – notably those from satellite warfare systems tested in the 800–900 kilometre range in the 1970s and 1980s – collide with one another. This debris now exceeds the orbiting mass of dust and ice and rocky or metallic material left over from the formation of the solar system or brought in from time to time by comets and meteorite showers.

Once the scatter of orbiting debris reaches a certain density, the likelihood of collisions increases exponentially and a cascade effect is predicted to occur, called the Kessler syndrome after the orbital analyst who first identified the possibility of such an event. This effect is expected to render the most useful zones between 250 and 1,500 kilometres from Earth too hazardous for spacecraft sometime in the next few years.

NASA currently tracks more than half a million manmade objects capable of doing serious damage to spacecraft. Travelling as they do at 1–10 kilometres per second, this includes pieces from the size of a marble upwards. Between twenty and thirty thousand of these tracked objects have a mass of 1 kilogram or more and, at 10 kilometres per second, something this size would destroy a spacecraft on impact and create a huge quantity of debris in the process. There are at least 100 million fragments smaller than a marble – like the paint flake that chipped a chunk half the thickness of the pane from a Space Shuttle window. Dust-sized particles continually bombard satellites with an effect like sandblasting. The body of a satellite can be shielded with foil or ceramic fibre, but solar panels and optical equipment, which must of necessity remain unshielded, suffer continuous damage.

The days are lengthening noticeably now – *days grow longer, cold grows stronger.* Rain mixed with snow continues to sweep through; as temperatures drop, we might get a proper snowfall. Like raindrops, the ice nuclei from which snowflakes form must have a particle of some solid material – dust, pollen, bacteria, salt, soot – as a substrate, but for reasons not well understood, ice nuclei form much more rarely than raindrops, even in freezing conditions. Rain is most easily seeded from windblown dust or pollen or salt.

Two favourable ice substrates are soot and some types of bacteria – mostly plant pathogens that foster ice formation and so gain access to their hosts via frost damage. This ice-seeding capacity seems also, through precipitation of snow clouds, to be part of these organisms' dispersal mechanism. Some of the snowflakes falling here will have formed around particles from the fiery re-entry of a rocket stage, some around life forms making their way around the globe – or around the universe; it has long been suggested that some bacteria could survive in the icy heart of a comet and seed life where they encounter favourable conditions.

From the unthinkable edge of things, dust blows in on the stellar wind and meets, hundreds of years overhead, debris from collisions, strikes, counterstrikes that ricochet through the generations in killing silence. Airless distances that give

worldviews their vantage become untenable. Certainties dis-
integrate under the bombardment of experience; they lose
power, become purblind, shatter to white noise and are pulled
back to the realm of breath. They burn and fall; in their wake,
water clicks into ice around seeds of char; salt tears form
and drought ends, for a while. Sometimes it's too much, the
burning and the ice; things lock up and die. Sometimes new
growth stirs, leans upwards. Survivors for now, washed warm
and shivering, we see it all begin.

Text

Salient: [– L. *saliens, -ent-*, pres. pple. of *salīre* to leap]
1. Leaping, jumping...of animals...of water...3. *salient*
point: in old medical use, the heart as it first appears in an
embryo; hence, the first beginning of life or motion; the
starting-point of anything.

Oxford English Dictionary

The waning moon rises later and later, nearer and nearer to
dawn, ever thinner, until, lined up between Earth and the sun,
only its unlit face is turned our way. After a pause it reappears,
a shining filament on the evening horizon.

High-pressure systems flatten the ocean and push away rain –
as the days continue to lengthen, we sit at the bottom of a deep,
still well of clear, dry air. It feels exhilarating after the darkness
of winter but this warmth, so early, also points towards the
season to come. Already the sun begins to burn as the layer
of ozone over Antarctica is destroyed with the return of light
and the hole widens to take in these latitudes. In the northern
hemisphere, fires rage and customary protections do not serve.
The shade of an olive tree is no longer a guarantee or even an
image of peace as the missiles come in.

But here, now, soft air moves and buds open. A grey shrike-
thrush investigates nest sites under the eaves and reports to its

mate – *wejo jo jo wikijowiki*! Narkies, waterhens with mad red eyes, fearless, chase off a feral cat, then gather beside the dam to make their mating and nesting arrangements. Night and day they shriek a chorus in tag-team crescendo – *na keena keena keena kee* – like a conference of crazed plumbers hacksawing pipes in concert.

Bees work the grevilleas for nectar and gather a sudden flush of willow pollen that ripens as catkins open and change from silver to gold in the course of a morning. A New Holland honeyeater carries nesting material – thin strips of honeysuckle and tea-tree bark for the cup, furry bud tips from the banksias for lining. Frogs are calling.

This place moves through me; it shapes me as I attend to it. I wait for what the body brings – sensory events that register like speech acts with 'sudden salience on the surface of the psyche', as Gaston Bachelard puts it in *The Poetics of Space*.[28] These words of place become part of a mode of bodily thought that greets the creatures of sound and touch, scent and taste and

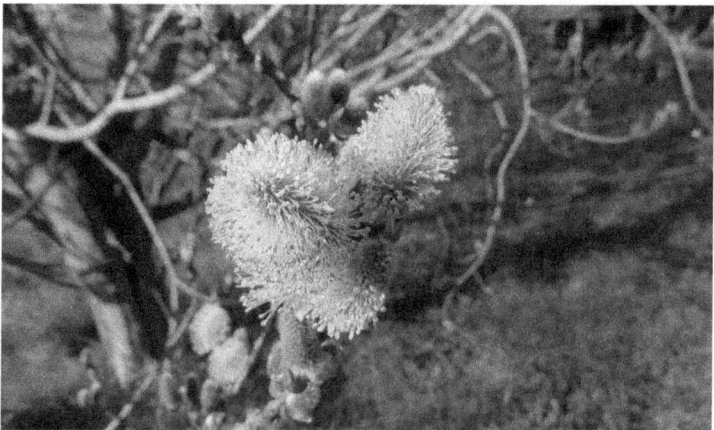

sight. I notice what brings itself to my attention, what leaps forward and stays with me. I let sensations connect, walk myself into rhythm until a beat begins – a word and a word and a word from the world. Attention and event – warp and weft of the text-cloth as a phrase begins to form. A life's work, to call out of the *here-now-only* stream that passes through me, part of a pattern of intelligences, speaking place and spoken by it.

My inheritance is a consciousness buckled by silences and frightened of the conjuring power of words. Like so many others, I was born into a family that was punch-drunk after a couple of hundred years of destruction, displacement, reinvention. Amnesia and fantasy; desire to pass, invisible; and desire to excel slugged it out in the production of identity. Hiding in the thickets of clannishness and religion, refusing to look at the devastation behind and around them, my forebears sought to protect themselves and those who followed.

My mother's tired body and baffled mind brought me in, sombre on sombre, to a world of interdictions and erasures; all that could not be spoken pressed, blinding, at our backs. In her shadow I squeezed through the gates and the air I breathed was fear – of speaking or hearing or thinking the unknown-unthinkable. Reverie was discouraged as tending to madness – that is, to a propensity to make connections that might run away into story, which could, and surely would, clutch and take its creator out into a dazzled hell-realm. This is where I come from, light threatening.

To work with my legacy I call on peripheral vision, developed in darkness and sharpened by anxiety, to acknowledge and give form to intensities that have gathered over generations, and to bring them into language. They take shape as images of precise particularity – creatures and weathers, their interconnections and patterns of growth and decay – and in doing so they become personal, lose the intolerable glare that till now surrounded them. As they step out of formless dread or longing into speech, they widen my sense of the nature and boundaries of psyche, becoming merely themselves – simultaneously subjective states and aspects of the world outside that help me make sense of things. Looked at sidelong, soul and its inhabitants turn out to be not less than everything – I in the world, the world in me, with its mortal dangers from which no shelter can be had, and also its rich portion of pleasure and joy.

Fog gathers in the valley and lifts on brightness; light burns through from inside, dazzles from outside as it goes and comes – just itself, *salient*.

Pass

scrabbling under my ribs, a bird has flown straight in,
dragged bark and debris, piled its nest on my heart-shelf

Daylight comes early now. Swallows hunt in and out of the
sheds and under the eaves and add experimental daubs to last
year's nests. Black-faced cuckoo-shrikes have made the journey
south; they swoop and *churr* and shuffle their wings as they
land to search the hedgerows for insects. Nests are everywhere;
fan-tailed and pallid and bronze cuckoos have arrived for this,
and migratory swamp harriers – a racketing din from ducks and
narkies and plovers marks a hen hawk's progress as she hunts
low over the dam and surrounding paddocks to feed the chicks
she's hatched in a nest in the long grass. In a good season like
this, many species have already raised one brood ahead of the
parasites and predators, but successive broods will be hard-hit.

Cuckoos coopt nests of other (often much smaller) species –
thornbills and wrens, silvereyes and flycatchers, honeyeaters
and robins – and lay their eggs among the host bird's clutch.
Host birds attack cuckoos and chase them away if they can;
some species build decoy nests or nests with false entrances. If
the cuckoo does make it past these defences, its egg is usually
not recognised as that of an intruder. When hatched, the young

cuckoo pushes out the host bird's eggs, and its hunger and distress calls bring the host parents and sometimes other birds rushing to it.

In a co-adaptive countermove, female blue wrens sing a 'password' to their eggs during incubation, and sing it more intensely when they know that the cuckoos have arrived.[29] The call is different for each nesting family. If a hatched chick doesn't sing the password back, the female refuses to feed it and abandons the nest. Wren eggs take about fifteen days to hatch, while those of Horsfield's bronze cuckoos, the wrens' most common parasite, take twelve. The mother wren begins to sing the password song on about day ten – this means that developing wren babies have five days to learn the song, while cuckoos have only two.

Snakes are also coming out of hibernation in time for the bounty of eggs and nestlings and young of all kinds. Their skins are dull and soon-to-be-shed – sometimes in ragged pieces, sometimes whole, inside-out, complete from transparent eye-scale to tail-tip; delicate, airy, they're soft and damp at first, becoming brittle as they dry. Today in the ceiling there was a sudden furious scrabbling and an explosion of activity away from a nest of rats whose sounds I've been hearing – a snake has made its way into the roof cavity.

And it's windy again – the equinox comes with a gale strong enough to lean on. As at this time last year – and most years – creatures contend with wrecking force just when they're most vulnerable, incubating or feeding young. Trees come down in ruin with all their occupants, roofs blow off houses, water tanks go bowling away. I walk with the dog on the easterly slope below the old house that burned, out of the worst of the wind. The dog scouts the pocked ground where orchard

once grew and springs over blackberry vines after a scent she can still follow even through the blustery air. She's young and I'm anxious in this, her first season of learning to cohabit with snakes. I showed her a cast-off skin and she bristled and backed away – that's a good sign, but I'm not sure that her caution won't be overridden by her desire to hunt if she comes across a live one. She'll have to take her chances.

In the late afternoon I fill and light a fire under the outdoor bath – probably for the last time this season as days warm and fuel loads dry. Now, just after sunset, the water is hot and I climb in. Remaining light picks out a column of insects that rises and falls in a dance blown ragged by gusts of the sharp nor'-wester. It's cool and delightful on my face as I lie in the warmth; I have to move my arms and legs now and then to circulate the little

scalding streams that rise around the tiles placed over the floor
of the tub where the fire cups itself to the bath's iron underside.
The water is stained tea-brown by waterweed and by the lives
and deaths of creatures – the platypus has swum in it, and so
have eels and swans, grebes and ducks that nest in the reeds and
rushes, and feed on its insects and larvae. Herons have stalked
its edges and snakes have curled beside it in the sun and swum
the shallows hunting frogs.

I'm looking up at fast-moving clouds, which here and there
shine red as last light hits their tops from over the curve of
the world. Cloud streams and spools in massing cumulus scraps
condensed over warming hillsides. Across the river, the peaks of
the second range are invisible; it must be raining there already. I
can hear each breath move through the treetops, up the forested
slope below the house then over open ground and into the
flowering blackwoods of the westerly windbreak; leaves and
stamens blow onto the water, and scraps of bark torn off by
foraging cockatoos. A bandicoot emerges from its daytime nest
and fossicks urgently in the soft earth; a blackbird rattles its
wickwickwick alarm or threat before sleep. All the birds call as
they settle on their darkening roosts – wattlebirds and wrens,
ravens and crescent honeyeaters, New Holland honeyeaters and
the spinebills that for months have evaded the New Hollands'
territorial bullying. A pallid cuckoo repeats and repeats its
upward trill. The first star shines in a gap, a gulf of air, and a
line of cloud advances, dragging its pelt of rain.

As darkness deepens, firelight glows red on the mud wall
of the house beside me; shadows rear as a gust flings out a
spray of sparks. Then the wind drops for a moment and smoke
drifts – incense of eucalyptus twigs and pine-cone kindling, a
branch of rosemary broken off in a storm and set aside to dry,

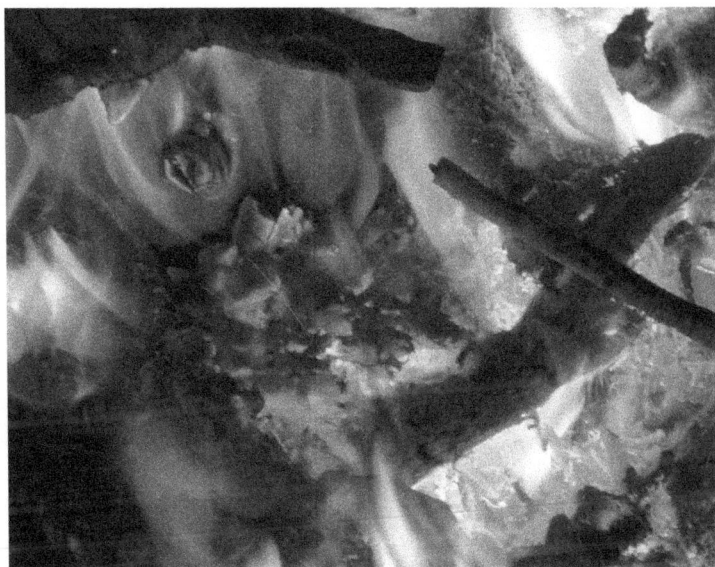

macrocarpa limbs trimmed from the hedge. Again the wind picks up and the smoke blows away. Full night comes down; I step out into it as the rain begins.

The dog runs circles round me; tracks of her wet paws and my bare feet intertwine on the paving of the verandah. I think about Newton's third law and how, with each step, we meet an equal and opposite force that presses up; it perfectly matches the touch of each toe, the pads of each foot as if, woman and dog, we're shadowed by other selves coextensive with the earth, joined at the soles, keeping pace everywhere.

And this is how it is, the world always there to meet us, touch for touch. The earth pushes back and lets us leap away; air and water take our imprint, carry the beat of wings and fins. We may gather mass to crush and be crushed; we may override the

133

secret mutuality at the heart of things, but we're formed by it, bone and muscle, all our mobility born of pressure returned. And when we lie down, each night the ground holds us up with the touch of a mother or lover – there we rest, and all through us, across the threshold of space and duration, matter resolves to chirruping chords that sing us and sing us in. Cuckoo and host, hunter and prey, this is our shared pass into life; our great fortune, to make our way out of the shell, out of the outgrown skin, to travel the falling, rising country of breath.

Thou

The cows themselves differentiate between the airs sung to them, giving their milk freely with some songs and withholding with others. Occasionally a cow will withhold her milk till her own favourite lilt is sung to her.

Carmina Gadelica[30]

The grass is growing and I'm milking a cow again after a break of years. In these parts, the domestic economy of having a house cow in the family goes like this: after a calf is born and its mother's milk comes in, the calf is left with the cow continuously for the first couple of weeks to drink as much as it can of the bright yellow colostrum – the *beost* or *biestings* as it's known in Europe, and here called *beastings* – without which it would die and which contains a kind of starter kit for its immune and digestive systems, along with growth factors and other nutrients. During this time the cow is milked only of the excess that the calf can't drink. After that, mother and calf are separated during each night – the calf is kept in a sheltered enclosure while very young and later outside at grass, with the cow close by in the night paddock.

The cow is milked in the morning, and afterwards the calf runs with her all day and takes the day-milk; towards evening they are separated once more. This has many advantages over the commercial dairying system in which cow and calf are permanently separated after about a week to ten days. Benefits for the cow and her calf are obvious, but it also unshackles the cow's humans from twice-daily milking plus feeding of calves, which is otherwise necessary. Once the calf is big enough to take all the milk it is even possible to have a day off now and then without distress for the cow, and without provoking mastitis and a diminished or dried-up milk supply.

When all is well, the milk routine is immensely soothing – the walk in predawn air to find the animals where they're bedded under the windbreak; the sound of their breath and their clicking hooves as they walk to the milking-shed; their huge warmth as I lean my head and shoulder into a flank; the clanging music of milk on metal, purring deeper as the bucket fills; the milky, grassy cow-musk that rubs off on my skin and clothes; the cow's meeting with her waiting calf and the creak

of new grass she crops as the calf begins to suckle. But the sore teat and protesting kick, the shit-caked hoof in the bucket, the sick calf, the milk fever, the freezing rain – these are part of it too. And death. Accident and disease take their toll among the cattle, and even the healthiest cow lives only fifteen to twenty years. Calves that can't be kept once they're grown are eaten.

Living and working with animals brings me face to face not only with the reality of death but also with the inescapable understanding that death is part of the fabric of the world. Every animal must kill something in order to live. In my early twenties, I was strongly attracted to the skills and concepts of self-sufficiency, as many of my generation were. Vegetarian at that time, I didn't think this through before I joined a farming community in which animals were killed for meat, and found it very confronting. Bringing a sheep to slaughter or beheading a hen, I quickly became aware that some of my resistance came from my own fear – of death itself and of the fact that, whether I eat plants or animals, to be alive is to be inextricably beholden in a death-for-life web.

Although I never get used to killing (any more than I get used to the knowledge that I will die), for me the problem around eating meat, as with eating plants, is how to find a way to acknowledge other lives and deaths without treating them as mere adjuncts to my own. If I am going to intervene so radically as to domesticate and kill another creature, how will I ensure that its life is a good one that meets its needs and desires? I've had very mixed success in this attempt and, passing the problem on or turning away, have many times eaten plants and animals without knowing what kind of life was lived to feed me. It's one of the ironies of the choices I've made that my desire to be more aware of the network of lives in which

I am embedded, to acknowledge the creaturely relationships that literally sustain me, has brought me into the realm and awareness of death-dealing as well as giving life.

The moon wanes to a lash, a splash returned to the spill that pours brighter each day along the morning horizon. As I go to milk, the birds begin – a wattlebird coughs in the hedge and from bushes near the door a wren complains about the porch light. The cow waits while I put hay sprinkled with cider vinegar in the headstall and cut up a few pieces of apple. Hot water to wash hands and teats before I begin; salve to clean and soothe and then the rhythm of milk and song; the rising foam. By the time I've finished and let her into the day paddock with her calf and hosed away spattered milk and shit and piss, the daylight world is about its business.

Then the walk back to the house with full bucket to strain the milk through gauze into bottles and tubs. Some goes into the refrigerator and some I use in the domestic alchemies of cheese- and butter-making – although this is not a transmutation from a base substance to a noble one, but of gold to gold. Today I'm making feta – starter culture is added to the milk for flavour and acidity, then rennet that sets the curd; the silky warm junket is cut and stirred and settled and the whey is drained off – later I'll use it to make ricotta. The drained curd is pressed and, in the case of feta, stored in brine. Another day I'll make haloumi – curd cooked in hot whey then pressed and brined – or cheddar – curd salted and pressed and set to dry.

Any kind of interspecies connection seems amazing to me – how each works with differences and also with common needs and desires shaped in deep time during a shared formation by landscape and climate. I'm interested in the social and temperamental bases for some species' consent to work with

humans. Many species can be tamed or trained but only a few
have entered into symbiosis with us – dogs but not foxes, cattle
but not bison, horses but not zebra, reindeer but not gazelles.

Sometime around 10,500 years ago when the first settled
communities appeared in what is now Turkey and Iran, people
in a few villages in the high valleys of the Tigris and Euphrates
learned to bring in *aurochs* – huge wild cattle 150–180
centimetres tall at the shoulder with horns spanning more
than 2 metres – and persuade them to live and breed alongside
humans. DNA mapping shows that all domesticated cattle are
descended from perhaps eighty *aurochs* cows in the region of
modern Dja'de in Iran and Çayönü in Turkey.[31] We've been
calling them in, singing to them ever since, our heads pressed
into their sides as we milk, our crooned words passing into
them through the bones of our skulls:

My heifer beloved, be not alone,
Let thy little calf be before thee;
My little black heifer thou! My little black heifer!
The same lot is mine and thine.
May thy little black calf not be lost to thee;
But mine only son beloved is beneath the sea.

My black cow, my black cow,
A like sorrow afflicts me and thee,
Thou grieving for thy lovely calf,
I for my beloved son under the sea,
My beloved only son under the sea.

Carmina Gadelica[32]

Like my mother and her mother before her who paid their bills in butter and cream, like my father lifting the full milk cans onto the train before school, like his father gored by the newly calved cow, and like his father's father before him who put down his buckets to die in the byre and only spilled one, like all the generations before them I enter this work.

Bless my little cow;
Bless my desire;
Bless thou my partnership
And the milking of my hands.
Bless each teat;
Bless each finger;
Bless each drop that goes into my pitcher.

Carmina Gadelica[33]

Brew

deep but dazzling darkness

Henry Vaughan, 'The Night'[34]

A young echidna blunders into the porch at the back door in its undeviating search for territory and food and a mate – I hear scrabbling and find it in a corner trying to bulldoze its way into the mudbrick of the wall, like a wind-up toy that has encountered an obstacle. Its spines, emerging from deep in soft fur like thorns from a moss-garden, are sparser on the back and thicker on the sides and around the head and tail. Black-tipped as if hardened by fire, they're sharp enough to go straight through thick leather work-gloves T puts on to pick it up and take it down the hill into the bush where it will find the ants that are its food. Ancient creature for which our house is a blip, an empty ant nest, an impediment to be dug through.

The days are warm, flourishing, then cool again. Though the first wildfires have begun in the drier parts of the island, in the night a southerly front comes through with rain and wild wind and by midmorning there's snow in the air. People are struggling with colds and flu at one moment and hayfever the next. I'm making elderflower and lemon syrup – a respiratory pharmacopoeia all on its own, with a handful of rose petals thrown in, *cordial*, because they are flowering too. The smell of steeping flowers and fruit fills the house. When it's ready I'll strain it into bottles and we'll drink it as a tonic, cold in summer for its taste of deep hedgerow shade and hot in winter for its summery smell.

Calendula is in full flower – the common, flat-petalled, daisy-marigold that is such a useful first-aid herb and alterant. Sticky resin concentrated in the flower heads contains antimicrobials, along with substances that help to promote the granulation of wounds. I pack the flowers into jars and cover them with brandy – its alcohol dissolves the resins and other non-water-soluble principles, and its water component extracts other substances. A tinctured combination of calendula and St John's wort is my go-to treatment for cleansing and easing the pain of cuts and grazes and beginning the healing process.

Roses and wisteria are at their peak. I see movement in the fringe of flowers outside the laundry window and think it's a bird, but instead find myself eye to eye with a mouse. Like tiny trapeze artists, a whole family is working the vine; they hold with their hind feet to sprays of blossom and hang, gripping the nectar-filled flowers with front paws to eat, swaying, suspended in the purple and white fall, eyes half-closed in ecstasy.

Everything rushes to fill up with juice before the scorching days when green withers and life sinks to its cool roots or burrows deep. Already it's dry underfoot, and any time now rivers of scalding air will flow south off the mainland. I check the bees; as usual the swarm under the greengage tree is furious – workers fall like sparks onto my hands and cling there, stinging. Unfortunately for me and them, today I've put on cloth gloves with only the palm and fingers dipped in latex in place of the rubber kitchen variety I usually wear, which the

stings can't pierce but which are also hot and fill with sweat. Bad move – the barbed stings go straight through the cloth on the backs of my hands, catching there and disembowelling the bees as they deliver their venom. I'm not allergic to bee stings but my fingers swell and itch as the poison works its way out of my system. I take homoeopathic *apis* and rub on cooling aloe sap, then an ointment I've made from comfrey, St John's wort and arnica, in a base of almond oil and wax from these same bees. Each swarm with its own temper and moods.

When I was a child it gave me great pleasure to make *mixtures* of all kinds, using dirt from the garden to which I added water and seeds and chopped leaves and spices from my mother's kitchen. It felt purposive, as if the result must have a use even if I didn't know what it was; as if the act of choosing and mixing were directed; as if my choices and their results were given, somehow, part of a *recipe* in its original imperative sense – *receive!* – from the Latin *recipere*. I've been thinking about this as I use my tinctures and salves and cordials, and as I prepare leaven for sourdough – a combination of rye flour and raisins and water and milk *kefir* – live yoghurt culture. The starter must be fed with more flour and water each day for a week until wild yeasts from the grain and fruit work together with yoghurt bacteria to make a living brew that will flavour and lift bread dough.

I like the thought that organisms cultured in this way may be integral to the creation of the miraculously self-propagating *terra preta* soils that form where people live for generations and cook and create ferments and return their scraps to the ground.

Drawn and driven, we compose each day from ingredients that walk or fly or are gathered into the ferment-space where every brew is received as gift and command. Organised around loves and resistances found or created, we wrestle an outcome, construct a narrative that calls in its own powers of choice and intent – every recipe enacted as a spell. We make a mess. And then sometimes, despite our self-undoing attacks, despite our thorny softness, our longing for what's sweet, we let ourselves fall into healing dark, that black seat of being with its residue of char. Relieved for a while from the heaviness of our intent, we and the whole mix we are in can be transformed, lifted and starred by wild leaven that comes to us from outside, unwillable.

Birth day

Begin anywhere.
John Cage, *Diary*[35]

At the solstice, soft rain blows in off the sea. Here Christmas marks the high tide of the year, and this year the shortest night coincides with moon-dark; across the black ecliptic, planets trace their apparent loops and progressions – now Jupiter turns back on itself, Uranus moves forward out of retrograde and Saturn enters the constellation of Sagittarius. Haymakers are in a stop–start frenzy of work and frustrated inaction. Too wet to mow, grasses continue to ripen; clouds of pollen fly and bleached patches appear in the paddocks as seed heads mature and leaves and stems dry, losing their value as fodder.

Six cows in the herd have calved this month – bad management on our part. One of them died giving birth and her calf with her; it's the wrong time – the cow too fat on summer grass, the calf too big. Much better to carry a pregnancy through the mild winter (no snow settling for more than a few hours, ever), lean and spry on hay and roughage, the calf compactly grown. And then new grass to feed on, udder springing milk for the calf to come. But this year we didn't bring the bull to them in spring or summer as we should have, and in autumn – late, that is – the neighbour's bull got through the boundary fence. T uses the blade on the tractor to deepen a stump-hole in the bush; he buries the bodies there, out of reach of animals.

The dog and I skirt warily around a snake that rests beside the track in intermittent sun, its skin rough and patchy, ready to slough; it moves its head to watch us through dull eye-scales. Cloud-herds trek south-eastwards, striking sparks as they go. There's still not much in the rain gauge but thunder rattles the windows and, with tremendous noise, a pine tree on the ridge south of here explodes in fire as its gathered charge meets a finger of lightning from the cloud above. Once a rare occurrence, now many wildfires begin this way.

The storm makes me think of how, as a child, I used to watch my father put on his wet-weather gear and go out into the rain to fix damage caused by lightning strikes on the transformers in his care as operator of a hydroelectric substation. Thwarted in mind and energies, there was often a crackle of anger around him. He drew it, too – he had a round burn-scar in the small of his back where, in his days as a linesman, a stray arc from a transmission cable caught him and earthed through his legs and feet, throwing him to the ground from 10 metres up where he stood on a maintenance platform. The impact cracked vertebrae in his back but also restarted his heart.

I sing in a band with a group of friends. S brings baby bandicoots with her to a practice session; three in a sock, eyes not yet open, they're furred and marked like moths. Warm moths. She takes a sports bag with her everywhere and inside it, in pouches made from knitted caps and bags and hot water bottle covers, an assortment of orphaned wallabies, bettongs, possums, bandicoots, along with bottles of their various milk formulae and a thermos flask of hot water to warm up the milk in its syringe-with-teat feeders.

The bandicoots drink 1 millilitre each, every three hours, day and night. Every now and then a wallaby child looks out and calls across the room to S in its soft, grating voice before returning to sleep or to eat the honey-myrtle flowers she's given it to keep it occupied. These are animals found in the pouches of mothers that have been killed on roads or attacked by cats or dogs. There's a network of carers who take them on. Many die but some survive to be released as adults.

We're practising to sing at a birthday celebration for Bob Brown, retired from politics after a lifetime spent challenging the ethos of might-as-right, of world-as-commodity. He served as a senator for the Greens from the 1990s till retirement – a shy man now free of obligation to be so much in the public eye. He's been an inspiration to many, somehow maintaining integrity while still entering fully into the mess of life as a politician. This seems all the more remarkable now as political parties spiral into frank endorsement of everything that's worst about humans. The prime minister and his minions declare, in relation to desperate escapees from Iraq and Afghanistan and Sri Lanka, that their major achievement has been to *stop the illegal boats* and to *detain* children and their mothers in tents on tropical Nauru, where they can be kept without free access to water, let alone medical care or schooling, out of sight, out of reach of the media, out of mind. And, anticipating a time when this will become politically inexpedient, making a deal with Cambodia. To the tune of 'O Susannah' we sing: *O we're going to Cambodia to send them refugees / and later on, the sick and old / and those who caint pay fees.*

Between days of overcast and drizzle, in clear, humid intervals, now, again, the bees swarm. The voice of a young queen about to hatch comes piercing, insistent, from the colony in the wall. The old queen flies and lands on a limb high in the windbreak; workers that have flown with her settle around her in a ball. This is my chance to catch the swarm and persuade the bees to stay in a hive, before scouts can locate a hollow tree or wall space and lead the queen to it. The limb is too high to reach with a ladder and we decide to cut it – it's one we had planned to take out anyway as it's crowding a chestnut tree growing in its lee.

It's a delicate operation, cutting just far enough through the branch so that it dips gradually downwards within reach. At some point there's a miscalculation and it drops with a crack like a rifle shot, dumping more than half the bees onto the

ground and the queen with them. She isn't sufficiently disturbed to fly so we put a box over the moving mass, hoping that the queen will crawl up into it and that the others, those on the ground and those still on the branch, will follow her scent and join her. I've rubbed the inside of the box with stems of bee balm – *Melissa* – and put in frames to which I've attached sheets of foundation wax. The smells of their favoured herb and the wax entice them in, and by evening they're all inside. Once it's dark we lift the box onto a board, close the entrance and move the hived swarm to the spot we've prepared, east-facing, close to clean water, sheltered from the hottest afternoon sun and westerly winds. The next day is warm and soon after sunrise the workers make their first orienting flights and begin to forage from the hive.

Every birth's an *anywhere* – chord, discord, dreadful and wonderful. My soul hums in its cup, its cave, in shadow, born in the brightest hour as long days tend towards night. So much depends on the place we begin – every life composed from what's at hand and every year another start as last year's music dulls and thickens and is shed. Mercy comes, and death comes; I close my eyes on black branches of the flash, shock that stops the heart, shock that jolts it in. Soul flies out; with or without consent, seedfall gathers.

Year 3

Philyra

Walking like an invalid, tenderly,
my wits return the standing wave –
layered cloud, water over rock,
clean shine of bone.
What I hear, I am saying,
this mouth any mouth, a little icon
opening on a corner of blue cloak or sky.
What I can't think, I am saying –
words sucked out by air that gulps
up and over mountains,
words pressed out by weight of nights
above the valley.

Clouds frayed invisible
make rainbows in clear sky, scraps
that fade and brighten.
Words too, the body's thoughts,
a reyny cope *against this light*
that burns my clothes,
shoulder and side
ash-white.[36]

My mouth holds many weathers.

Not sick but carrying,
we stumble sometimes,
cry out and hear a new voice call.

Everyone talking now.

At the start of the new year, on this summer's first hot night, I sleep out under the flowering linden and all night its perfume drifts around me in the warm wind. Ringtail possums go their ways in treetops whose branches have been shaped by their passage, pausing to chirrup-whistle warnings about my presence in the nightworld. A brown bandicoot digs soft ground under the tree; mosquitoes keen outside the net I've rigged. Well before sunrise, bees begin to work the blossoms. Disturbing dreams are said to come to those who fall asleep under the linden but I remember none, unless the whole night with its light of a waning moon and its wind and whispered conversation of leaves and creatures is a dream. When I get up it's already 24 degrees Celsius at 5.00 am; after milking I go back to my sleeping platform in the shade and spend the morning reading in leaf-light, then retreat indoors when the temperature climbs into the 30s. A high thin haze slides in from the north; the sun dulls but still the white sky glares, too hot.

Among deciduous species, lindens seem like ur-trees to me – satisfying in shape and texture and colour and perfume, in leaf and flower and branch. *Lipke, linde, lenda, lentus – lithe.* In the forests of Asia and North America they're markers of ginseng habitat. All though Europe, towns are named after lindens, and from earliest times they marked shrines – to Laima, goddess of fate and fertility, and, later, to the Virgin. The tree's shade was believed to elicit truth and inhibit lies, and this power was invoked during legal cases that were tried, and their verdicts declared, *sub tilia* – under the linden.

In Greek the word for linden is *Philyra*, name of one of many water spirits associated with particular rivers and springs, daughters of ocean deities Tethys and Oceanus. The nymph Philyra mates with Chronos – god of time, constraints, form and structure – who comes to her as a stallion. Afterwards she gives birth to the centaur Chiron, healer and prophet, teacher of medicine and music and the art of hunting with a bow. In the earliest versions of the story, she takes her child to the slopes of Mount Pelion where she raises him and trains him in his work.

The linden tree embodies Philyra's gifts of nourishment, healing and delight – its nectar is beloved of bees; its beautifully scented flowers, leaves and sap are medicinal. It also embodies her capacity to transmit her knowledge, since its inner bark can be used to make paper. Patron of papermaking, writing and perfumery, she passes her skills to her son in his role as culture-bearer to humans.

Chiron's gift of music is also received from his mother, whose name, according to T. K. Hubbard, means *lover of the lyre* – φίλος λύρα.[37] Germaine Guillaume-Coirier goes further, suggesting that Philyra's musicality, like her healing skill, is an aspect of her capacity to hear, distil and record, and that the name may be closer to φίλοςὖρον – *philosyron* – *lover of the swarm* – from the Proto-Indo-Germanic *swer*, meaning *humming* or *murmuring*, cognate with Latin *sussurus*.[38] Philyra recognises, nourishes and transduces the living murmuration of things.

Linden wood, which doesn't warp as it dries and can be worked flawlessly smooth, is favoured as a surface on which to paint icons. In a myth that parallels that of Philyra and Chiron, the Virgin Hodegetria – she who shows the way – tutors not only her divine child, but also the physician and icon-painter St Luke the Evangelist. Luke is the Greek-speaking culture-bearer of the Christian era, to whom the Hodegetria recounts details of her life. Alone among the gospels, the work attributed to Luke tells intimate stories of the Virgin's pregnancy, of the birth of her child and of her experience of parenthood. Luke's legend also insists that he painted several likenesses of the Virgin, on wooden panels that devotees believe to have survived, working their miracles, to the present day.

After frightening heat and fires on the mainland, from the middle of the month it rains and rains – the wettest January here since 1916 – blowing soft and soaking from the north-east. Feathery heads of ungrazed browntop bentgrass beside the road hold droplets like tethered clouds until the wind swings west and south, stormy. It brings down trees whose roots lose their grip in the softened ground; huge branches fall from the old pines as the weight of saturated needles grows too much for rot-weakened limbs. As the days shorten towards autumn, this drenching brings relief from the expectation of fire.

Sheltered from the rain, newly fledged wrens scutter like mice in the dry underbrush of a garden bed along a north-facing wall of the house. They were hatched in a nest tucked into twigs of a small koromiko growing at the foot of latticework that supports climbing plants. The chicks' confidence increases by the hour as they flutter-hop further upwards into tendrils of jasmine and branches of shrubby wintersweet, while adults from previous hatchings crowd around with grubs and encouragement. These are the first wren chicks I've seen this summer, in a season of many snakes and cuckoos.

The cherry harvest is over and the apricots are ripe. Linden flowers and willowherb leaves dry in baskets; nettle roots and hawthorn berries tincture in jars of sherry. The first hard cheeses begin to mature. Preparing foods and medicines from what's at hand, I learn skills conceived in this meeting of place with galloping time.

Shapeless potency finds form and complexity is born – the arrow's moving point describes a line; the line describes a curve; *lithe*, we attend and learn the care that transforms curve to cup. Somewhere deep, a murmur draws the swarm and tempts the leap, to touch and leave our trace in flesh and fruit, on paper and on wood, where the god of place looks out, where we look out from our work as it gathers like a wave, dissolving.

Trill

In the night courtyard, ripe fruit and rotten –
find the clean flesh, find the stone;
in darkness where a seed might split,
see how soul limps out,
shakes its curled wing,
claps the air.

A sound that belongs to warm evenings at this time of year – the trilling of mole crickets – *Gryllotalpa* species, pale brown, about 5 centimetres long, with a soft abdomen and short forewings. They're damp-ground burrowers with front legs adapted for shovelling dirt; the flightless males sing from their burrows – a long, trilled monotone – and the winged females fly in, following the song.

A male has dug in near a dripper at the base of a tomato plant in the polytunnel to broadcast his trill; the polythene pipe of the dripper system adds its resonance to the already powerful sound.

Crickets sing by rubbing a rasp-like section of one forewing against a ridged patch on the other – it's a tiny chirp. To amplify it, mole crickets make a bulb-shaped hollow at the base of their burrow, joined to a flared mouth by a narrow chamber in which the cricket sits, facing inwards, to sing.

In a study of the physiology of these *singing burrows*, J. Scott Turner[39] has shown that the crickets' structures have the same properties as a well-designed musical instrument such as a trumpet, where the hollow at the base of the burrow corresponds to the musician's mouth cavity, the constricted area where the cricket sits corresponds to the mouthpiece, and the flared opening of the burrow forms the mouth of the trumpet. The cricket's body acts like a trumpet mute, squeezing the frequency of the sound into a narrower, more far-reaching range. To create a shape that matches the resonating frequency of its song, the cricket modifies the burrow in response to 'test' chirps made while digging.

Turner has calculated that, in this way, some species are able to convert up to 34 per cent of the muscle power expended in the trill to sound (compared with a power-to-sound conversion of about 2 per cent for the best audio speakers). He argues that the burrow acts as an extension of the animal's physiology.

The song of the cricket in the hothouse is painfully loud to my ears at close range but has, at the same time, a strange, muffled-then-clear, *diminuendo–crescendo* quality. This species turns its body through 360 degrees as it sings – a revolving auditory beacon that sweeps the air with a beam of sound the females can home in on. But female crickets are not the only creatures attracted by the song. There's a species of flower wasp, *Diamma bicolor*, whose shining, titanium-blue, flightless females seek out mole crickets in their burrows, paralyse them by stinging and lay their eggs on the body, which becomes a living food supply for the wasp larvae when they hatch. This species parasitises mole crickets only. The adult wasps themselves, both the winged black-and-white males and brilliant females, feed exclusively on nectar and act as pollinators for a wide range of plant species.

At the start of the month I check the bees and come away disappointed – very little comb has been filled and capped. But now the stringybark eucalypts begin to blossom. Twenty metres up, the canopy of the old tree outside my workspace shines palely inside a halo of sound, as bees and wasps and honeyeaters and parrots work the blooms and send down a sifting litter of stamens; the air-map of the garden is marked by creeks and runnels of honey-scent. This flowering is a response to the rainy summer – seeds, which need to have their hard cases cracked by heat in order to germinate, will be ripe in time for the next fire season, and the heavy fuel load created by new growth will have had time to dry.

Now evenings hum as flights of insects of many kinds hatch and converge to mate. Forest ravens and grey currawongs congregate to feast on pasture grubs and their adult morphs, mostly moths and cockchafer beetles. Quolls and bandicoots do well too – everywhere their droppings glitter with fragments of chitinous wingcases and exoskeletons. Over the course of a few days around full moon, summer corbies – *Oncopera intricata* – emerge in their tens of thousands, one of the many *ghost moth* species that occur throughout those areas of the world that were once part of the Gondwanan supercontinent. They crisscross low over the pasture soil from which they've hatched; the sound is an echoing drone like the engine of a heavy, propeller-driven plane, and if I crouch to find the skyline in fading light I can see moth-bodies crowd the air just above the ground. If I walk the darkening roadway I'm accompanied by bats that use it as an unobstructed flightpath and echolocation substrate, flying back and forth along the stretches that belong in their territories to feed on hatchling moths.

We're feasting also. The first tender figs ripen on a young tree in the orchard. The last of the Moorpark apricots sweeten to incandescent orange, weeks later than those that grow down by the river because of our couple of hundred metres' elevation; the first apples pop with juice, tart stripy Gravensteins that won't keep but taste marvellous after months of sad, mealy coolstore fruit. Little yellow-and-russet Beurre Giffard pears are ready to pick on the old hawthorn-grafted tree in the paddock. Late-season raspberry canes poked into a corner of one of the polytunnels on a whim have grown 3 metres tall, staggering under the weight of their fruit; they find the support of old tomato trellises, or collapse as the berries fill with juice. Blackberries ripen by the roadside and in the paddocks.

It's dark now when I set out to milk and the cow is still bedded down on grass that's flattened and partly dried by her body heat. She comes sleepily to the manger, chewing cud; the calf rouses itself too and waits close by – it calls to its mother and the mother replies. As light grows, the contact-calls of young parrots – *tink-tink, dedink-tink* – chime back and forth, far into the quiet air as they feed on fruit in the hedgerows.

There's a fantastically expansive feeling about these high clear skies and cooling days. Tension breaks as heat subsides and the threat of fire recedes. And then, unmasked by the lift of buoyant air, sadness rises too as everywhere the ideologues sing from their burrows – so small, so loud in their season. Facing in, soft bodies buried in the machine, they rasp their thin monotone and the culture-horn, the language-and-technology-horn brays it louder; and everywhere their ruin runs to find them where they hide.

A season, a season, year on year, no rest in the flowering, fruiting, dangerous world.

Fruit

the angel of place bellowing through
out of the ground

Dry pasture has no goodness left; the cow makes little milk and I leave more and more for the calf who waits impatiently for its mother each morning. When a storm crosses the Kimberley coast of the western mainland, tree frogs begin to chirp – always a hopeful sign – and soon rain does come, not much at first, but once there's moisture about, more follows, warm mist and then rain – steady, soft, heavy. The sound of it builds around me like time, near and distant, and afterwards the bees work furiously in steam and sunlight. A few days later, thunder wakes me, a wall of sound like black mountains to the west. Bands of cumulus sweep in, and needle-tailed swifts ride ahead; I hear their whistling flight before I see them as they arrow through. Moving at more than 100 kilometres an hour, they dip low then arc upwards and are gone over the horizon in seconds. They sleep on the wing, following rolling humidity across half a hemisphere for the insects they favour.

Morning grass is dewy again where it's still green in the shade of apple trees whose branches are propped to hold the weight of fruit, but the paddocks are brown underfoot – the

ANGELA ROCKEL

164

rain hasn't done its work yet. From bare patches where turf roots have been eaten by thousands of caterpillars, clouds of heavy-bodied moths continue to emerge from sunset to sunrise and fill the air over the pastures with their echoing drone. All night, bandicoots and quolls fossick for hatchlings and leap after moths that make the air. Well before first light, ravens congregate to talk plenty and scramble-hop after the fat insects swarming low.

A sense of relief lingers for weeks after the fire season has passed. Everyone who's lived here for any length of time has experienced the wildfire terror directly or indirectly. Everyone knows a story of hiding in a creek bed as flames go over, or of packing a suitcase and running to open ground – a ploughed paddock, a beach. Stories of houses burned and people and animals lost, or miraculously saved, found bewildered on a strip of green around a dam. Everyone has a memory or a story of sifting through rubble where, in windless corners, soft ash feathers to dust, the past all simplified.

Fog in the mornings then bright, warm, clear air. Wasps and honeyeaters finish off the last, little, insipid Chinese pears. I offer some to the two horses that are visiting to eat grass in the orchard but they're not interested. T brings in walnuts – the first in years to mature before white cockatoos come by, as they do each autumn on the rounds of some neuronal map laid down through generations of the flock. Cheesemaking is over for the year. I use the ricotta pot to boil tomatoes for paste and their acid dissolves the milkstone that has hardened on its sides.

I pick mid-season apples before the parrots really get to work. In the house a smell of apples and pears, and of walnuts drying by the stove, their green husks peppery, astringent. Around the valley, pickers arrive to bring in the apple crops; young

165

women and men from all over the world walk the roads to their orchards, to their ladders and picking bags and fruit bins, or sit outside the pubs and hostels where they're staying, to talk and eat and flirt in their spare hours. Scare-guns boom in the early mornings to frighten off birds from the orchard rows. Along with starlings and parrots and white cockatoos that gather to eat, currawongs come down from the mountains for the sugary harvest, their calls clinking like jingled change or a bugled chorus, according to their kind, grey or black.

Rats and mice move into wall spaces and ceilings after their summer in the long grasses. The wedge-tailed eagle pair are overhead every day with their fledgling, feeding on an abundance of roadkill that's there at the end of each summer, after the breeding season and when animals are attracted to green grass in the roadside ditches.

Young parrots chinter in the hedgerows, a sound that belongs to this season only, and the ground along the track is littered with cracked husks of hawthorn seeds where they've fed. Then dust and husks and dead leaves and the abandoned nests of summer are whisked up and away in the first gales of the approaching equinox. Everything is shaken loose, thwacked like a rug before it settles, gold and blue, quiet.

Sitting in the small garden between house and windbreak I can hear cows breathe outside the fence, and smell the white, musky rugosa roses planted along the house-wall. Marvellous light and warmth, tiny air movements. A wolf spider with her many young on her back labours through the grass beside me. Circles of the garden labyrinth are almost swallowed in creeping thyme; the aloe leans across the entrance with its bitter hands, its bitter healing sap, sharp humour.

Eclipse season – first, over the Arctic, the lunar disk slides in front of the sun, then here in the south, the whole night hemisphere watches Earth's shadow cover the full moon. We sit rugged up against the cold to see the yolk-sac, blood-sac as it reddens, darkens. Thin cloud slides across then clears, and stars burn. The Pleiades' dense glow sets in the north-west; further north Orion hangs head-down, club dangling.

Just to make space for myself was the reason I wrote at first; now I do it to wake myself up, my tongue stumbling on the edge of freedom, here with ghosts in the deep-scuffed circle under the tree in this place that keeps speaking itself again, again.

On the ground

...the fiction of knowledge is related to this lust to be a viewpoint and nothing more

Michel de Certeau,
The Practice of Everyday Life[40]

Cold silver days. First frost blurs the pasture hollows; first thin snowfall greys the sawtooth ranges across the river, from which mist rises every night to fill the valleys. Fires in logged-out forestry coupes send their plumes to yellow the light of clear afternoons and blue the rain-fogged tail of a cyclone that lags over the island.

Edible field mushrooms push up among grazed pasture grass on westerly and south-facing slopes, pink-gilled, some with brown tops, some silver-white. We eat them fried with butter – their taste is as good as their wonderful smell. Beneath the pines and birches, brilliant *Amanita muscaria*, poisonous and hallucinogenic, appear from their complex of underground threads like the visions they provoke. Their rounded caps echo the breasts of scarlet robins that begin to emerge from occult plumage and put on brightness to pair and nest. Hedgerows fill with their songs and with metallic-percussive contact calls that crackle between them like sparks, like sticks tapping a code along the strained wire of a fence.

Raven pairs scramble like fighter jets to harass this year's eagle chick as it passes over territory after territory. The chick learns, when it wants to come down to hunt and scavenge and rest, to tolerate and evade them. Currawongs feast on apples; ripe quinces and clingstone peaches fill the house with perfume; walnuts are dried and ready to eat and I use some with the last of the basil to make a batch of pesto. Stamping down the first bucket of grapes from our few pinot vines, I set the juice aside so that wild yeasts can begin their work. The brew froths crimson; after a few days I strain off skins and stalks to let the ferment finish in a jar.

I've been working in the garden labyrinth, sweeping the brick paving at the entrance, weeding paths, cutting back overhanging foliage and clearing fallen leaves. I also cover with earth the skeleton of a quoll that came to one of the paths to die, months back, after a fight.

Even with these clearances, though, I still can't see the whole pattern. All plans dissolve at ground level, where the straight progression of the high clear view is deflected, directed by hungers and tensions that wind far back. And on the ground, everything that grows and lives and dies in and around the pattern makes its claim, adds its imaginings. Whether I walk in plain darkness or smoky daylight; whether I blunder, uneasy, under the black sun, the red hallucination of eclipse, still I put one foot in front of the other and the ground talks back. The conversation breaks up old habits of mind and body as it moves on inward-leading and outward-leading paths, their turns and counterturns, their unexpected meetings and partings. Old battles, old wounds have their way and will be remembered, but in these courses scar tissue drags and unravels on an inbreath. Out of nowhere, unwilled, distant points connect; scarlet feathers flare as the cold deepens; juice can turn to wine.

Warm

Straightway after the rime dripped,
there sprang from it the cow called Auðumla;
four streams of milk ran from her teats,
and she nourished the earth.
She licked the rime-stones, which were salty,
and the first day that she licked them,
there came forth in the evening someone's hair;
the second day, their head;
the third day, all of them was there.

Prose Edda[41]

Out of the windy cold and dark comes a new addition to the household – a young cow, Elsie. She's a mulberry Jersey – dark-coloured – with a black face, pale around the mouth. She has ochre-brown ear tufts and topknot and white horns that curve outward, then in and up to their black tips in a spiral known as a *crumple*. The dark ochre colour of her ears and forelock continues along her spine and upper flanks, shading to brown-black lower down, stippled white in places, as if splashed with milk. The fronts of her legs are black, their backs shaded grey-fawn, like the legs of a deer. Her two-toed hooves are shining black; she has a long, black curling tuft to her tail.

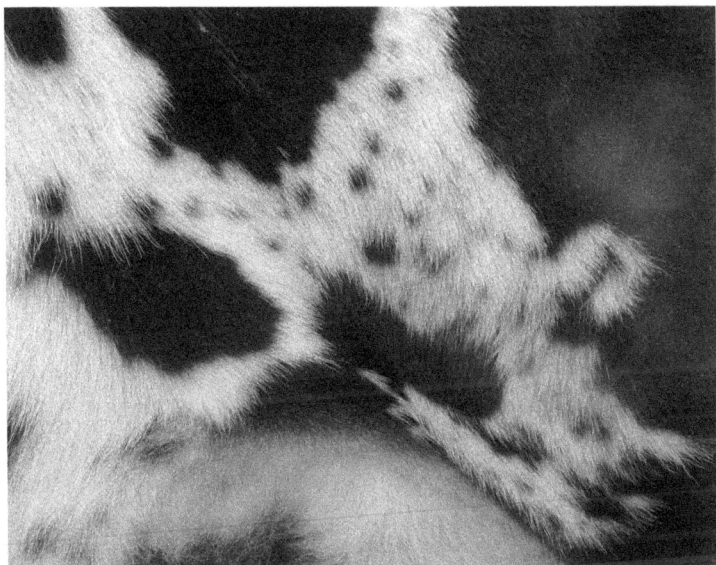

At the moment the cow and I are negotiating the correct amount of bran that will keep her happily eating while I milk. I am encouraging her to finish what's in her manger, a longitudinally sawn 44-gallon drum, before I give her more. That way, when we finish there's no leftover feed that will bring (more) rats to nest in the barn. So far, so good – when she's scooped up the bulk of what I give her, she fidgets and leans hard into my leaning head; I hold still and continue to milk; she acquiesces and seeks out the food that's been pushed to the ends of the drum.

Winter storms have formed early this year over the Southern Ocean. They smash against the island, bringing weeks of windy rain from north-west, west, south-west. In the river, water-muscles flex over sunken snags as trees fall and are swept along in the swollen stream, their roots loosened. The waverider buoy off the west coast records waves of 10 and 12 metres, then there's a day of 14, 16, 18 metre readings, then more 12 metre days before the sea begins to settle. Wind brings down branches from the eucalypts and sends blizzards of leaves from the apples and plums and pears; it loosens dead needles from the pines and combs them all one way along the track. But the birches and chestnuts still hold their leaves for the moment, and the oaks will keep theirs till new growth pushes the dry brown aside in spring.

Riding the sweep of cold air, three eagles hunt low over the paddocks, hoping to flush some creature from where it crouches out of the wind. As they pass overhead, each one turns to look at the dog as she runs beside me. But she weighs 30 kilograms now and would be too much for them, unless she was injured and had no one by her. Sometimes the adults park the youngster in a tree and go off. The chick hunches into its pale shawl and calls urgently, piercingly – *what seek what seek what seek what seek* – till they come back with something for it. Under the tree, one downy feather, wide as my hand, and the clean-picked bones of a narkie with only the scaly feet and legs untouched.

Deep puddles gather on the track to the house. I take a spade and dig channels into the wet ground to let them drain – water-play that's as satisfying now as when I was a child. Happy to be out of the weather, each morning the cows steam and drip an elliptical outline of their bellies on the concrete floor of the milking stall. The new cow licks her red calf as it suckles, roughing its coat this way and that till it looks like a child with its cheeks scrubbed bright, its wet hair combed straight up.

And at this lowest ebb of the year, the friend who, when we were both in our twenties, taught me to milk, goes into

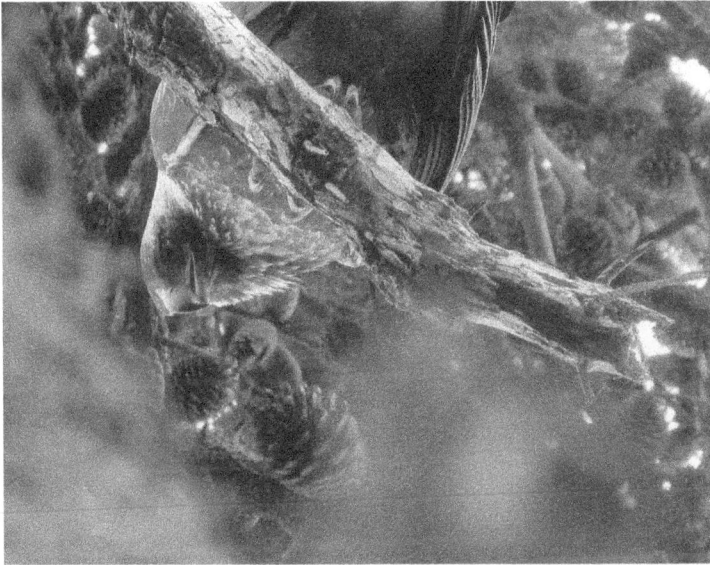

hospital for heart surgery – a long, complex operation to repair several kinds of damage, some congenital, some incurred over the course of her life. During the operation, her heart will be stopped, her blood diverted and her body temperature lowered to about 20 degrees Celsius – below the point at which a person would normally die of cold. At this temperature the heart is protected from damage that would otherwise be caused by lack of oxygen during the hours it takes to complete the various procedures, and so is the brain. When the work is done, the heart will be restarted and my friend's body will be slowly warmed.

When word comes that she's going to theatre, I walk into the labyrinth and take with me the thought of that heart and all it must undergo. When I reach the middle, from the box in the human sector I choose some chalk and the little bottle of hawthorn heart tonic I keep there. In the empty circle of the sixth lobe I draw a double spiral like a galaxy and put a few dark red drops in the centre.

She is going far – may she safely return to us.
You bright-eyed riders overhead, look away, pass quickly on.
You have no business here – she is hurt but not alone.

May she consent,
like Fráech in the coils of the serpent,
to the grip of the cold, the merciful knives,
so that what was lost may be restored.

And you, Auðumla, when the work is done,
lick her back to life, breathe on her –
out of the saving ice bring her into the salty world once more –
she has life to live, she has a child in her care, she is wanted here.

Let the heart-storm settle; let her come to quiet air.
Sinews bind up; bound up, may all hurts be healed.
May she slip cleanly back to the world,
smooth as a calf that slides to an easy birth,
warm as breath and milk.

Lick her into life, Auðumla.

And my friend does come back, and her heart does heal.

Under foot

Cadmus settled in Ogygian Thebes, and there he killed the
Aonian dragon, guardian of the spring of Ares. Athene tore away
the teeth from the dragon's jaws and bestowed them as a gift upon
Cadmus and Aeetes. And Cadmus sowed his half on the Aonian
plain and founded an earthborn clan of warriors, of all whom were
left from the spear when Ares did the reaping.
Apollonius Rhodius, *Argonautica* III, 1179–87[42]

I thought the eagles had gone, as if, recruiting them as images
of my fear for my friend's safety, I'd conjured them away – *you*
bright-eyed riders overhead, pass on. They were here, winding
their triple gyre high and low over the valley, and then the air
was empty. And two wedge-tailed eagle bodies were found,
dumped under a piece of plastic beside a road a few kilometres
away (I thought it must be them, surely – their territories are
huge), with the bodies of a sparrowhawk, a brown falcon,
five Tasmanian devils – one a female with young in her
pouch. Someone had baited a carcass and waited to see what
would come.

I searched for the eagles each day. One night I dreamed I saw
three, then four, then more each time I looked, until there were
seventeen weaving a cat's cradle of flight in the gulf over the
river. A couple of days later as I crossed the high paddock beside

the house I heard ravens call the eagle-warning – *aaaouurrr?* *aouuaaaarrr?* – and over the trees appeared the upward-curving wingtips of one, two, three – *four* wedgetails. Has the young one found a mate? Is the new bird a widow or orphan of the two that were killed?

Most days I walk south–north and back again along the road that passes our gate, following the ridge that forms one side of the river valley. Usually the dog comes with me; she trots ahead to check the wallaby/quoll/devil/cat/bandicoot/dog/narkie/horse-and-rider scents, and to seize fallen pine cones as part of a throw-and-chase game. Her paws print the fine brown dolerite gravel used to maintain the road, but under that in places, the hard, knapped-stone surface of an old macadamised wagon-way can be seen.

Over the years, I've become fascinated by this original road, made after the establishment of the local road trust in 1856. First its various locally quarried stones caught my attention – pieces of close-grained, green-black sanidine porphyry studded with oblong feldspar crystals; chunks of mudstone layered with marine fossils; pebbles of white quartz and blue-grey lace agate from ancient river gravels. Later I came to notice more and more the texture of the surface under my feet, its stones cusped and packed together like worn molars. I watched its changing look in shifting light and weather, silvery brown-grey when dry, and in rain, vivid yellow and brick-red where its rocks were burned to make them easier to break.

The road-building method pioneered by the Scotsman John McAdam in the early nineteenth century was revolutionary. In place of axle-breaking, rider-dislodging rubble-rock causeways or packed earth that alternated between bog and baked wheel-ruts (some roads were ploughed to make them usable after winter), McAdam developed a simple alternative. He used a cambered soil substrate with ditches on either side, onto which was laid a 20 centimetre (8 inch) layer of rocks no larger than 7.5 centimetres (3 inches; i.e. smaller than the iron wheel rims of the time). Men were to sit and break these rocks with small hammers, before carefully spreading them, shovel by shovel, onto the cambered surface. The passage of iron-shod road-traffic was sufficient to pack the rocks thus spread to a durable crust. Not since Roman times had roads been pushed through so efficiently – wheeled transport could now bring commerce, religion and the military to areas previously scarcely passable on foot. From the 1820s, macadamised roads began to be built throughout Britain, and soon throughout the British empire and the rest of the world.[43]

177

In Ireland during the famine of 1822, roadworks were begun in order to provide employment, and to 'bring in' within reach of the military, areas where there had been unrest. At this time, labourers were partly paid in cornmeal, and these road-building schemes kept many from starvation. In the Great Hunger of the 1840s the work continued, but now government policy forbade the use of food as payment, arguing that it would interfere with market forces.[44] Workers on those roads would have experienced a bitter irony in McAdam's construction method, which came with the recommendation that men should check whether they had broken the stones to a suitably small size by putting them in their mouths – any stone that wouldn't fit was too big. *Who among you, if a child asked for bread, would give them a stone?* During the 1840s many workers starved while waiting to be paid, sometimes lying down to die beside the roads they worked on. Sometimes they were paid but still starved, having received insufficient money to buy the food that was available. Some roads were abandoned, unfinished, to be reclaimed by grass – the *green roads.*

My mother's father was born in the 1860s near Skibbereen in West Cork where many famine roads were built. He came from a family that avoided starvation by working for the interests of their landlord – albeit one who did not remove himself during the famine and was in fact bankrupted by the road-building projects he initiated. My grandfather's family became landowners themselves by buying one of the land parcels that was sold as part of the bankruptcy process. Still it was not enough to live on – by the 1870s, only one sibling remained in Ireland; all the rest were sent to Aotearoa New Zealand to try for a new life. By a turn whose irony could not have been lost on him, my maternal grandfather was obliged to work on the Aotearoa New Zealand roads to pay his way. And as already narrated, my father's grandfather served part of his prison sentence building a military road in the fallout of the Land Wars in nineteenth-century Aotearoa New Zealand.

The first wagon roads in Tasmania were built by convict labourers. Later the road trusts continued their work. Precursors to town councils, the trusts used a system of tenders in which local men made application to form and maintain sections of road, often near where they lived.[45] Where I walk each day, several different styles and preferred materials can be seen – the stones in some stretches conform to McAdam's recommended bite-sized chunks, but in other areas much larger pieces have been used. I can imagine the dark humour that might have informed the choices of men transported here from Ireland during and just after the famine years – *Pass me a hammer and I'll break my bread, so. And I'll have it in bigger pieces, now.*

T's great-grandfather would have been among those workers. And during the hungry years of the Great Depression in the 1930s, his father and uncles laboured on roads that were pushed through to the west coast of the island, breaking stone alongside city men, indoor workers whose hands blistered and bled. I inherit the ease of the roads and in me their networks spread – their art and science and politics, their shame and coercion. Bread for stones, stones for bread; ground sowed with broken teeth from which an army rises.

At last there's a pause in wild weather. A huge winter high, created at this time of year by cold air circulating from the pole, forms over the Southern Ocean to the west and everything slows, stills, clears to intoxicating brightness. A friend arrives on the first sunny day to help me build a shelter for our outdoor oven, using a piece of galvanised iron salvaged from a water tank damaged by a tree-fall. Till now I've had the clay dome covered with a plastic sheet held down by an old polythene tarp, laboriously tied in place when the oven was not in use; the plastic wore into holes and let in rain as it flapped against the gritty surface in windy weather.

The oven is constructed in three layers – pure clay on the inside, baked to a kind of earthenware in the heat of the flames, an insulating middle layer of sawdust mixed with a little clay, and an outer layer of sandy clay that is less brittle than clay alone. When the fire is lit, cracks open in the sides as the dome expands, and if water gets in it seeps through to the middle layer of sawdust mix. In the first season after I built the oven, toadstools appeared from the cracks and the whole thing gave off a damp, mushroomy smell as it heated. Now that it's properly sheltered, I refurbish the outer layer and fill the chinks with mud. Better air circulation around the outside means that windblown rain dries quickly. It's a delight to have easy access and to know that I can cook outdoors even if there's wet weather coming.

I set sourdough to rise in the evening and slowly, slowly the ferment does its work, bringing the flour to life; by morning it's ready to bake. I arrange kindling and light the oven, burning small sticks for a quick, intensely hot fire. When I think the heat is sufficient, I rake out the coals, wipe the oven floor with a wet mop, put in the loaves and seal the entrance – steam stops the crust from hardening too fast, and the loaves rise freely as they bake.

But the bread of empire is costly, no matter that I handle it with love and that the seeds from which it comes retain their holy innocence. It's costly to the people whose land was taken to farm the grain and it's costly to the earth from which it comes,

in ways that can remain out of sight over the edge of the world while the machines of agribusiness and big transport are still able to hum.

The story I've inherited is that, once grain was domesticated and grinding technology existed, the city was always on our horizon, inevitable, with its religious and secular hierarchies and their fortifications, with its roads unrolling and armies on the march to secure and hold territory. The wastelands the city creates, its slave labour, its diseases of contagion and of malnutrition due to reduced variety and availability of food – these things, it was put to me, were unfortunate collaterals of the shining prizes of civilisation. And here we are still, the planet's dream or nightmare, building empires that map our fears and desires onto the world, squandering its waters and its soils.

Now, though, we understand that this trajectory is not inevitable. Grindstones more than 30,000 years old have been found at sites around Australia;[46] Bill Gammage, in *The Biggest Estate on Earth*,[47] and Bruce Pascoe, in *Dark Emu*, have documented how Australia's Indigenous peoples farmed local grain varieties sustainably over large parts of the semi-arid interior for tens of millennia without recourse to empire building. They were baking loaves 15,000 years before the Egyptians.

Can we sow some other crop than dragons' teeth? Can we learn a just relation with what's underfoot? Would the earth accept our tenderness at this late stage? We, too, are the planet's thoughts – perhaps it can change its mind.

Page

capable of being in uncertainties

John Keats, *Letters*[48]

Working at my desk at night, I disturb a little bat; I hear wings and think a bird has found its way in, then recognise the sound and see the dark, glove-leather sheen of fingered webbing as the bat makes puzzled rounds of my head in the glow of the screen. It's a *chocolate wattled* bat – they hibernate for a shorter time than the other seven species that live on the island, but even so this is early for it to rouse from its sleep, tucked into a fold of curtain or wall-space cranny. All the bats here are small insectivores – microbats of the Vespertilionidae family. A couple of species have adapted well to living around humans, making use of buildings as roosting places and feeding on insects attracted to their lights. The walls of my workspace are porous – the flittermice have made themselves at home.

I once found a sleeping bat on a footpath in the middle of Hobart. It was at about this time of year – someone must have put on a seldom-used coat that had been chosen by the bat as a hibernation roost; the bat was carried along until it fell out, there in the street. These creatures are tiny, covered in fur that's thick and ravishingly soft; holding the sleeping animal in my

hand, its few grams' weight was imperceptible – all I could feel
was the faintest warmth as my own body heat gathered in its
pelt. Its face was almost invisible, deep in a ruff of fur; along
its sides I could see the arm-bones and shirred skin of its folded
wings. I wrapped it loosely in a shirt and kept it in a quiet place
while I worked. Walking back to my car after dark, when I
lifted a corner of the shirt, the bat stirred and flew off. How
far from its roosting place had it been carried? Did it survive
until spring? All the species here hibernate through the coldest
months, and to be disturbed at the wrong time can mean death
by starvation.

On the mainland, bat lyssavirus – a form of the rabies
virus feared throughout history for its symptoms of delirium
with terrified aversion to water, followed by convulsions,
paralysis and death – has become a cause for concern among
those who come into contact with the big fruit bats of the
tropics and subtropics.[49] Several people have died after being
scratched or bitten. There's a vaccine but not much hope of
cure once symptoms appear in the unvaccinated. As settlement
encroaches and the forest fruits and blossoms these bats feed on
become scarcer, they move into orchards and parks; as seasonal
patterns alter, they're also extending their range further south.
Occasional strays cross Bass Strait and make it to Tasmania,
although there are no colonies here, so far. But the virus has
been found in one species of microbat on the mainland, so it's
possible that animals here could carry it.

It snows – big wet flakes mixed with rain at first, then the rain
stops and the snow continues, falling in silent showers through
the night. But the ground is sodden and all that remains in the
morning is a crusted glaze on the grass, though the lower peaks
and passes are white and the mountains gleam. By late morning

it's gone from all but sheltered pockets in the high country. Thirty years ago, we used to get two or three falls each winter that lasted a day or so, but now that's rare and some years pass with none at all.

With the snow, the black cockatoos are back – *they'll tell you when bad weather's coming, yes, and where from too – they'll be flying out of it, away.* A flock of sixty or more makes the rounds of pine hedges and wattle gullies along the valley and their signs are everywhere in shredded cones and chunks pulled from fallen timber, torn apart for the grubs that live in dead wood. Three young birds, their feathers still greyish, not yet grown into glossy black, sit in the prickly wattle outside my workspace and eye me, unconcerned, as they strip bark from a rotted limb. They keep up a continuous conversation – it's a sound I love, a mixture of hissing creaks and a kind of nickering wail, keen and directed out of some wild will, untrammelled.

And mixed with these cold days, wafts of balmy air and the smell of working ground – grass in the paddocks has begun to grow and buds are moving. Green rosellas feed in flowering wattles, showering the ground with nipped yellow sprigs. The call of the first pardalote falls, *drip-drop*, into the still air of afternoon from high in a eucalypt, and the first quail answers from the cover of grass and tangled weeds under the lucerne hedge, *sip here? sip here?*

The platypus has appeared in the dam again now that winter creeks and roadside drains are running. I think it follows the water uphill, treating farm dams along the way like billabongs in a river. It stays for a while then moves on, perhaps retreating with the water to permanent creeks in the valley below. Now at twilight it surfaces and goes under in smooth, rolling, purposeful dives, stirring up mud and turning the dam turbid in search of its invertebrate food. Its arrival reminds me of my self-divided turmoil on returning from Ireland, and how consoled I was by the creature's ease of movement back and forth between the worlds of light and dark, land and water.

Around the anniversary of the Irish pilgrimage I have this dream: *I am standing on a quay in West Cork with a little town at my back. I am watching seals sunning themselves on rocks some way offshore. Complacently, my dream-self rehearses the selkie stories in which certain seals, benign shapeshifters, are able to shed their skins and leave behind their oceanic life at will, to walk on land as humans, with whom they sometimes fall in love, though often at great cost. But as I look, I realise that by some reversal I'm using the wrong word and that these creatures are not selkies but kelpies – water horses, also able to take human form but at best tricksters and at worst intent on taking humans – the unwary, the greedy and naïve – with them into the water to be drowned and eaten.*

I took my familial blindspot, my cushioning ignorance, with me into famine country in Ireland and in return the ancestors showed me faces I hadn't bargained for. Working in the dark, we scare up what's been sleeping; into the dream-space and the space of each moment, uninvited, come *uncertainties, mysteries, doubts* – furies that can tear us apart in payment of blood debts incurred generations back.

In the light of the little lamp, the space of the page permits a meeting with these rouselings. And if, as part of a writing practice, I can sit with what approaches, if I can tolerate grief and anxiety for the necessary interval (days, months, a lifetime), perhaps a curse can be transformed; perhaps I might find a way to honour the furious dead, let them speak, hold the tension between worlds to find what redress is required then/there and now/here. But there's a seasonality to this process that can't be ignored – periods of shutdown in the face of wintry forces, periods of choosing life on land over entry into the cold and dark, times when I'm infected by a horror of the watery realm and its fearful work, acknowledging all that is damaged and destructive. And then there's a shift and again the work becomes possible.

Early or late, ready or not, change comes. Something wakes us; *our dwelling is plucked up and removed* and we take to the air, the water, the road, zigzagging up into the darkening sky or over the rise and down to the west-flowing winter creek. Drawn or driven, impelled by necessity, we add our inscription to the immense tracery that elaborates itself everywhere.

AUGUST

Gods

Rulers want their go-ahead. High and wide,
two eagles circle right and tear their kill –
that will do for a sign. And once war is let loose, all
that lives is game – the daughter, gagged, goes down.
But there's another law, another
lawkeeper who hates the ones that feast on fear.
In time she'll bring them low.
Speak your grief, let justice come.

Aeschylus, *Agamemnon*[50]

Early in the month, squalls blow in from the south-west where lead-coloured cloud gathers thick. One day towards evening, sleet begins to fall with the rain and, by morning, stillness and mirrorlight announce snowfall, the whole world blanketed down to the sea and everything holding still, delighted or horrified under the blessed touch. Every twig is a balance that weighs airy white, every forest clearing a brilliant sheet, signalling *here! here!* Long before I go out, birds have been up writing their four-toed lines, and wallaby tracks already fill with fresh flakes. Schools are closed, commuters stay home. All day, snow showers bluster then fall silent, drifting down. They're interspersed with blue sky and sunlight that strikes the coming clouds purple-black.

Under tall trees downslope in the bush-run where the cattle are sheltering, T finds an eagle feather. It's draggled and muddied by the trampled ground where it fell. Longer than my forearm, the edges are uneven, with a deep indentation about halfway along one side – at first I think some creature has chewed it. Then as I look more closely, I see that it's a primary feather – not chewed but notched, wide at the base and narrowing to form one of the distinctive, separable 'finger' points at the tip of each outstretched wing.

The quill is thick as a pencil, pale at the base, shading brown-black along its length. It's ragged and the shaft has begun to split. It will have been used till it started to break up, then shed in sequence with other feathers along the wing in a *wave-moult* pattern, which doesn't leave wide gaps that might compromise the bird's ability to fly.[51]

Confined by cold, the bees are quiet. In my workspace, rats are nesting in the wall where the swarm is – they scutter there and I hear the young ones mew. Chewed comb and dead bees fall from the wall cavity into the downstairs space of the milking stall below my feet. I will set traps for the rats; I don't want to use poison – owls and quolls sicken and die when they eat the dead and dying animals.

The dog hasn't seen snow before – she rushes through the powdery world making star jumps, snapping up mouthfuls of strangeness and tossing it into the air. Cattle stand chewing cud, bodies steaming, melted flakes glistening in their coats. I'm only milking one cow now – the young Jersey, Elsie. The other cow, Maggie, is resting before she gives birth in the coming months. Elsie is, I hope, in calf too – we brought the bull to her when she came into oestrus and if so, she'll calve in autumn. Now, as I lean into her flank each day to milk, I'm singing not just to

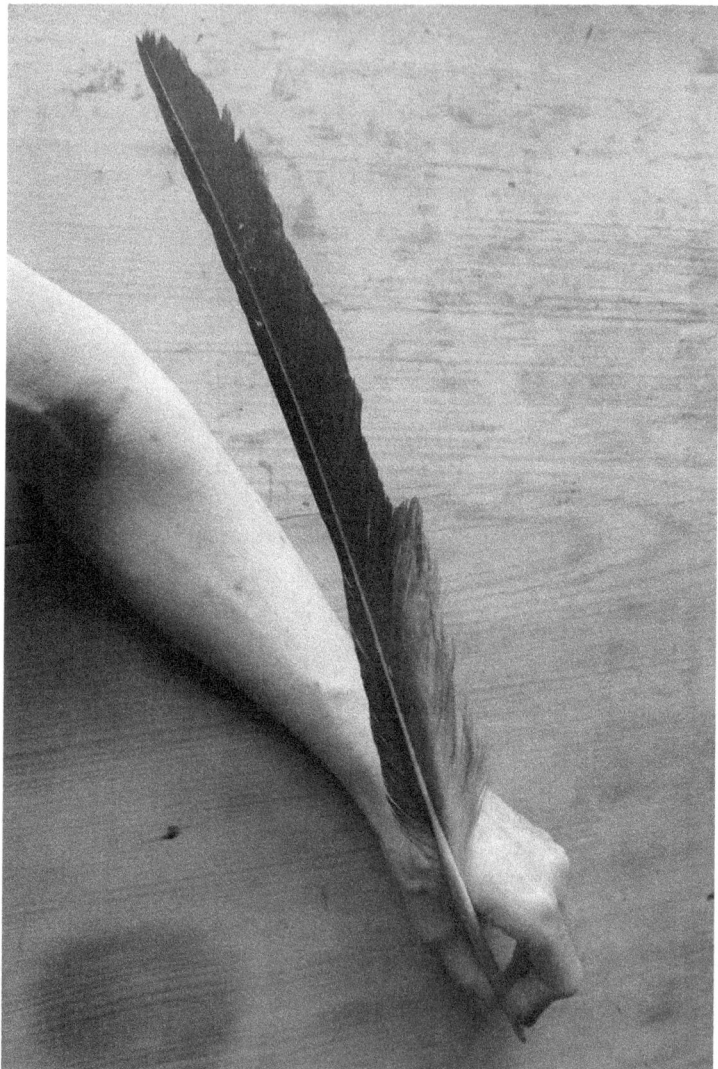

her but perhaps to her calf as well, a cluster of dividing cells that hangs like a star above my head in the dark hoop of her pelvis.

For three days snow showers continue, then the fronts that brought storms from the Southern Ocean move on and the sky clears. Snow melts to slush and clear nights bring hard frost that turns the puggy mud on pathways and around paddock gates to stone. Ice shines right to the treetops, though here on the ridge this doesn't happen often – usually the cold air slips downhill to pool on the valley floor, while (relative) warmth is trapped above it under a layer of dense air. But now and then, freezing fog draws up from the river and spills over the valley rim; blades of ice build from the western edges of things. Cobwebs hang like little chandeliers; every needle on the pines, every leaf on the eucalypts is limned ice-white. My face and fingers burn as I walk, fast, to the top of the hill. From the green-white blur of frosted leaflets, silver wattle flowers shine acid-yellow; the surfaces of farm dams are glossy with cold, as if the water had thickened, *gelid*.

Then everything softens and, as if primed by the freeze, willow catkins break silver and a yellow smoke of pollen blows from the pines. Branches of the cherry plums are crowded white with blossom in a recapitulation of snow. Courting grebes and coots arrow across the surface of the dam or splash and call in preening dances. A little flock of white-eyed ducks arrives, and two swans, glossy black adults, feed for a day or three then move on, down to the river flats.

Nesting has begun and, in the still air, a feather drifts down. Wattlebirds pull strips of bark from the grapevines and tea-trees; yellow-throated honeyeaters land on the backs of cattle – or dogs and cats or the heads of humans – to take hair for nest-lining. Honeyeaters of several kinds fight for feeding rights in the winter-flowering grevilleas, while others search for insects under loose bark in the eucalypts.

Moss shines as if lit from within in answer to the low sun still tethered to the northern horizon, but the days are lengthening and pasture begins to grow. When I bring the cow in each morning, she strays to snatch mouthfuls of new grass from ungrazed places outside the paddock gate. All winter she has rushed eagerly to find the sweet meal I heap for her in the half-drum feeder, but that taste palls now beside the delight of fresh green. Leaves and flower buds emerge from the tips of the elder tree that grows beside the doorway and she reaches for them, wrapping her tongue around the twigs.

With the first warmth, blowflies and bristle flies wake and find their way inside. A week of daytime temperatures above 13 degrees Celsius brings the bees out to forage for pollen in the

willow catkins and tree lucerne flowers – food for this season's brood. Despite the rats, the wall swarm seems vigorous, the workers unaffected as they come and go. Maybe my traps aren't needed.

Manipulated, manipulator of environments, disposed and disposer of lives, hesitant, uncertain, I make my interventions – a predator wired for reflection, every move held up to the light of irony and another view. In me, in each of us, in households and nations, the old dramas play out still – blood debts linger in actions and reactions, tensions and conflicting impulses to which humans have given the names of gods. And everywhere, as always, the large is figured in the small – a city is built where a heifer lies down to rest; a war is foretold by the stoop of raptors, by the death of a hare. Meshed from the start, I harm and protect, I feel pity and I feast, and the furies will have their due – no action without its consequences. From footprints that cross and recross, from curlicued vines on a trellis-stave, through lens-droplets and in the opacity of milk I read my story.

Span

Use the strength and range you've found
to reach across and hold the tension
of the gap. There, in you,
is where the unknown works things out.

Rainer Maria Rilke,
'As once the winged energy of delight'[52]

It's the spring equinox – for a moment, light and darkness match each other, then the days continue to lengthen, brighter as the sun arcs higher. All through the month, waves of blossom follow one another – almonds and cherry plums, apricots and peaches, then greengages and damsons, and later the first pears and apples, the first elderflowers. This despite alternations of snow with the beginnings of warmth. The mountains throw up clouds as they lift warm air and it collides with the cold above. Thunder booms up and down the valley – each charge meets the ground at a single point as a lightning bolt, while above, the opposite pole discharges horizontally throughout the ionosphere, unboundaried.

As spring advances, for once we manage to check the bees early, looking into boxes, removing jellybean-shaped queen cells from the bottoms of slides and burr comb from the tops. The workers are bringing in plenty of pollen and all the hives have healthy brood. Among the bees of the newest swarm I catch a glimpse of the long, pointed, shining body of the queen as she moves across the face of the comb to lay her eggs in cell after cell. I put a queen-excluder above the brood box where she is – a sheet of zinc with holes big enough for workers to pass through but too small for the queen – so that later in the season I can take honey without killing brood or injuring her.

In the mornings before milking, before breakfast, half asleep, I move straight from my bed to a mat in the next room and begin a practice that comprises a series of movements and stillnesses, different each day. Between worlds, focus still soft, I reach into myself like a child putting on clothes, feel my way into arms and legs, lift through the joints of my spine, turn this way and that to find the scope of movements that belong to me. It's a way of becoming present as I wake. The night's stiffness and contractions begin to limber.

The movements I practise belong to one of many styles of meditation in which gestures work like a syllabic language – each combines with others to create a syntax of experiences through which body and mind inform one another and in the

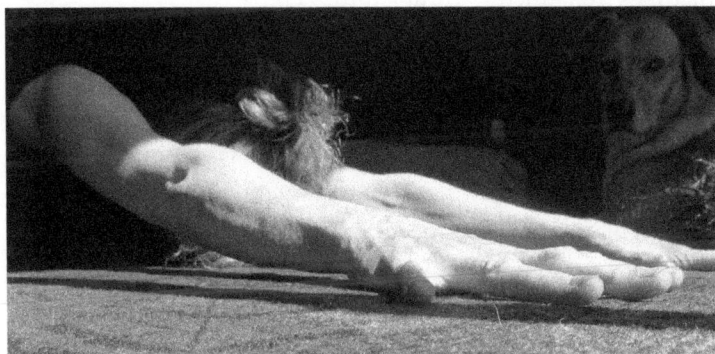

195

process, collapse their distinctions. Between and around each movement-word and movement-sentence is stillness-silence, in which sensation-thoughts can resonate.

Often these practices have developed as defensive or offensive training regimes for religious or secular troops during times of upheaval, with the aim of achieving combined stability and mobility – strength and flexibility of body-mind. Practice styles are passed on through lineages of teacher-practitioners who develop a metalanguage of observation and instruction, alongside and arising out of their practice.

I began in my twenties because I wanted to find a way to manage back pain and, later, shoulder injuries. Showing up on the mat, paying attention again and again, I became aware, first, of how much of me, with the exception of areas of injury, was blank, without sensation. Slowly, over years, some of the blanks began to fill, often with what initially felt like pain. Eventually I began to be able to distinguish, in some measure, between sensations that signalled damage and those that were merely intense. Though unwelcome, injuries that are not completely disabling can be great teachers – I understand my back and shoulders more thoroughly now than I understand some places that have remained untroubled thus far.

Everyone who develops a practice must renegotiate the distortions of history and culture and personality to which instructional language is subject, and everyone expresses the movements and sequences differently, via their particular aptitudes and resistances, fears and attractions. My own practice has been shaped by a need to work with long periods of restriction relating to injuries and my own fears. I began with, and from time to time revert to, a default pattern that swings between intense anxiety and disembodying escape.

Coming to my senses time after time, I am able to experience how bodily and mental and emotional pain and anxiety and happiness fluctuate and are so interconnected as to be indistinguishable from one another. I begin to be able to tolerate better my own shifting affect and to realise that it is not in itself a cause for concern. And now, in a moment of relative freedom, it pleases and amuses me to do handstands before breakfast, while I can.

In winter darkness or as now in spring light, this is how I begin most days – I lie down, sit, stand, turn myself upside down. Yellow wattlebirds clear their throats in the grevilleas outside the window. A young shrike-thrush, juvenile feathers still speckled all over, learns by trial and error to calculate the undulations of its flight. A warm, windy day shakes open the leaves of hawthorn and elder, hazel and birch, while in the gullies, swathes of silver wattle blossom begin to fade as the greenish flush of blackwood flowers begins. The shining cuckoos arrive, and the harrier hawks.

And across the world, in the violent air, war gathers and strikes, strikes again, and the people stream away; or here and elsewhere, old age the tiger leaps, or sickness or accident, and our life goes back to the world. In the silences before and after, we step into the space of our work, reach and hold the tension as we find the shapes of family, history, culture – ours and others' – their freedoms and terrible limits, their collisions and intersections. What we knew is overturned; we see back to beginnings and understand how things seeded long ago cross through us, seeking recognition. We respond; something works itself out, something is handed on, discharged.

Manifold

Each day the soul spins its tangible dream.

The cattle are shedding their winter pelts. They rub themselves on posts and branches to rid themselves of the thick undercoat and coarse guard hairs as the silky-fine summer coat grows in. It gives them a tender look, like a baby's head or a fern frond unfurling. On backs and flanks, tufts of the thicker hair still cling.

The young cow, Elsie, has had enough of her calf and has kicked him off. He's well over a year old now, taller and heavier than she is. I went away for a fortnight and left them together, thinking that she would be happy with this arrangement – but when I got back he was weaned and her udder was empty.

By chance, the other cow, Maggie, who we thought wasn't due till November, calved the night I got home, so there's milk again. She's a stocky Jersey-Angus cross with a black coat; she's calm, unflappable – but not keen, as Elsie is, on being scratched behind the ears or having her coat brushed. She stands quietly during milking but at other times responds to touch with a toss of her head – *Be off!* – and an irritable shuddering of her skin, as if a fly had landed there.

Over the first weeks the calf stays with Maggie day and night. We bring him into the milking stall with her each day so that she knows where he is and isn't anxious for him as I ease the pressure in her udder, taking the milk he's still too small to keep up with.

I freeze excess colostrum produced in the first few days so that I have some on hand for calves who are orphaned or rejected or, as sometimes happens, simply forgotten or not recognised by young heifers who've given birth for the first time. The proportion of colostrum lessens rapidly, and after ten days the milk has paled to its ordinary hue.

In cattle-herding societies, colostrum has always been used as a tonic for invalids and as rich food for children, the elderly and the immunocompromised. In recent times it has been prescribed with some success for AIDS-related digestive problems. If gently heated it sets, and the recipe for *beastings custard*, sweetened and spiced with nutmeg, was one of the first things passed on to me by a neighbour who saw my ignorance and took me in hand when I was learning to milk.

Everything is growing, leafing, extending itself into bud and blossom. In the hay paddocks, grass leaps out of the ground; in the garden, long strands of cleavers and vetch and fumitory insinuate themselves through any growth that will support them. The fishy smell of hawthorn blossom mixes with the cold sweetness of late-flowering narcissus on south-facing slopes. Oaks are clothed in gold-green and the stringybark eucalypts are freshly tipped with red. Even the sombre pines have sprouted bright new needle bunches among which tiny purple cones are forming.

Nesting continues and day after day wrens and robins and shrike-thrushes fling themselves at reflective surfaces – windows,

199

wing mirrors of cars – challenging the rivals they see there. Tiger snakes are active, hunting nestlings – much more substantial than their usual diet of frogs. They seem especially attuned to the presence of blackbird and sparrow nests, and ignore the attacks of parent birds to work their way intently through vines under the eaves or hunt high among twiggy branches. Mobbed by wattlebirds and honeyeaters and tracked by the agitated buzzing of wrens and thornbills, they carry on undeterred.

Against the steady light of the waxing moon, a solar flare sends an aurora pulsing across the night sky. Extra energy entering the planetary system brings stormy weather that adds itself to the already blustery conditions around the equinox. Internet connections drop out; phone lines fail. I'm edgy and irritable and have to bring myself back again, again, again, to the slow pace I need in order to think, and to the quiet that will enable me to work with the animals without communicating my disturbance to them.

I went to Aotearoa New Zealand to see my mother. She's ninety-eight now, frail and beginning to be aware of moving between worlds. *I think I must be going to die soon,* she says. *I can't seem to remember that my mother is not alive.* She gestures towards photographs of the dead and the living pinned to the wall opposite her bed – *I feel she's here with me. We used to call her Nellie – there she is, with all the others! They're all here. It's comforting.* Then, pointing to our reflections in the mirror next to the photographs: *And who's that in the doorway?*

Often she seems content: *I can't imagine what's in store for me but I know it will be wonderful.* At other times she's full of grief, inconsolable: *Something's wrong!* she weeps, and, worried about her effect on me – *This won't be helping her!* – she tries to distract

herself, grasping at words from the television – *Oh they said 'rescue'!* – or from conversations in the hallway – *Fruit and ice cream. Who said that? Yes, please, that would be sharp and lovely!* Next day, smiling, she greets me calmly: *It's you! I thought you said you were going. Off you go – I'll stay here with Nell.*

And through all this – mind and physicality altered, bird-boned – she's still completely, recognisably herself. Not-this, not-that, manifold, the soul sounds out its chord and every soul its once-only variation on the creaturely, human, ancestral theme. Winking in and out, each night we hang in the darkness that comes before and after; each day we're born into the flourishing and afflicted world that at once feeds and feeds from us, inoculates and weans us from itself. Sometimes it's possible to hear and bear the discord – then, from all that's given, each night, each day, turning, we compose our reply.

El Niño

Lully, lulla, thow littell tine child,
By by, lully, lullay, thow littell tyne child,
By by, lully, lullay!

O sisters too, how may we do
For to preserve this day
This pore yongling for whom we do singe
By by, lully, lullay?

Coventry Carol[53]

Suddenly it's dry, hot. Pastures are still green but stinging heat gathers and already the grass is yellow in places where the soil is thin, or where trees take up moisture close to the windbreaks and at the edge of the bush. The hay crop is sparse; farmers are selling stock they won't be able to feed. It's reminding me of how things were in the drought of the early 1980s. Rain gathers in the mountains but does not reach us – it stops on the other side of the river, falling like a curtain there while we watch, tantalised.

It's the start of an El Niño event whose influence might last a year or go on for the best part of a decade. Rain-bearing patterns of atmospheric convection move east – torrential rain falls in the central Pacific and on the west coast of South

America (where the effect was named after the Christ Child because it's usually strongest in December); in eastern Australia, by contrast, drought may set in.

The El Niño occurs when the prevailing east–west trade winds falter over the equatorial Pacific. Warm water, no longer driven westwards by the wind, spreads into the central and eastern ocean, which is usually kept cool by an upwelling of cold water, drawn from the depths along the coast of South America to replace warm water that is being pushed away. This warming sets up a feedback loop that causes the winds to drop further, as the pressure gradient that generates air movement from cool to warm regions diminishes.

On the Australian mainland, the eastern states continue to dry and fire warnings heighten from *extreme* to *catastrophic*. Wildfires begin. Here, though, halfway through the month it turns windy, cloudy, buffeting from the south-west, west, north-west so that the frames of north-facing and south-facing windows creak as air sucks past them. Showers, cold enough to fall as snow on higher ground, bring a couple of centimetres of rain that alternates with fierce sun – the hay thickens. Ironically, this respite from drought is a result of higher than usual temperatures in the Indian Ocean, which suck up storm systems from the south and bring moist air across from Western Australia.

At a local level, weather systems are full of apparent paradoxes and contradictions like this one, where warming to the west brings us rain and cooling protection from fire. And further south, the East Antarctic ice sheet is melting more slowly than the West Antarctic sheet because the east of the continent, which was previously the driest of cold deserts, now receives more precipitation as a result of generalised change elsewhere.[54] And locally colder weather, such as extreme winter cold recently

recorded in East Antarctica, creates ideal conditions for chemical reactions in the stratosphere that destroy ozone molecules. As a result, the ozone hole was near record size when it formed this spring. Systems interact in unexpected ways.

UV intensity increases as the ozone hole begins to break up over the pole and the area of weakened protection spreads north. Peak intensity is usually reached in December–January here, and after that the effect lessens as the region of thinned ozone begins to be replenished. In the intense light of our star, the flowering season rushes ahead. I've been collecting ingredients for teas from among the plants that are ready to harvest: a daytime mix of antioxidants, alteratives and cardiac and respiratory tonics – red clover, sage flower, nettle leaf, calendula, elderflower, rose, lemon verbena; and a second mix containing green oats, mallow, linden and chamomile flowers to drink before sleeping – nervine, demulcent, digestive, soporific. They both taste good.

Against localised climatic aberrations, the background shift is ever warmer. The oceans – chief stabilisers and therefore also chief modifiers of Earth's climate – take up more than 90 per cent of the heat that accumulates in the global system, forming a planet-wide energy bank that is an engine of change, slow to warm and also slow to cool. A growing body of research has shown that, to a depth of about 700 metres, water temperatures have been rising in the surface layers of the oceans since the 1970s.[55] Conditions in the abyssal ocean, however, are so extreme that it's enormously difficult to go there or even create remote-sensing devices that can withstand the huge pressures, hundreds of times greater than at sea level, and work in that cold and utter darkness.

Around the turn of the millennium, more information about the deeps began to become available, after the Argo Project[56] launched 3,500 free-floating sensors that were able to monitor ocean temperatures to a depth of about 2 kilometres. Their findings, along with feedback from individual probes dropped to the abyssal seabed, have confirmed that the deeper ocean is warming too – at a much slower rate than the surface waters but still measurably. This is especially noticeable around western Antarctica. Warming may be occurring there because of increased glacial melting in the Amundsen Sea, where the release of fresh water decreases salinity and therefore also decreases the density/sinking of water to replenish the cold depths.

Western Antarctica is one of the few 'feeder' zones for an immense system of deep, slow, cold currents[57] through which about a third of the world's seawater circulates at any given time, driven along the *thermohaline* gradient from cold/salty (and therefore more dense) to warm/less salty (and therefore less dense). This convective cycle begins where sea ice forms, dropping most of its salt as it freezes. Beneath the ice, highly concentrated brine accumulates, very cold and dense, which sinks deep, dropping quickly to a depth of about 2 kilometres, and begins to flow along a series of pathways like rivers within the sea, taking with it dissolved carbon dioxide and picking up nutrients as it goes.

Eventually these deep rivers warm and rise a little, through prolonged contact with areas of geothermal activity on the sea floor or by mixing with adjacent layers of warmer water, or they are forced upwards by geological barriers or the shallowing of the ocean. In places they cross over themselves, warm above cold, forming patterns like gigantic cloverleaf flyovers. When the warmed water finds its way back towards the poles, the cycle begins again. Carbon and other dissolved nutrients and minerals in the cold, upwelling water are taken up by phytoplankton – minute organisms that produce more than half the world's oxygen and form the foundation of the ocean's biomass and food cycle.

Deep currents are slow, slow, though they may move a little faster as they warm. Radiocarbon dating of isotopes from samples taken at different parts of the flow suggests that it might take 1,000 years from the time water first cools and sinks till it comes back to its starting point. If the formation zones of cold currents continue to warm, regulatory systems that have been in place since the last ice age will begin (have already begun) to recalibrate. We don't know how that might play out.

Faced with a need to adapt, fear and necessity and self-interest shape the way we use available information, and also the stories

207

we tell ourselves about what is happening and our part in it. Predictions about the effects of changes to deep ocean currents range from accelerated warming, to the onset of another ice age, to the cancelling-out of the former by the latter. We gather our data and drink our chosen mixture down, in hope that it will wake us or offer a means of healing or help us to sleep.

Meanwhile, for a time, the oceanic ruminations of the planet go coiling under still, taking with them our outbreaths, the bodies of the sea's dead and all dense matter washed and blown and jettisoned from land. Benign and poisonous, all is dissolved. Water that sank to the floor of the abyss a thousand years ago comes round at last into the light with its freight of carbon and silica and salts, marked and taken up by plankton blooms, those starbursts that give us breath and feed the life-web.

And sooner or later, we too go under and return to our mineral selves, whether through collective or singular self-undoing or murder, or when the body or the age is stricken or wears out. Then from our dissolution something else can come, as yet unknowable – all that we were, monstrous and salutary, taken back, rocked and cradled to another birth.

Joy and sorrow cake

*Disturbance in the soul is perhaps more prosaically understood
as persistence in the memory.*

Ross Gibson,
Seven Versions of an Australian Badland[58]

In the first weeks of December, strong westerlies continue to
rake the windbreak trees and bring down nests. A gust pops
the roof out of one of the polytunnels with a crop of tomatoes
inside, heavy with green fruit. All day the split plastic wallops
in the wind but in the end not much damage is done – a willow
windbreak takes the brunt and though some branches crack, the
trees lift the worst of the gale up and over. In a different year
the windbreak might be gapped, the crop thrashed and broken.

Hunkered down in the house, I look through the book where
I transcribe favourite recipes (or better still, get the people who
taught them to me to write them in) – things made by family
and friends alongside dishes I've found for myself and enjoyed.
Buckwheat blini from G, my friend and mentor of many years;
J's pear and whiskey cake; JH's tomato relish; A's fruit cake.
And from my mother, the recipe for *German flat cake*, given to
her by my father's mother, who in turn received it from her
husband's (Highland Scots) mother, via *her* German mother-in-
law, my great-great-grandmother. It's a sweet yeast cake in the
tradition of *Freud-und-Leid Blechkuchen*, sheet cakes made for

weddings and funerals – quick and easy to prepare and serve to crowds of people:

1 oz [30 g] block of compressed yeast [I use sourdough starter]; 4 saucersful flour and half a teaspoon of salt; 1 saucerful softened lard or beef dripping [I use butter]; 1 saucerful sugar; 1 saucerful sultanas [I use currants]; 1 tablespoon mixed spice, 1 tablespoon flour, 1 tablespoon sugar – these three combined for topping. Start yeast in a cup of warm water or milk with a teaspoon of sugar. When yeast mixture is frothy, add softened fat and combine with flour, salt, sugar and fruit. Add extra water or milk as needed to make a soft but not-too-sticky dough. Leave to rise for an hour [longer for sourdough]; knead once or twice during this time then roll out into a rectangle about ¼ inch [½ centimetre] thick and leave to rise again for half an hour on a baking tray. Brush with milk and sprinkle with spice/flour/ sugar mixture just before baking. Cook in a medium oven till brown, being careful not to burn the fruit – about 20 minutes.

At home we used to cut it into strips and eat it warm, with butter melting into the gritty topping of spice and sugar.

My great-great-grandmother emigrated with her husband and two young sons from Prussia to Aotearoa New Zealand via the Barossa Valley in South Australia, where they landed in 1848, late among successive waves of Lutheran migrants encouraged there by the South Australian Company. Born in 1822, H was a household servant and seamstress, a city girl from Königsberg (Kaliningrad) on the Baltic coast (though, like most, her family had peasant beginnings in the countryside close by), daughter of a soldier, married to a soldier. In Australia, her Barossa Valley neighbours were earlier arrivals from rural Silesia, who followed a stricter form of Lutheranism and thought her *unsociable*, a *conceited hussy* who *dressed different*. For her part, she mocked their country accents, and when her embroidered underwear gave offence, responded that *the real scandal was that any woman should report such a thing to the church elders*.

At twenty, in service to the family of one of her father's regimental officers, she was taken far from home to the garrison community at Potsdam to be an on-campaign amusement for a wealthy, much older officer. He gave her *frequent small gifts of jewellery* and set her up in *a neat comfortable cottage in the suburbs* – then in the spring of 1844 was posted away and left her to her own devices. Though he continued to come and go from the city, she never saw him again, and, evicted from the comfortable cottage, pregnant, she took in needlework and sold her small gifts, piece by piece. And so she lived for three years after the birth of her son, my great-grandfather. When she became pregnant again, the Garrison Court and church intervened and her father was approached to help find a potential marriage partner. From among the soldiers of the Potsdam garrison, her father put forward the name of a man who had worked for him in Königsberg – and who may in fact have been the second child's father. My family now carries his surname – one thread in a mostly Irish and Scottish plait.

Despite the silk and lace and jewelled locket of an affluent moment, her face, in the image I have of her, made in about 1866, looks haunted to me, traumatised, watchful, like the faces in so many portraits of the time, when, as Ross Gibson puts it in *Seven Versions of an Australian Badland*, 'the camera was still unfamiliar and people had not yet learned to mask the emotions that set their nerves and muscles ajangle in front of the deadpan lens'.[59] It's the face of a woman who, during a time of war, had survived on her own with a child in a garrison town, who had entered a forced marriage with a man of *violent disposition* and had unwillingly emigrated with him to Australia, then sunk in the brutality of its own frontier war. There she endured the loss of her third child in infancy, blaming the baby's sickness and death on her husband (*niedrige Kerl!*), after he forced her to help bring in a harvest during stormy weather, leaving the baby and the two-year-old outside in the care of my then five-year-old great-grandfather, who was unable to find shelter. She went on to give birth to four more children.

In 1866 the family had been six years in Aotearoa New Zealand, where another war continued. In the coming decades she would live through the deaths from disease of children and grandchildren, and her husband's bankruptcy and subsequent death by poisoning (accident? suicide? murder?), after strychnine was mixed with the chloral hydrate to which he was addicted and which he used to self-medicate the *lunitic fever* of his ungovernable rages. Her eldest son, my great-grandfather, embroiled in his stepfather's financial ruin, would be jailed for forgery.

I think about the family story through these blustery days of hay harvest and its attendant anxiety. By Christmas the winds have died away; it's hot and perilously dry. Hay's cut and scattered, raked and baled — so thin — less than half the usual crop. For many years now, we've used round bales — they weigh between 300 and 400 kilograms and need specially adapted tractor forks to move them around, but each one is like a well-constructed hayrick that sheds water. And so the panic is gone, that once was there every year when we used the smaller, 20–25 kilogram rectangular bales — would it rain and turn the sweet crop to poisonous slime or heat it to spontaneous flame in the shed; would friends and family be free to help bring it in, with their own harvest to attend to; would we be free to meet our obligation to help in return?

And in fact it does rain this year, the day after Christmas, soft, steady, miraculous, with the bales still out in the paddocks. With the mercy of water, ready to start again having lost its nest in the devastation of wind, a brush bronzewing pigeon paces outside the window, bobbing its head and calling to its double in the glass – *oom oom oom oom* – or perhaps looking for a way to reach nest sites it sees in shadowy corners of the interior, dim like the scrubby thickets where it makes its flimsy platform of twigs. In the freshened air after the rain, I spend an afternoon picking flowers for *Blütentee* inside the perfumed tent of the linden, in whose shade only truth can be told.

We're made from their ingredients, the ancestors – they're in our bones and skin, in the hue of our moods, in the taste of our hungers and fears and generosities. Though they try to show us only their strengths, we're also the memories of their wounded and wounding lives, their bitter weddings, their funeral feasts; they persist as our disturbances. Rough-grown and fine, they store themselves up in us and we roll them out, make our story from their pieces, tell the happiness and grief of their souls as we shape our own.

Year 4

Counsel

[W]hen I die, I can breathe back…to the world all that I didn't do. All that I might have been and couldn't be. All the choices I didn't make. All the things I lost and spent and wasted. I can give them back to the world. To the lives that haven't been lived yet. That will be my gift back to the world that gave me the life I did live, the love I loved, the breath I breathed.

Ursula Le Guin, *The Other Wind*[60]

A couple of hundred metres upslope from our house, across the paddocks, is the house where my husband grew up, and where his brother now lives. It was built around the turn of the twentieth century, from horizontally overlapping eucalyptus weatherboards in the local style. Its wooden joists sit on brick stumps, and because it's on a slope, there's a gap of nearly a metre between the floorboards and the ground on the downhill, northern side of the house, diminishing to a few centimetres on the uphill side. The underfloor space is enclosed by boards, and in the deepest parts by stone and cement walls, with a gap left in one place to give access under the house.

A few months ago, a female Tasmanian devil moved in and has made the underfloor her den. She hunts at night and comes back in the morning twilight to feed her half-grown cubs, calling to them – *hmm hmm mmh hnh* – as she walks to where they wait, deep in the narrowing space. On warm days, while their mother sleeps, the cubs, about the size of large housecats, come out to sun themselves on the grass beside the house when they think nobody is looking.

Tasmanian devils, *Sarcophilus harrisii*, are marsupial carnivores that once occupied the whole of the Australian mainland but are thought to have become extinct there about 3,000 years ago. In Tasmania, their numbers are decreasing for the usual reasons relating to loss of habitat, but also at present because of a cancer called Devil Facial Tumour Disease, which is communicable from one animal to another for reasons that are not currently well understood. The disease most often affects the face and jaw and is passed on by biting during fights over food or when mating. Now new strains are being discovered, one of them just a few kilometres from here.

Attempts are being made to identify pockets of greatest genetic diversity and to breed disease-free 'insurance' popu-lations on offshore arks – literal islands off the coast, or zoos and breeding programs on the mainland and overseas. It seems likely that the female denning under the house is also part of a more informal ark project, where healthy rescued animals (orphans of those killed on the roads, for example) are released into 'clean' areas.

The local disease-free status has not come about because there's a population that has resistance here but because devils were hunted out many years back – or rather, their main prey species were shot for meat and/or killed off as pasture and cropland competitors. When I first arrived in the 1980s there were no wallaby species in evidence here, and T, born in the 1940s, had never seen any in the area. About twenty years ago, we were amazed to find, here and there, tracks of pademelons and Bennett's wallabies, and then increasingly frequently, to glimpse the animals themselves. Now they're everywhere, in large numbers, along with eastern grey kangaroos, and the devils have a food supply – mostly in the form of roadkill carrion. This abundant source of meat is a trap for carnivores. Of several dozen devils released recently from a captive breeding program, many have already been killed by cars.

Each night I think of that devil mother out in the summer dark. These have been smoky weeks, sun and moon red, with a smell of burning and the far side of the valley almost invisible in the haze from dozens of fires started by lightning strikes to the north and west, which have razed stands of alpine and rainforest species such as pencil pine and deciduous beech. Now and then throughout the month, the wind swings southerly and drives the smoke away; after days of low skies and stinging air, I step outside one evening to find clear twilight and a pale moon overhead, but to the north a pearl-dark wave stands over the ranges behind the city. By morning the wind has dropped and smoke flows south once more to drown these hills. We hold our breath and check the fire pumps and hoses as eucalypts exhale their oils and paddocks dry to crisp yellow grass and bare earth.

This is a semi-arid landscape and its plants and animals are drought-adapted. Some of the small bird species have raised several broods this year, and the bronzewing pigeons, which feed on fallen seeds of wattle and tree lucerne and pine, have nested continually since late spring. The pigeon that bobbed and called outside the window at the solstice hatches two chicks this month and loses them both – one falls from the nest early and the other survives till it's nearly fledged before something takes it. Now she's sitting on eggs again.

219

In the first days of the new year I take honey from two of the hives. That's very early – usually at this time the workers have only just begun to bring in nectar after a frenzy of pollen collection to feed new brood, and there's no surplus honey till February. Late summer is the usual collection time in these parts for a beekeeper like me who doesn't feed sugar syrup but leaves a good portion of honey in the hive as overwintering food. But this dry year the bees too have made good time, their foraging uninterrupted by rain and all the pasture and bush and garden plants still blossoming in their season – eucalyptus and wattle and willow, clover and blackberry, tree lucerne and grevillea, apricot and plum and cherry, apple and pear and quince, and all the vegetables and weeds that flower and go to seed.

I was taught to use (and inherited equipment for) the Langstroth hive system favoured by commercial apiarists. Its basis is a brood box in which the queen lays her eggs, with honey boxes placed on top, from which the queen is excluded. Rectangular wooden frames are suspended vertically within each box, with foundation wax fixed into each frame.

Recently, some beekeepers have been trying a different approach – the *top-bar* system, which I'm learning about and would like to try; frames are arranged horizontally in a single, longitudinal row, with more added at either end as needed. The queen naturally gravitates to the centre of the hive space to lay eggs and so the comb at the outside can be taken without killing brood. Comb taken is not returned to the box in this system, and though this adds to the worker bees' load, it approximates more closely the pattern of a wild swarm, which creates new comb regularly and so keeps ahead of disease. Comb in a top-bar hive is easier to access and can be removed in small quantities, an advantage for me as honey is much denser than water and, when full, a Langstroth box is heavy – 25 kilograms or more.

Picking and drying greengage plums and apricots, brining olives and cucumbers and onions, eating the first, early apples, Gravensteins sharp with juice, as the last of the old crop withers and rots, I'm still thinking about the ancestors – how they persist in and through and around me whether I'm acquainted with them or not; how I must find means to understand and live the known-unknown I have from them. In this place, wailing and laughter rise up out of the ground: fragments of family story – voices of the disappeared who could not be gathered for mourning – *mum was taken and sent into service here; her mother's name was Minnie – we don't know what happened'er*; voices of those who lived bereft of their birthright – *we always knew mum was dark but she never said nothing about that; I reckon she thought she protected us that way*; voices of those who made a life and went on – *but the old ones used to visit her, you know, and yarn and drink tea there by the fire.* These things stay with me; they bring comfort and grief and counsel as I set them down next to one another. They let me find questions, help me to wonder about how suffering becomes contagious and how it is transmitted across the generations. About gifts, adaptive responses passed on despite or because of terrible circumstances. What can be kept, and how?

And now, in the last few days of the month, lightning storms travel from the north-east – first a line of dry strikes that start more fires, and in their wake a downpour. At first the water sits on top or runs off soil that has become so dry as to repel it, and in the north of the island there is flooding. Here, though, it begins lightly, wetting the dust enough to let the showers soak in. It's such a relief, though there are still nearly ninety fires burning and weeks of the season to go.

Smoky rain drifts and clears and settles in. This is the breath the ancestors breathed. Now I feel, hear, see them, now I don't.

Hunted

Slow cloud builds,
light and shadow move over the house;
change comes
falling in drops warm as blood.

I've moved my workspace. An editing job that sprawled over many years and covered all the shelf and table surfaces in my writing room above the milking stall has come to an end. Although I love it there, it's hot in summer, cold in winter, and I've enjoyed sitting out the last of the heat in a room that's better insulated while I slowly unclutter and reclaim the other space.

Now my desk faces out into blackwood trees planted against the westerlies when we built the house. Sleeping quolls scratch and mutter in the ceiling cavity above my head; fantails and finches and honeyeaters come and go in the windbreak foliage and black cockatoos check dead limbs for goat-moth grubs. The wind is dry again and under the evergreen blackwoods, discarded leaves gather in drifts on the pale mudstone soil and pods split to offer their glossy black seeds on crimped, vermilion tethers. Life has retreated to the roots of bleached grasses. Air pours through the windbreak with a sound like river rapids or surf on a beach of many sandbars. In its lee, a little whirlwind sweeps up dirt and leaves and wanders a second or two before it lets fall its handful of dust.

Such is my longing for rain at this time of year that from the drought in me comes a dream of a purple-black thundercloud, many breasted, lit by the yellow sun of these days, and a strong wind that brings closer the cloud and its downpour. When I wake I think of Ephesian Artemis and the famous statue from her shrine in what is now Turkey, its upper body garlanded with breasts or gourds or eggs or balls or the rounded cells in which queen bee larvae develop, her belly and thighs and back carved with images of lions, bulls, goats, griffins, bees.

Lady of the beasts, deity of death and fecundity and of the hunt, Artemis precedes settled life and agriculture. She eases the births of humans and animals and protects their young but also brings sudden death to women and girls, and she tracks and kills with bow and golden arrows the animals in her care.

She's known by many names but I connect the thundercloud presence in my dream with her epithet *Celadeine*, from the Greek *kelados* – the roaring of water or wind, cognate with *clamour* and *call* and *claim* – Artemis Celadeine of the storm-voice, who loves the sound of the hunt, loves to capture what she seeks.

The stone statue from Ephesus, copied throughout the Greek and Roman worlds, was a replacement for a much older, eighth-century BCE wooden *xoanon*, which was probably largely featureless in itself, plank-like, with rudimentary arms and head, but adorned, bound with cloth woven with animal motifs and hung with jewelled tributes and attributes. In the 1980s, hundreds of drop-shaped amber beads were found at the level of the site where the original wooden image is thought to have stood before a flood destroyed the old temple in the seventh century BCE.[61] These beads may have formed part of the garlanding that was reproduced in stone on later statues.

Eventually the first cool days do come, and some rain, though not enough to put out the wildfires that still burn across thousands of hectares of fire-sensitive forest and alpine herb fields; they won't recover any time soon, dependent as they are on high rainfall for their growth and health, and vulnerable as soon as they dry. Climate modelling that predicts that the rainforest will disappear seems to be accurate so far. The worldwide wave of extinctions and adaptations continues.

Restless with the grief of change, I prepare ingredients for a salve – for burns, as it happens, but also for cuts and abrasions generally. First, in olive oil I steep flowers of that weed of dry places, St John's Wort, *Hypericum perforatum*. Left on a windowsill in the sun, resins and oils are released which turn the infusion deep amber-red.

225

St John's Wort is nervine, anti-inflammatory and vulnerary, and used topically is especially helpful for easing the pain of damaged nerves. Into the infused oil, over a bowl of hot water, I melt beeswax rendered from honey cappings, and beat into this mixture a brandy tincture of common daisy-marigold flowers, *Calendula officinalis*. Calendula is antimicrobial and promotes healthy granulation of injured tissue, decreasing scarring. It's good for treating wounds that are slow to heal. Beeswax has its own healing properties and also serves to emulsify the oil and alcohol mixture and set the ointment as it cools.

Hawthorn berries are ripe, ready to tincture in sherry as a heart tonic, and friends have come to pick fruit from the elder hedge to make jams and syrups that can be added to hot drinks for winter colds and flu – if I'm lucky they'll give me some when it's done. Some days have the feel of autumn already, clear and still; green rosellas call to each other in the fruit trees and hedges, and among the stubble of hay paddocks where cows have been let in to graze, ravens stalk, turning over dried dung pats in search of insects.

The road becomes a threshing floor for wattle and tree lucerne pods blown onto its surface from overhanging branches; under the tyres of passing cars and tractors, seeds loosen and empty husks are winnowed away to the roadside. Parrots and bronzewing pigeons settle to eat.

On a cool day, I curl on my side in a patch of sun to read. The dog looks over my shoulder for a while, hoping to stare me into a game, then lies down behind me with her paws against my back and goes to sleep. At some point she begins to dream, yelping, her breath ragged, and I feel her gallop up my spine – I've become the ground of her chase; she ranges the earth of me.

The Celadeine is on the move, with her lightning strikes and her fires that flush out prey. She shocks me out of life-by-rote, sends me running, patterns wrenched by her exigencies. *Live!* she says. *Wake into your creaturehood – heart and wits and innocent cunning, while I come for you.*

The shaky isles

Quake swarms rattle the crockery; volcanoes throw up clouds of ash; steam rises from roadside ditches – these things are commonplace and mostly go unremarked. But every now and then the ground thrashes and glares like a hooked marlin, or a mountainside bulges and weeps a smoking flood and everything changes. Then you remember that the air itself is tagged with a sulphurous warning – caldera below.

I'm thinking about my eldest sister, whose birthday was at this time. I began to write the poems that appear below after sitting with her during the months before she died, in Christchurch where she had lived most of her adult life. The poems use images of the convulsive geology and landscape of Aotearoa New Zealand. Just as I finished the sequence, a 7.1 magnitude earthquake struck 40 kilometres west of Christchurch, followed six months later by a 6.3 magnitude aftershock that hit the city directly. One hundred and eighty-five people died, and large areas were destroyed or made uninhabitable.

In catastrophe, the soil – the solid body, the structure of things – becomes porous, becomes fluid. It behaves like water when the big quake comes, reimagines itself. Some land sinks and some is raised up.

During my sister's illness and after her death I thought a lot about hope – about how some individuals and communities find ways to sustain it without denying the reality of disaster. Again and again it seemed to come down to small gestures, movements of tenderness in the patterns of ordinary life. These are moments that can sometimes enable even the tortured to survive, as Michel de Certeau describes it, *by maintaining (perhaps we should even say 'enduring') the memory of comrades*, and of another reality.[62]

After my sister died, I went with other family members to the glacier country in the west of Te Wai Pounamu, the South Island. There you look up to where mountaintops should be, and then you must tilt your head further back as you become aware of presences halfway up the sky. Their emissaries, the ice-rivers, grind their way down to the sea. It's somewhere I can imagine coming, like Jacob on the run after his latest misdemeanour or like a soul at death, to wrestle with my angels.

Worse than useless, to try to hold onto the moment before change comes with its grief – like grasping the mane of the *each uisge*, the water horse of my Scottish forebears, which drags its would-be captor under and eats all but the heart and liver. But to relinquish that grip is to step, bereft of the story-spells that worked before, into a charged field, wordless.

The space is dark, in which language reassembles itself, if it ever does. Samuel Beckett describes it in *The Unnamable*, where, he says, *[at] the threshold of my story, before the door that opens on my story...it will be I, it will be the silence, where I am, I don't know, I'll never know, in the silence you don't know, you must go on, I can't go on, I'll go on.*[63]

1 Water

There's a spotlight of late sun on the roses outside the church. They're
white and red with the blue of a thundercloud behind
but I turn away, bend towards a screen.

There's a wall of black water out where the land begins to drag.
Lean closer – you can slam through that glassy door
to where scraps roll, lethal.
There'll be time on the other side for salvage
where logs, frayed timbers, creak in their chains as they're towed upriver;
there'll be voices across quiet water.
Then the boys will have work, those ones
who smashed the windows of all the cars in the car yard.

But now the young mechanic steps towards his wife and child,
breathes them in,
and that breath is the ark that will carry us over.

2 Fire

In my fiftieth year the ground turned hollow underfoot –
eyelid, eggshell, door into burning black.

She said she had pain. I listened into silence and now I fall
and fall to the place where she lay, life boiling off her,
dying sun under my feet.

She was walking ahead and she was hit –
smashed bone, jagged nerves of her foot and leg –
and a black star gathered there
from the broken motes of her blood.

I put my hand on the ground of her
where it swelled tight as a drum on ravening darkness. Down, through,
in another world there's a burning river. Shore to shore mirrored
I look across, fire scouring, watch her burning down.

From deep under you wake –
there was a sound but you don't know what it is.

I couldn't put out those fires, so small before I got perspective
I thought I could reach across to smother them.

3 Ice

When you see the glacier you hardly know what it is,
stepping down among its towers, sheathed in its own light,
into the red shade of the summer forest, the world.

You have to go to it then across striped stones of the riverbed;
you have to get as close as you can, shivering in your thin clothes,
taste its breath, feel its tremor work the valley;
see the angels clamber in their boots and gear.

When the cry has gone up and they come
to shine a torch along the dark streets of your brain,
this is where they should look,
here under the ice cliff where you fought and won your blessing.
Now you're climbing years compacted blue –
stones, stories that broke your back and were your treasure too,
abandoned on that track, everything delivered at last,
everything rolled and offered down in the springing stair.

4 Earth

The body shapes itself anew each day –
tears seep and tunnel, rage strops its claws
inside and out. The body forms, resolves
and forms again –
its integrity, its symptoms
scored across and through.

A wormhole – an opening and something
dissolving there. Tears bore inwards,
build a scab to hide their tracks –
that mark on my cheek like a leaf, like a little fish.

Each day the soul spins its tangible dream –
something tries on a life.

5 Air

Hot light,
wet light of an eye that snaps open –
these islands jag through.
Ground down like old teeth
they erupt again
and the eye of the fish rolls in its milky film.
Shaken,
we stand on its slippery back
and breathe.

Tracks

A whole mythology is deposited in our language.
Ludwig Wittgenstein[64]

Wasps and bees and tiny vinegar flies materialise around the sweetness of bruised and rotting fruit as late apples ripen and thump to ground. Currawongs call from the windbreaks, metallic, chiming-percussive, and the sound carries far in still air as they fly in to eat, with honeyeaters and silvereyes and green rosellas. Since reading Michael Pollan's *The Botany of Desire* I've been fascinated by the thought of our apple varieties, *Malus domestica*, descendants of the wild, immensely diverse *Malus sieversii* forests of Central Asia, whose seeds made their journey west along the Silk Road to the great port cities of Lebanon and Syria and Turkey and so into Europe and its colonies. Pollan describes a visit to a kind of apple ark in Geneva, New York State, which aims to preserve some of this diversity. There he finds orchard rows in which 'no two...trees look even remotely alike, not in form or leaf or fruit',[65] grown from wild seed gathered in remnant forest in Kazakhstan. Many fruit forests were cleared as part of a deliberate policy during the Soviet era, and some of those that survived outside the Republics have been mined, bombed, torn apart by decades of warfare.

The days continue warm and dry though the equinox is weeks past and the sun's arc is low and declining. The house smells of quinces, and beeswax from oilcloth I've been making to wrap loaves and cheeses, and the steam from a pot of tomatoes cooking down for paste, and the last of the basil, gone into pesto with parsley and garlic and almonds and pieces of hard cheese from last spring which continues to mature, sharp and crumbly.

Grape-and-damson wine ferments in 5 litre jars that came from the chocolate factory north of Hobart in the days when their flavourings still came in glass and they gave the empties away. These jars are among my household treasures, reused and stored from year to year along with other objects that I handle with affection and gratitude – plates and cutlery from a set brought to us after our house burned down, given by a neighbour who had lost her own house in the 1967 fires; a dozen 2 litre glass coffee jars with screw-on lids from another friend who gave them in full enjoyment of her own largesse and our shared understanding of their perfect utility. Now I use them to store honey and to tincture herbs and ferment vegetables and kefir.

Then sadness. The young Jersey cow gives birth and her calf is dead. One evening she's restless, pacing, awkward, all angles around the big, lopsided curves and full udder of late pregnancy, turning to look at her belly and calling to it with the low, intimate, crooning groan used for a newborn. I think she might calve in the night but when I get up to check she stands chewing cud in the moonlight, no sign of labour beginning. At dawn the same, then halfway through the morning, she pushes out a water-filled bulge of membrane and lies down, waves of contractions coursing along her body. The front feet of the calf appear but after that, no progress. T manages to get hold of them and, with each contraction, pulls to help the calf along the birth canal. It comes easily, a beautiful curly-haired black heifer, limp as water, lifeless. The cow turns to it and begins urgently to lick away and eat the membranes of the amniotic sac and the placenta, nuzzling the body and calling to it. Her udder is distended and hard – with no newborn to relieve her we must act quickly to take milk.

We put the dead calf in a wheelbarrow and the look of it curled in the bowl as if asleep is like a punch to the heart. We bring it to the milking stall and the cow follows alongside, murmuring to it. But then as we ease the milk from her she stands to eat hungrily, not glancing back, and when we've finished, she walks by the body without a glance and goes to sniff for a few moments at the scuffed ground and spilled waters of the birthing-place. Soon she loses interest and doesn't call, grieving.

Next morning she comes to the stall as if nothing has happened, though her body knows, making bucket after bucket of milk – first the sticky, yellow beastings, which pale day by day to creamy white. She moves slowly, still, and wants only to eat and rest and stand to be milked and massaged with the balm I made in summer from calendula and hypericum and beeswax, healing and soothing. Her rough winter coat is growing in, its summer sheen eclipsed, but her eyes are bright, her breath sweet.

Perhaps the waters had already broken that first night and the calf died in the long hours when labour didn't go ahead as it should have. Perhaps if I'd intervened the little one might have lived. Or perhaps there was some heart or lung or brainstem problem that meant that she couldn't, in any event, survive her birth.

Daylight saving has finished – it's dark at six in the evening. I begin to milk before sunrise and each morning the electric light disturbs two or three bees from the swarm in the wall – they hurl themselves irritably at its glare until we put a shield around it. Now there's milk to drink and milk to ferment and milk to give away. The house smells of fresh curd settling in buckets, silken at first then firmer, rubbery as the whey separates and is ladled away to make ricotta. The dog waits for a chance at the compost bucket with its gobbets of leftover curd. The rhythm of milking and working with milk – morning, evening, morning, evening – sets the shape and pace of the day.

And in ruined Syria as the month ends, a hospital is bombed in Aleppo, killing the last paediatrician left in the city, along with other medics and dozens of patients. Gone the power to bring in the future alive; gone, stillborn, the sense of past and futurity of place; gone the houses and their loved objects, the trust between communities. In the city where Abraham milked his white cows and gave the milk to travellers passing through, there near the end of the Silk Road where faiths and their sects once coexisted peaceably and all the diversity of the world was welcomed in, the old storm god of the Amorites makes his camp in the citadel once more, Hadad of the bulls, who warred with his brothers. What are the stories that would have made meaning of all this in the language of the Melukerdee? How does palawa kani construct this world?

In an essay called 'The corn-wolf: writing apotropaic texts', anthropologist Michael Taussig quotes Ludwig Wittgenstein:

> And when I read Frazer I keep wanting to say, 'All these processes, these changes of meaning, – we have them here still in our word-language…If what is hidden in the last sheaf is called the Corn-wolf, but also the last sheaf itself and also the man who binds it, we recognize in this a movement of language with which we are perfectly familiar…'[66]

Taussig comments: 'For me that is the anthropological project: becoming aware of that presence in our lives, in our writings, and in our institutions, so as to neither expose nor erase but conspire with it, as does the wolf.'[67]

Such is the power of language and our need to make meaning, we come to believe that stories jump out from events, thus the city (or household) as source of milk offered freely to all (on condition of a death); the city (or household) as focus of a punishing rain (which feeds the corn). Writing, I notice the tracks that stretch behind me, leading in and out through the world of my life; I hear a rustle in the stories I set down.

Run

*And one day towards the end of the year...three drops of the
charmed brew flew out of the cauldron and fell on the finger of
Gwion Bach. And by reason of their great heat he put his finger
to his mouth, and the instant the three drops touched his tongue...
he foresaw everything that was to come...and Caridwen saw that
all the toil of the whole year was lost...and she went forth after
him, running. And he saw her, and changed himself into a hare
and fled. But she changed herself into a greyhound and turned
him. And he ran towards a river, and became a fish. And she in
the form of an otter-bitch chased him under the water, until he
was fain to turn himself into a bird of the air. She, as a hawk,
followed him and gave him no rest in the sky. And just as she was
about to stoop upon him, and he was in fear of death, he espied
a heap of winnowed wheat on the floor of a barn, and he dropped
among the wheat, and turned himself into one of the grains. Then
she transformed herself into a high-crested black hen, and went to
the wheat and scratched it with her feet, and found him out and
swallowed him. And, as the story says, she bore him nine months,
and when she was delivered of him, she could not find it in her
heart to kill him...*

'Taliesin', *The Mabinogion*[68]

Autumn high pressure systems swing south – we no longer sit under the blue dome or bowl at their centre but are clipped by gales at their edge. Moisture-laden, they bring an end to months of dry. Rain falls – proper, soaking rain, wind-driven at first as each front passes, then steady, quiet in the aftermath. It turns the mornings silver, misted, sometimes frozen, the branches and leaves heavy with droplets. The passing brightness of first snow whitens the highlands.

This year's nests have had their cover of leaves blown away: silvereyes' hammocks of twine and moss and goldfinches' lichen half-spheres lined with thistledown show up in the outer twigs of the hawthorns; blackbirds' heavy, mud-lined bowls fall and the grass domes of thornbills, decorated with spider egg sacs, are combed from tussocks and blackberry thickets by the wind. Under a big eucalypt at the edge of a gully lies a cup of shredded bark and spiderwebs lined with pademelon hair, arranged so that the rim looks like the hood of a fur-lined parka. It belongs, I think, to a scarlet robin.

The ground is muddy underfoot, greasy and chopped where the cattle walk their habitual ways or where paths converge. Roadside culverts are full and water runs into the dam, its level rising steadily to cover the fringe of rushes and willowherb, small loosestrife and senecio that began to grow on mud exposed as the waterline sank. The platypus has reappeared from the permanent creek in the valley floor, gorging along the way on worms that have surfaced from deep in the subsoil with the wet; now it dives and turns in the water, smooth as an eel, in search of larvae that flourish in the nutrient-rich run-off. Two swans have come to feed once more on waterweed.

There's a feeling of relief – the ground is still warm enough for grass to grow; wallabies graze on green shoots in paddocks and on roadsides that have been bare; bettongs eat the fruiting bodies of fungi that form in bush and pasture soils. Black cockatoos wheel along the rainy wind to feed on pine cones in the hedges and banksia seeds in the garden by the house. The cows no longer wait all day by the gate to be fed but have their heads down, eating.

The first thing I noticed when I came to this eastern part of Tasmania from Aotearoa New Zealand was the rarity of permanent creeks – no sound of water trickling in folds of the country. The river that is central to the landscape here is fed from the western rainforest and the mountains – it runs through this semi-arid rain shadow as an emissary from another realm. In dry years, El Niño years like this one, we stand in sunlight on our parched hills and watch rain falling over the forest across the valley. Town water is piped from there and almost all farms rely on dams to water livestock, orchards, crops, and have rainwater tanks to capture roof run-off for household use.

This is a good place for apples and pears. In the early 1960s, those who had orchards increased their acreages to grow fruit for the United Kingdom, before it joined the European Economic Community in 1967 and produce from the colonies became surplus to requirements. As part of that pre-EEC expansion, my husband's father had a big dam dug to irrigate new plantings of apples. It's elliptical in shape, about 150 metres long by 45 metres wide and perhaps 6 metres deep in the centre. Semipermanent springs feed into it from the slope above, and it gathers run-off from ditches along the ridge road higher up.

When I first arrived in the late 1970s, sags and bulrushes had colonised the shallows but the deeply shelving wall was still open to wind and wave action – the water was opaque yellow, coloured by clay particles washed and blown in. There was insect life, enough to support two or three pairs of grebes that nested in the reeds, and wood ducks that hatched their eggs high in the forks of a big eucalypt a few metres from the water. Narkies raised their chicks among the rushes and shrieked their hacksaw choruses back and forth in the night.

About twenty years after the dam was dug, pondweed appeared, *Potamogeton* carried in by birds. As it became established and grew its long strands in the shallows around the edge, the water cleared. Then, quickly, a whole new series of creatures arrived. Several more species of ducks began to visit and nest, and nesting pairs of coots settled in. Swans came to graze on the new weed.

The cauldron of the dam empties and fills and empties, and I with it. As water seeps, bandicoot-self, I dig down with snout and paws and worm-wise I uncurl from my dry knot deep in yellow clay; I eat and am eaten. The world runs through me, and the words of Gwion Bach:

I've taken form after form without restraint – believe it.
I've been a hand of claws, narrow and sharp;
I've been an eagle and the course of her hunt.
I've been a flame that leaps a firebreak,
a shiver of panic that runs through a herd.
I've been a dam that swallows a creek,
and I've been a baffled fish downstream.
I've been an upwelling spring,
a drop in a rainshower,
foam in a flooded ditch.
I've been a word in a phrase of the first tale,
and for a year and a half I was torchlight on rapt faces.

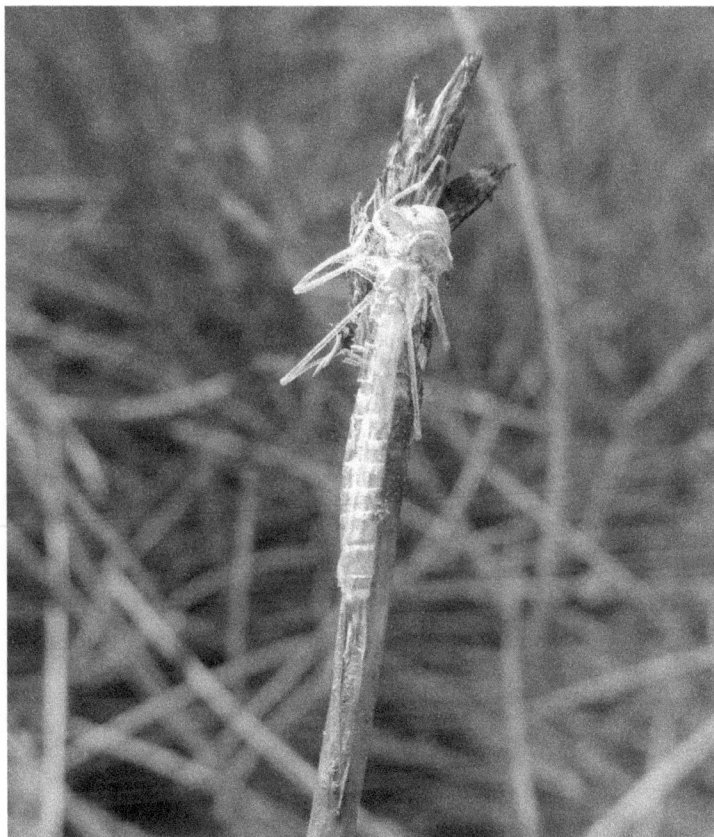

I've been a shield that fends off snarling,
a corner out of the wind.
I've been a knife in its sheath.
Nine years caught in the lines of a song,
I've been fog and starlight.
Yes – what am I without these stories?

After the *Kat Godeu*, Peniarth MS2[69]

243

JUNE

Currencies

There was once upon a time a widow who had an only
son named Jack and a cow named Milky-white. And
all they had to live on was the milk the cow gave...but
one morning Milky-white gave no milk...So Jack took
the cow's halter in his hand, and off he started. He
hadn't gone far when he met an old man, who said to
him...'Well, Jack, and where are you off to?'...'I'm
going to market to sell our cow here.' 'Oh, you look the
proper sort of chap to sell cows,' said the man; 'I wonder
if you know how many beans make five.' 'Two in each
hand and one in your mouth,' says Jack, as sharp as a
needle. 'Right you are,' said the man, 'and here they are,
the very beans themselves,' he went on, pulling out of his
pocket a number of strange-looking beans...'I don't mind
doing a swap with you – your cow for these beans.'

'Jack and the Beanstalk'[70]

After a week of hard frost, a big, strange, warm wind pours
down from the north-east, bringing rain that floods all the
river basins in the north of the state. There, in a town at the
estuarine confluence of two rivers, suburbs go waist-deep, then
deeper, but when the flood peak comes, it coincides with low
tide, and the levees hold. Outside the levees, people climb onto

the roofs of farmhouses, crops go under and herds are swept away. Here in the south there's no flooding, but the ground is soaked and the warmth keeps the grass growing, just when I thought it must surely stop. Bees work madly in the flowering lucerne hedges and in the grevilleas round the house.

Wind blows from the east so rarely here that trees come down, pushed from the side where the grip of their roots is tenuous in the soaked ground, and limbs crack, unbalanced by saturated branches braced in a different direction. The roads are littered with twigs and leaves, and with buds from silver wattles, soon to flower. Green needles are torn from the pines and clumps of beard lichen, heavy with moisture, lose their grip and dot the ground below like stranded deep-sea creatures; rockpile mosses cushion up.

A day later snow falls from skies that look black against the magnified flare of sunlight fingering down through gaps between squalls. Reluctant to leave the warmth of the kitchen, T husks the *Phaseolus* beans that have been drying in their pods since autumn – haricots and flageolets and romanos, and frost beans – climbers named for their cold tolerance and ability to produce right into autumn. He piles their creamy, green-white and crimson-and-white riches in bowls on the kitchen table – more than a thousand beans for each seed that was planted. Hugging the fire like him, I toss carrot and ginger and greens in chilli-hot rice-flour paste for kimchi and set it to ferment in crocks, then go out to the cheese shelves, turning and scrubbing the hard rounds to keep them from mould in the damp.

The second cow has calved, and despite the cold and wet the two are making abundant milk, and since Elsie has no calf to drink half of what she produces, I need to set curd and make cheese every day. I'm running out of room – soon I'll have to beg shelf-space in the cellars of friends. This year I'm making cheeses in the style of cheshire and camembert and feta. When I first learned to milk forty years ago, these options were not available. It was very difficult to get rennet – the enzymatic setting agent that causes milk protein to separate from the fluid whey around it and form curds; it was even more difficult to obtain the cultures that produce differences in flavour. I used to add a bit of yoghurt to the curd and hope for the best.

From inside this eat-some, save-some economy, I understand stories that didn't make sense to me as a town-born child – how substances and objects and processes come to represent *worth* of various kinds when life depends on them. Milk can stand for subsistence and beans for profit via their astonishing self-multiplying power.

Versions of 'Jack and the Beanstalk' began to be written down from the mid-1700s, when enclosure and deeding to single owners of the commons and open-field farms of the old manorial system was well under way, alienating lands formerly shared by entire communities of subsistence farmers. While famine was never far off in a subsistence regime if crops failed, good years were a time of plenty. Enclosure, however, meant certain starvation for tenant farmers, now unable to access common grazing or grow a row or two of crops for food and rent – and so the landless poor became available as a vast pool of factory labour, which enabled the Industrial Revolution.

With enclosure came more efficient farming systems and the means to produce a surplus for profit. This in turn brought access to new, high-yielding seeds, *far-fetched and dear-bought* – such as strange-looking beans from the Americas – *Phaseolus* varieties that would replace the old *Vicia faba* broadbean crops grown by the poor of Europe. Jack and the Beanstalk is not just

a weaning-tale of a boy sent away by his mother at the end of the milk, not just a story of a boy and his little sprout, growing, which gives him power to obtain gold and its agency. It's also a story of the end of one social order and the beginning of another, where a cow and her milk is worth less than a handful of *improved* seeds. Jack's trade is the story of my ancestors too, there in the plantations of Ireland and in the colonies of the Antipodes.

The full moon at the solstice comes with cold rain and ravens gathered in parliament around road-killed carcasses, and the creaking calls of young black cockatoos begging pine seeds in the windbreaks. The planet leans towards the light once more but it will be weeks before the days seem longer. Here and there, pale flowers of sunshine wattle, *Acacia terminalis*, gleam like coins in the bush understorey and then one day, by ordinary magic, an egg with its secret gold appears in the nest box of the henhouse.

Everywhere, during peace or just down the road from a war, before the revolution and after it, people go on trading their currencies.

Brightness

There's a solitary brightness
without fixed shape or form.
It knows how to listen...
It knows how to understand...
It knows how to teach.
That solitary brightness is you.

Linji Yixuan, trans. John Tarrant[71]

Mud, mud and a watery sheen on the ground; a stream flows from the outlet of the dam and clear water runs in the roadside drains; the ground is full. It's the wettest three months since written records began to be collected for the island early in the twentieth century.

Snow falls from the curled crook of a storm deep over the Southern Ocean, then rain and more rain, wind-driven, that blows itself out in snow again, showers drifting across the river all day. All the catchments are saturated and, with snowmelt added to rain, at full moon the town upriver floods at the bridge where the flow turns tidal; shops and houses are awash, but no one drowns and no animals are swept away, as happened in the north of the state last month.

The mountains keep a shawl of snow but the ground is too wet to let it settle here; even on days that are sunny, every grass blade is tipped by a droplet of water, every curve is a filled cup. The cattle seek dry ground on which to bed down, even if it's in the wind. And the dog, who would usually rather be outside, running, is willing to stay near the fire. There, turned hard into herself, she sleeps.

Out of the darkness, snow flares into the light that spills from the open doorway beside me as I milk and disappears as it touches the ground. I tuck myself into the cow's pocket of warmth where she stands steaming, eating hay and cut-up apples from the manger, melted snowflakes glistening in her coat. The smell of her milk, her own smell, different from that of any other cow, rises around me as the bucket fills.

Moisture-loving creatures that can tolerate cool temperatures are out and about – a few hours after a walk in the bush, the dog begins to sneeze violently, shaking her head, and eventually a gleaming, chocolate-brown leech emerges from her nostril, fat with blood. There's no bleeding from the nose despite the anticoagulant the leech injects to ensure free flow of its meal, so it must have attached itself far enough up that the trickle runs back down the dog's throat and is swallowed.

Daylight comes perceptibly earlier now, and lasts longer – a few minutes at the beginning and end of each day – though it's still black-dark at morning milking. And despite the cold, spring sounds begin – in the hedge a grey robin calls *here! com'ere!* and in the orchard a scarlet robin sprinkles a glitter of notes over its territory. From the litter of twigs and seed pods under the blackwoods, a bronzewing pigeon begins its one-note homing signal, *oom oom oom*, to bring in a mate.

The hen eagle stands in the paddock, tall-shouldered, her feathered legs planted square like the chaps of a gaucho, talons digging the soft ground, while a circle of ravens keeps a respectful distance around her. She turns her massive head with its hooked face to watch me as I pass, with the dog beside me, on the empty road in the snow wind. Her mate flies overhead, playing the air in deep upward arcs and dives to announce that this place is part of the range of a nesting pair.

Silvereyes huddle in blackberries along the fence line – mouse-sized feather-balls, they shuffle close in a row among the thorns. They used to migrate to the mainland each year in the cold months, most of them, but more and more overwinter now, somehow making enough heat to move about each day in search of insects, down among the dead leaves and grasses.

The platypus seems to be here to stay. It cruises the waterweed in the shallows of the dam, keeping an eye on me when I sit nearby, happy to come close if I'm quiet, swimming away if I stand or move abruptly. It folds and dives and creases the still surface of the water, pushing up a bow wave. One evening at dusk, when it's far off at the other end of the dam, I think I see a second smooth head and body appear alongside it. Perhaps it's a diving bird, but if it's another platypus, maybe they'll mate and dig a burrow – away from the dam wall, I fervently hope, so that it doesn't, as I've heard sometimes happens, breach the structure and let out the water that makes our living here possible.

Now and now and now the year rolls on. As an adolescent in the 1970s, in reaction against the heaven-and-hell deferrals of my culture, I tried to learn to *be here now*, hugging that phrase, with its own cultural baggage invisible to me then – the idea of the necessity of ego-loss (when I and most of the people I knew didn't have an ego that was sufficiently robust to lose); the idea of detachment (which I understood at the time to mean not involving myself in the mess of life).

251

Bright in my darkness, dark in my brightening hours, unable either to accept my people's religion of exile from paradise or to experience the present that was available to me, I rushed towards each moment, but meeting it, looked over its shoulder to see what was next. I feel tenderness for that girl I was, who felt herself to be a failure, and who teaches me that curiosity and urgent longing and all the transient weathers of the heart and mind are also *here*, *now*, each day's one-and-onlies. I receive from her as a gift what she struggled to win through effort. Some things fall to the hand when they're ripe, or when we're ripe. As my future foreshortens, the present steps towards me – moments both past and to come – and of necessity I turn to it.

Now the dam shimmers with all its lights and lives; one day it will surely empty. Brightness and its dark go on.

River

Yo vide una garza mora dándole combate al río
Así es como se enamora tu corazón con el mío
Yo vide una garza mora dándole combate al río
Así es como se enamora, así es como se enamora
Tu corazón con el mío, tu corazón con el mío
Luna, luna, luna llena menguante

Simón Díaz, 'Tonada de luna llena'[72]

I saw a black heron battling upriver
Just like your heart...

The moon, a yellow coracle, noses its way through the windbreak and, setting, touches and then goes down over the sawtooth ridge of the first range to the south-west. A quoll stirs in its den in the ceiling and rattles away over the iron of the roof on its night's hunt, making a run for shadowy ground, skittering out from under the eye of the owl that waits in the darkness of the hedge.

Willow catkins push free from brown husks; their luminous silver gathers light till the wind shakes them loose into gold. Plovers scuttle low and furtive away from eggs and chicks that crouch, perfectly camouflaged, in cow-footprint nest-scrapes, and pairs of ravens chase each other in close formation; their feathers squeak on the clean glass of the wind. In gullies scoured by fires twenty, thirty, fifty years ago, wattles that came up thickly from heat-cracked seeds cover themselves in lemon-coloured blossom that froths for weeks before it browns, subsides.

My mother has died. She lived her life in currents of love and rage, terror and wonder, struggling, enraptured and at war with her would-be lovers, her god, her family. Now she has gone on, reclining at ease in a coffin like a little boat.

From childhood and throughout much of her life, she was beset by anxieties that contorted her mind and heart, and which arose, as for so many, from intergenerational trauma suffered during what Doris Lessing called these *centuries of destruction*. At times their grip broke and she surfaced to experiences of freedom – the moment of the kingfisher; the moment of the morning star – which she described, nonplussed, as a collapse of oppositions, a widening of her sense of self, in terms resorted to by mystics across the centuries. Her predecessors had been wrenched by the desperation of living through the Great Hunger in Ireland and by the guilt of having survived it; deracinated by a forced move to the other side of the world and frightened by the violent realities of a new country in the throes of its own colonial war. They were stupefied by the amnesia that distance makes possible, and captive to fantasies that rushed to fill the blanks left by memories pushed aside.

Wracked, they clung to religion as offering continuity with home and the possibility of another realm, and as a way of ordering their lives against inner and outer collapse, overwhelmed by strangeness or by escape into the familiar relief of alcohol. Their beliefs were frightening, rule-bound, designed to terrorise a community in extremity away from

tearing itself to pieces. Their faith was also consoling in its promise of a god who identified with the experience of human suffering; its stories were vivid, passionate and affirming of a rich inner life.

This was my mother's legacy. Her father was an alcoholic who died when she was six, and then the Great Depression came. She once recounted to me a memory of standing, when she was about ten years old, with her mother in the yard of one of a succession of houses to which they had been forced to move seeking ever lower rents, and of her mother turning to her and saying, *I think I am going mad*.

My grandmother's respite from the distress of her life wasn't alcohol but the threepenny cinema talkies, and she would take my mother, her youngest, with her. My mother's childhood was divided between fantasies of eternal damnation and dreams of a Hollywood ending, with wedding. Forbidden to risk the former by attending the *godless* state-run secondary school, she opted for the latter and was tormented for the rest of her life by a longing for learning she felt she had missed. Evading the furies as outside forces, still they came after her from within.

When we were children and adolescents, the atmosphere of our house was imbued with the tension between her hungry intelligence and her fearful religious formation. My mother was a sometimes inspired and, often in those days, dangerous interlocutor and guide, by turns encouraging and terrified of our possibilities, as one by one she ferried us in. But in her seventies, she threw off painful lifelong mental and emotional habits and stepped into her own authority, deciding for herself that a love which created human complexity would not be quick to condemn it.

She sought and found an intellectual and emotional framework for her insights in conversation with family and friends, and in the work of an eclectic mix of writers, from Teresa of Ávila to Annie Dillard; from Fleur Adcock to Pauline O'Regan. In the end, what remained for her was hope in the possibility of transformation, in this life as much as in the next, as she had experienced it in moments of intuition and awakening.

Tiny, worn, in her hundredth year she was ready, impatient even – *though life is sweet* – to join her eldest daughter and her own mother – *they're here, with me!* – and the ancestors who, more and more frequently in the last few months, appeared in her room to visit, waking and sleeping – *I wish I knew their names; they're here because I'm going to them soon.* One day, with my sister beside her, she took a breath and a breath and went deep in and didn't return.

The night before the funeral, while our half of the planet was in darkness, on the daylight side the moon passed between Earth and the sun, and like the shade of a boat on the floor of a sunlit sea, blocked its light along a course over Central Africa and Madagascar and the Indian Ocean. Lined up together like that, the sun's mass is added to the moon's pull on the oceans and on the crust and core of the Earth – caught in a tidal warp, all that tries to settle and harden must groan and give. And just off the coast of the North Island of Aotearoa New Zealand where we were, the seabed buckled along fault lines of the colliding Pacific and Australian Plates, and an earthquake that measured more than 7 on the scale jolted the island and shook the town awake like a rough hand.

Pulled up by the sun, night-time river fog drifts in a clear sky over rooftops and paddocks where restless life jumps everywhere as a new season begins. Around the tatters of last year's silvereye nests, bunched leaves with embryonic flowers at their hearts sprout from the tips of elder twigs; thornbills and wrens and honeyeaters are making new nests in grasses and shrubby thickets along fence lines and in the bush understorey. A blue wren, brilliant in mating colours, pursues his mate through the garden, a single red anemone petal in his beak.

When I was about sixteen, I had a numinous nightmare in which, thrown into a muddy river, I was pulled under then spat out on a gravel bank at its edge. Beside the water was a jar, shoulder-high, with a plug of rags in its mouth. Pulling out the cloths, I was hit by a stench of decay so strong I almost fell. Inside the jar was a mummy, wrapped and bound in foetal position. As I looked, I heard my mother's voice warning me away. Unable either to obey or entirely to disobey, I lifted the bundle out of the jar and put it in a box of ice.

In my mother's last months, as she turned inward, she read less and less until her sole text became the aphoristic shorthand of a loved perpetual calendar, given to her years earlier by my sister. She used it as a means of orientating herself within the year, as a jumping-off place for rumination, and as a mode of communication – *Here, listen to this!* For the day she died, the reading was: *When we remain ignorant of the forces swirling around us, we suffer the consequences of our unconsciousness, affected by intensities over which we seem to have no control.* I receive it as a final assertion, a counter-imperative to the warning she gave me in my dream at sixteen, an affirmation that it might be necessary and possible to face some fearful things that have been put aside.

And, like a reply from the world, on returning to Tasmania I found that, while I was away, our household freezer had come unplugged and everything in it had thawed. Unsystematic, I couldn't remember what was there, but when I looked what I found was not a lot – bones, mostly, and broth made from the bones, and colostrum kept from calving time, to feed to an orphan calf should the mother die or reject it, and some fruit left over from summer. The smell was fresh – of blood and milk and sweetness – food for the very old and the very young; food for the soul on its journey.

There are many reasons why a sixteen-year-old, or a sixty-year-old, or a family group, might turn away from *the forces swirling around* – ancestral matter that washes and takes us down, that tinctures and binds bodies and minds and patterns of behaviour. But rotting or fresh, these leakages and bloody remains of bones and milk, of our horrifying losses and crimes and vulnerabilities, are also our inheritance and promise of renewal – poison and medicine that forms and informs us, spit of the moon passed down through the stream in which we battle and which carries us along.

Morning

And for all this, nature is never spent;
There lives the dearest freshness deep down things;
And though the last lights off the black West went
Oh, morning, at the brown brink eastward, springs –
Because the Holy Ghost over the bent
World broods with warm breast and with ah! bright wings.

Gerard Manley Hopkins, 'God's Grandeur'[73]

A little wattlebird has made her nest beside the door and I hear her murmur to her chicks and mate. It sounds like tenderness, though these birds bully and chase away smaller honeyeaters and other birds, and their call is harsh. Their feathers are subtly striated in browns and greys with white and black accents, and there's a band of soft russet across the middle of each wing that's only visible in flight.

Soon after the hen began sitting, I peered into the nest and saw two pale elongated eggs splashed with the same reddish colour as the wing-band. In the cold of a westerly gale or in steamy warmth she sat tight, tucked into the shelter of the honeysuckle, until the ceaseless carrying of nectar and insects by both parents announced a hatching. Now, a couple of weeks later, I hear their panicked calls and find feathers on the ground under the nest. One chick, almost fully fledged, crouches very still in the bottom of the cup. Later, in a clatter of wings a collared sparrowhawk flies from a nearby branch, tearing at its bloody fistful.

Everything dissolves in rain, in sleet-flecked mud, in a blur of wind that brings down trees whose roots have lost their grip in soaked ground. Grass grows wildly and the cows, up to their hocks in black ooze, graze its luscious tips and shit green. Hawthorn hedges brighten tree by tree; apple and pear and cherry orchards pulse into flower as gusts free buds from their sticky husks in blow-bloom surges that show the words' shared origin.

All month, air from the tropics hurls upwards and strikes down here as gales and storms. It breathes out its moisture in shapeshifting clouds, which lift from time to time to admit dazzling sunlight that angles across the mossy grass of south-facing slopes and gullies to glitter, prismatic, through beads of dew breathed back by every leaf.

From stands of rushes circling the dam, frogs call in deafening waves that rise and fall like the sound of a stadium crowd. It's the mating Olympics – sometimes it goes on for hours, sometimes days, before all falls silent. These are froglets, *Crinia signifera*, that grow to about three centimetres at most and are often smaller but project an astonishingly loud call, percussive, like the sound of the wooden clackers we used at football games to cheer on the players when I was a child.

I plough through pugged mud to get the cows, feet mired at every step, and the dog tiptoes beside me from one grass clump or peaked clod to the next as she tries to keep her paws dry, and fails, and shakes them and herself in exuberant distaste, and grins back at me, and runs on.

Soaked by a rainsquall, I come inside and crouch to reset the fire. Shivering, urgently turned towards my task, it seems like hallucination when, close in my ear, the disembodied voice of a bird sounds, as if the tongue of flame from my struck match had spoken among the kindling leaves and sticks. The metal tube of the chimney has conveyed the voice of a green rosella perched on the rim of the flue, dislodging soot and talking quietly to itself.

Parrots of all kinds like to investigate the deep interior hollows that form in burnt-out trees for use as nest sites. One year our neighbours heard noises in the grate of a fireplace they'd closed for summer, and removing the board from the opening, found a clutch of rosella chicks blinking from the ashbed. Given half a chance, creatures are resilient and adaptable. On Bruny Island off the coast from here, swift parrots, critically endangered by habitat loss as a result of forest clearing and selective cutting of older trees for firewood, have begun to use nest boxes and artificial hollows created for them.

This adaptability can extend to a sense of futurity – zebra finches of Central Australia sing a song to their eggs that tells their unhatched young of a hot season to come. Hatchlings that have been sung this song put on weight less quickly and grow to become smaller adults than those that have not had the warning, and their reduced body mass means they are less likely to become heat-stressed, because their surface-area-to-volume ratio permits easier cooling. They are also, as adults, able to tolerate hotter nest sites and raise more young than chicks that were not sung the heat-song.[74]

Blue gums are flowering and the air under the trees is aromatic, the ground littered with glaucous blossom caps and creamy stamens. In the understorey, love creeper scrambles to tether its blue clouds among brown-and-orange pea flowers and yellow goodenia; above them, white flowers of daisy trees and wedding bush and stinkwood and kurrajong fluoresce in shade and sunlight under the forest canopy. They're rushing to make seed because the fire season is on its way.

In the dark of my heart I touch these things and gather them under. Whatever morning is, it's not the end of death or sorrow; still the light appears, some principle as strong as death, some other reality that comes to us again, again, not as protection but as witness and companion through all the jumpy shifts that take us from drought to flood. It might be that, as Zen teacher John Tarrant says, *empathy is the most spectacular manifestation of the mysterious light in everything.*[75] So the Holy Ghost, Sophia, the Shekinah, broods and broods in us, in all our cunning stupidity and innocent hunger, and so we hatch a world, a way of being, open like a cupped palm.

Strike-slip, slow-slip, transform fault

Yes, I have an ulcer, for Chrissake. This is Kaliyuga, buddy, the Iron Age. Anybody over sixteen without an ulcer's a goddam spy.

J. D. Salinger, *Franny and Zooey*[76]

Roses – deep-red tea-roses and single yellow roses with a scent of apples; spherical pink roses with golden hearts whose cupped petals hold a smell of peaches; lemon-scented, apricot-coloured floribundas; musky-astringent white rugosas; crimson gallicas. Shaded from afternoon sun, lily of the valley and Solomon's seal, and along the western wall, purple wisteria.

Cherry plum fruits begin to shine yellow-green among the leaves in the hedge below the dam – a row of perhaps fifty seedlings that came up in a shovelful of earth from beneath a friend's tree. Each tree's fruit will ripen its own colour, in a range from yellow through orange to scarlet and the red-black of old blood.

Snakes and lizards bask in morning sun and retreat to cooler spots in the afternoon. Blue gums hold their starry canopies aloft as each tree conducts its own cantata for insects and birds that arrive to work the nectar cup at the centre of every flower. Bees swarm and the smell of ripening honey is fanned through the garden by workers as they drive off moisture before sealing the comb.

These few perfect days come each year in the interval between frost and wildfire. It's warm but not hot enough, not dry enough yet to scorch the grass that ripples like a pelt with every breath across paddocks closed up for hay.

Towards the end of the month, the first cut begins and the green swathes, luscious, lie to wilt a day or two before the tedder comes to scatter them for drying and later the rakes spin their teased-up windrows ahead of the baler. The distinctive hay smell of coumarin, one of the chemicals released by bruised grasses and clovers, rises in the warm air.

I watch a pair of ground-nesting swamp harriers shadow the hillsides and follow overgrown fence lines to flush out small creatures – what place have they chosen this year to raise their chicks? I hope it's not in the long grass of a hay paddock – I saw the hen hawk land in the standing hay on the next farm over, near where a pair settled one season a few years ago and were overrun by the mower. We looked for a nest this time but saw no sign – perhaps she was hunting mice.

The cows are still milking freely while the rich grass lasts – as well as cheese I skim cream to make butter. Hard cheeses from early in the season are ready to eat now; the first have the earthy taste of winter about them – hay and the meagre pasture of cold months; later there's a headier mix of new grasses and weeds and foraged leaves from the elder hedge.

White butterflies and diamondback moths begin to fly – time to use the last of the spring cabbages before they're chewed up by caterpillars. I inspect them for grubs, shred and sprinkle the leaves with salt, then pack them in a crock to ferment with grated ginger and daikon and carrot, using whey from the latest cheese as a starter.

In Aotearoa New Zealand a quake unzips the north-eastern end of the transform fault where the Australian and Pacific Plates grind past one another along the length of the South Island. Strike-slip fault lines along a 150 kilometre stretch of coast release pent-up energy as tremors jump from fault to fault, gathering momentum as they go, with horizontal movements of up to 11 metres and uplifts of 2–6 metres along the shore, leaving previously fully submerged rock reefs and their life forms high and dry. The energetic contagion stops short of the Cook Strait waterway that separates the two main islands. Even so, at the southernmost tip of the North Island, buildings in Wellington, the capital city, are damaged by shockwaves.

And now it's clear that these sudden releases aren't the only way change happens. A recently discovered slow-slip phenomenon,[77] only detectable since the advent of GPS technology, shows that in addition to quakes that can be felt by humans and recorded by seismographs, significant movements also occur silently over extended periods that cumulatively have the effect of magnitude 6 and 7 events. Sometimes, as in recent weeks, they follow a big quake; sometimes they precede it.

Shunted from the south-west by the Australian Plate, the islands of Aotearoa New Zealand, where they're not stuck to the Pacific Plate, are moving northwards and eastwards, by rupture and by stealth. After a relatively quiet period of sixty years or so, since 2009 the area of the plate collision zone on which the islands have formed has become active once more. In the 1950s, 1960s, 1970s while I was growing up in the North Island, though there was evidence everywhere of geothermal activity, there weren't many quakes – sometimes light fittings would swing or crockery would rattle on a shelf but that was all. I never felt the roar coming up through the soles of my feet or the lurch of ground like a choppy sea, described by my parents who lived through the Hawke's Bay quake and its aftershocks in the 1930s, and by my sister who lives in Christchurch and experienced the 2010 and 2011 quakes and their aftermath.

For those who have been through events like these, each new quake is retraumatising, and each reminder of the sensations of a quake – a heavy truck passing in the street, a wind gust buffeting the house – can bring a sense of panic. Twenty and thirty years on, my mother still startled at the buzzing hum of the fridge motor turning itself on – it sounded to her like the low noise that preceded a big quake.

It's hard to refrain from setting geology alongside geopolitics and my own internal world – everything same, same, different – a moment of quiet, a tremor, a moment of good governance, an overturning. A strike-slip tyrant of the Age of Iron, a slow-slip resistance. Tension builds, change comes – a remote shock may bring a silent shift, a silent shift may bring sudden catastrophe. When all the lives in the twitch-zone are shaken to pieces, another change must happen.

Talking backwards

*What can be said
with the whole packed weight of the world
pressing in?*

A few days apart, in the first week of the month I catch two bee swarms while they're still settled close to the hives they've come from, as scouts look for a new place. The first hangs from a low branch in the pine windbreak and T points it out to me. I have a fresh hive box with new frames and foundation ready for this one. The second is close to the house – I hear the background *muu* of the working swarm grow to *rahhhh* as the queen flies with thousands of bees around her, their sound intensifying, gathering as she lands in a young banksia outside the kitchen and they clump to her, clinging to one another, quietening.

For this swarm I have no home prepared and decide to put the bees back into the hive they came from – the old queen has taken most of the workers with her and left just a few behind with a newly hatched queen. As I did for the first swarm, I shake the warm, thrumming mass into a cardboard box in which I've put a few stems of bee balm. Then I put a couple of layers of newspaper over the top of the original hive-box, sit an empty one on top, shake the swarm back into it and cover it with the hive lid. By the time the workers have chewed through the sheets of newspaper from above and below, they will be accustomed to each other's scent-markers and there won't be much fighting. But one queen will kill the other.

When I remove the empty box and the remains of the newspaper a couple of days later, there's already an oval of new comb suspended from the lid, and inside the hive there's comb that's filled and capped – the season has begun early again. I check the other hives and find the same thing. Every year is exceptional now. I don't know how to interpret what's in front of me; I don't know how to respond. Ancestors and teachers and all those who went before crowd around to see what comes next in this haunted landscape where we go for our lives, seeing just where our mismanagement has taken us. In the fallout of empire, this is what conquest looks like.

ANGELA ROCKEL

Hay harvest goes on in starts and stops throughout the district, interrupted by rain. Newly cut swathes of grass fall cleanly aligned in one direction and repel water like thatch – a certain amount of rain simply runs off them – but rain on a crop that's been scattered can ruin it, soaking in and creating conditions in which mould flourishes, toxic and abortifacient. This year, drying is slow in any case because growth is heavy after a rainy winter and spring – so different from last season! In clear intervals, squat cylinders of hay or silage begin to drop from the machines and the drivers practise their skill, parking each bale so that it doesn't roll away on sloping ground.

Before Christmas, days of heat signal the start of the fire season (already long begun on the mainland) then, after the longest day, in the dark before daylight, rain falls with a sound like gravel on the roof; the smell of it blows in, falling through dusty leaves onto dry ground as a river of rain-bearing cloud from a cyclone in the Torres Strait pours down across Central Australia. It brings flash floods to the desert – waterfalls leap from the rock at Uluru – and continues south, over Bass Strait, across the island and out into the Tasman; warm rain falls steadily for a night and a day, a night and another day, followed by steamy warmth. Mist condenses in scarves around the hills and rolls in off the sea. It's marvellous, enlivening, forestalling fires, freshening the world.

For the cherry harvest that's about to begin, though, it's a disaster, and the valley echoes with the *duf-duf-duf* of helicopters hovering over the netted orchards to blow the fruit dry before it cracks. Haying stops; mowers and rakes and balers return to their sheds or sit dripping, abandoned in half-mown or partly baled paddocks. Cloud builds and lightning flicks *on-off, on-on-off* above the mountains and out to sea, too far away for thunder.

The house-surrounds smell of wet vegetation and of damp earth, exposed on the north-west side – the fire direction – where we've cleared away wattles planted as windbreaks when we built here thirty years ago, in what was then bare paddock. Put in because they were fast-growing, the trees were a poor choice – prone to wind damage and never long-lived, they were beginning to fall in a dry tangle of dead limbs and long grass – tinder.

In one of the apple trees, fantails make their elegant cone-cup of rootlets bound with spiderwebs, a single fine strand of orange plastic twine wound into the rim. One egg appears but after that, no more; leaves fall into the cup. Perhaps it was a cuckoo-decoy. For a while I don't see the pair, then they are in and out of the dense foliage of a tea-tree near the dam. Down in the gully below the house, pairs of satin flycatchers and their fledged chicks call and hunt insects in the canopy of stringybarks and white gums and wattles along the bed of the winter creek that's only now beginning to dry. In among the bracken and goodenia and blackberries of the understorey, pademelons and barred bandicoots wait out the daylight, sleeping, grooming.

Who am I talking to? Out into rainy sunlight I turn towards the living; back over my shoulder, into the years, into the ground, I turn towards the dead; into the space-before, I call out what I hear, what I see and smell and taste. Honey drips floral-fragrant, dusky, from the strainer into the tank. Dreamy, chewing cud as they walk, the cows lounge to milking along the track they've made through grass that's grown belly-deep. First linden flowers open. The swathe-labyrinth winds inward to the equinox and out again into darkness. I'm talking backwards. In the battle after the battle I'm asking: What might treaty look like? What would be its terms and who could speak?

Year 5

Six swans

*When the Great King, their father, knew the sorrow that had
come to him, he hastened down to the shore of the lake and
called to his children: 'Come to me, Fionnuala; come Aodh; come
Conn; come Fiacra.' They came flying to him, swans, and he
said: 'I cannot give you back your shapes till the doom that is laid
on you is ended, but come back now to the house that is mine and
yours.' Then Conn said: 'May good fortune be on the threshold
of your door from this time and for ever, but we cannot cross it, for
we have the hearts of wild swans and we must fly in the dusk
and feel the water moving under our bodies; we must hear the
lonely cries of the night.' And they rose into the air and flew away
calling to each other with the voices of children, but in their hearts,
the gladness of swans when they feel the air beneath them and
stretch their necks to the freedom of the sky.*

'The Children of Lir'[78]

*Sibling bonds offer us our first exit from domination and received
truth; they are an important corrective to hierarchical deference,
submission and obeisance.*

Sue Grand, 'God at an impasse'[79]

Still cool, the wind still moist. Where hay has been cut, instead of tawny stubble, new growth shows through – white clover and perennial ryegrass and red clover and the pale uneven squared-off shoots of cocksfoot. Wallaby lawns emerge as close-cropped green interstices among bleached heads of pasture grasses gone to seed in a season when the cattle couldn't keep up. Centaury, a relative of cornflower, pushes up its strappy leaves and clusters of small pink bitter blossoms that nothing eats.

In the last days of the month the wind drops and cloud lifts on warm stillness. My hands are stained red-black with the juice of boysenberries and blueberries, late and sweet; a second crop of eating grapes ripens and again a blackbird builds her nest on top of the vine. The first sauce tomatoes come in; I bring them to the boil then let them cool and strain out skins and seeds, and simmer the remaining pulp with a splash of oil till it's reduced by half. Flowering herbs steep on a windowsill for this year's batch of ointment; hawthorn berries fill out and blackberries colour on north-facing slopes; elderberry bunches darken around a fantail's nest in the hedge at the vegetable

garden – chicks teeter on the nest-edge, too big to stay, almost too fat to fly.

Six swans come and go on the dam. They arrive in a storm of wings, feet thrust forwards, water spraying ahead of them as they ski in. As they settle, their woodwind voices carry in the startled air; they lift and shake white pinions and fold them away so that only their dark body-plumage shows. Grey feather-edges and dark wingtips show that they're young birds – a family of this year's cygnets travelling together. A few hours feeding and they're gone again, wings smacking the water in decrescendo till only the tips meet the surface and they lift away, leaving a doubled trail, a reverse perspective. Next day they're back again.

Despite their size and the drama of their movements, at times the swans appear and disappear as if by magic – one moment they're head-down, quietly pulling up waterweed, surrounded by ducks and grebes, then I look away or turn a corner and come back to find no sign of them, water and sky empty of their dark shapes. It makes me think of those stories in which a group of children fall under the spell of a sorcerer and are transformed into swans or geese or ducks and fated to wander until the conditions of their release are met.

In the stories, ensorcelled children, wrenched away from their known world by ignorance and malignity, are forced to become aware of their former immersion in the certainties of the family mind, and of the freedom that comes with their exile into wildness. Through the shared plight of their sibling connection, they help one another to survive, and in the process find both their creaturehood and their discrete humanity, separate from the tribe.

It's not just in childhood that we're vulnerable to the spell of some mindset or mood, by contagion from outside or eruption from within. It's a life's work to respond with resourcefulness to forces that grip us while we're unaware and send us out to live to their bitter ends the consequences of our sleep. And part of what's required of us is to form allegiances, imaged in the stories by the siblings' faithfulness to one another, that can help us find our way back, though all is changed. It may be that, coming back, we bring disturbance with us – a reminder that the spell is only ever partly undone – like the youngest brother in the Grimm story of the six swans who is left with one human arm and one swan's wing, when the sleeve of the enchanted shirt woven to bring him in remains unfinished. And it may be that disturbance precedes our return, like the Children of Lir, who come home but no longer recognise the changed landscape of their birth.

Now, more than a month after the equinox, the light fades sooner but there's still a luxurious sense of space in the days. No hurry to milk the calfless cow in the evening – it's not fully dark till after nine. As I squat next to her, sunlight spills into the milking stall, and with it the sound of working bees from the swarm in the wall to the west above the doorway, the concrete beside me alive with their shadow-traffic. Stretched out in the warmth, the dog stirs and makes to snap then thinks better of it, as shadows crisscross her closed eyelids.

At twilight the sound of deep summer begins – mole crickets call from creek banks and patches of damp ground, each male singing into the embouchure of his trumpet-burrow. Going downslope in the forest for one last walk before dark, I stop with the dog beside a pool in the winter creek, dried now to a puddle of yellow silt. Still she throws herself in and lies panting and licking it up and comes out happy, gloved and bellied in stinking grey underslime. Overhead, ravens gather to mob a young eagle that's settled in the stand of white gum that grows only here in the moist soil of the gully – they call relentlessly, crowding in, and the eagle sits hunched. In the understorey, coprosma berries glow darkly in the half-light and sticky wattle gives off its varnish smell in the warmth. Retracing our steps uphill, I stop by the dam to throw sticks for the dog as she swims the mud off her. The swans were here but I don't see them now. On the road, six travellers pass by, walking.

Blown from our course by something that feels inhuman, we follow the ravelled skeins of complexity and lay them out as tales that map our predicament onto the world. Through the many-in-one of storying, we look for ways to track what's lost, and so we call and bring home the heart's scattered flock.

Presently

And now I became aware of perhaps someone else, it was only the faintest light and shadow as it were sketched on the air, a ghostly chiaroscuro walking familiarly with the rest of us as of by right. This sketchy figure was in truth familiar, uncertain of feature as it was: it was immediately recognizable to me as an early state of my death…a fully-grown duplicate of me but not yet fully defined, not yet fully realized, and therefore it was to me as a child to be looked after…

Like any parent I wanted the best for my death…walking beside me he was scarcely more visible than breath on glass but the manifestation of him was continually more detailed and refined although his face was obscure. He was not as yet ready to speak, perhaps he never would speak, but he looked at me with a look that said plainly, 'I know that I can trust you to do the right thing.'…When the time came I did the best I could.

Russell Hoban, Pilgermann[80]

Early one morning a hundred or more ravens congregate in the high windbreak and begin to call angrily, throwing themselves out into the air then settling back among the branches, flying out and settling, their row deafening – there's an eagle on the sloping ground of the paddock below them. It hop-walks uphill to the hedge, ignoring their hurled curses. Is it injured? It jumps to a low branch, wings extended, and balances there, then flies to a eucalypt a few metres away. Though the ravens are big birds, it makes them look inconsequential.

The first apples begin to ripen, a few crisp Gravensteins that will soon go mealy but taste marvellous now, months after the last of last year's keepers ran out, and with this, a silvereye once again practises its signature on the air – the same flourish repeated over and over to signal a territory and a nest. I thought there wouldn't be much of a crop on the pears and apples but as they start to colour I see quite a lot of fruit, hidden till now, same colour among the leaves. In the rest of the orchard, though, there's very little – the young apricot was stripped of its leaves in a single night by ringtail possums and the fruit didn't develop; there's a handful of plums on the greengages

and prunes; two figs ripen, delectable, on the young tree by the cow bail.

Leaves on the sweet chestnut and some of the vines are starting to change colour already; I collect them before they get brittle and store them away in brine as wrapping for soft cheeses. Some of the pears and quinces and hawthorns, some of the cherries and plums, look like winter already where, as happens each year, sawfly larvae, slimy and stinking, have skeletonised their leaves. It doesn't seem to affect the vigour of the trees.

In the polytunnels, zucchinis have nearly finished, cucumber vines are loaded but are slowing, *rocoto* chillies are ripe-hot. Paste tomatoes ripen and sit simmering in pots. The hens are still laying, so I make pasta – eggs and flour mixed and rolled paper thin, the yolk-yellow sheets draped over broomsticks in the kitchen to dry; dropped into boiling water, it's ready in a minute to eat with tomatoes and basil. Late potatoes have to be chipped out of ground that set hard – they were planted at the end of months of rain.

Wild fruit is plentiful – blackberries plump and soften in earnest, their red, unripe clusters darkening on the tips of the canes as if burned. I gather and share handfuls with the dog, though later when they come away more easily, she'll delicately pick them for herself. Flocks of young starlings rush to settle and feed in the elderberries. Their feathers are still greyish; next season they'll grow into full iridescence, sparkling-dark as the fruit they're eating now. The cherry plum hedge glows red and orange and yellow, and the cows clean up the fruit as it falls; damsons purple in the hedgerow beside the old house site, though they're still hard and eye-wateringly sour until the last days of the month, when the yellow flesh begins to soften and sweeten a little inside the still-tart purple skins.

Bees are loud in the forest canopy, foraging an abundant flush of stringybark eucalypt flowers that pour their honey scent down through the branches, while in the understorey, thickets of prickly currant-bushes, *Coprosma quadrifida*, are still covered in tiny red berries, with apple-berry, *Billardiera longiflora*, twining through them here and there, hung with brilliant purple-blue fruits the size of little olives.

Eucalypts are shedding their bark in sheets and ribbons as they grow in girth, and fuel piles up around them. It's the fiftieth anniversary of wildfires that burned through the district; throughout the island many lives and livelihoods were lost. On the mainland a terrifying heatwave presses from the central desert out through the eastern states, but here, the dice roll differently and cold air is sucked up from the Southern Ocean; here there's snow down to 900 metres the day after the worst of the heat to the north. Then sleety rain; we put on extra clothes and light the fire. Morning chill and river fog in the valleys announces autumn, with the sound of young parrots in conversation, their voices like wet fingers on glass.

Then days of still, clear brightness. Ravens fly down, the eagle forgotten for the moment, to stalk the yellowing paddocks, probing for pasture grubs with the look of nineteenth-century dignitaries, heads down, conferring. Fattened on the roots of grasses, flights of moths and beetles – adult morphs of grubs that evaded the ravens – emerge from their burrows at twilight in their tens and hundreds of thousands. Beetles fly to the house lights and are hunted by bats; moths, also hunted, keep low to the ground so that the earth itself seems to hum with their steady, E-natural bass drone.

As a small child, following my father around at his work, I would ask for this or that and often he would answer, 'Presently.'

At first I thought he meant 'I'll give you what you ask for, as a present,' and was delighted. He had to explain, then, that the word meant 'soon', but quickly I learned that he was saying, 'Not now; not yet.' 'Soon' only came if I could settle, make a nest for myself in the present of *presently* – if I could hear, see, touch what was already there so that I was no longer waiting. It was the beginning of an apprenticeship in the plasticity of time, and of connecting with the world. Eventually, being present became interesting for itself, not just as a way to tolerate my boredom and agitation and longing and impatience. Experience not deferred but here, unfolding.

At this other end of my life, *presently* does mean *soon*, as it must have done for my father, tired and in pain and not much younger than I am now, with a toddler at foot. Even if it's *not now, not yet*, the reality of my death gains definition, perhaps as a process already begun or simply because it is coming closer. Presently I will go in.

On a south-facing slope where forest and pasture meet, corded roots of eucalypts, exposed and scarred by the passage of cattle, reach out into the grasses that grow over the rocky bones of the hillside, making for water that soaks the earth of a gully clumped with rushes. *Presently* I trace the knotted bark of the roots and the dusty hollows between; *presently* I smell damp soil and understand the steady upward draught of moisture into the leaves above; *presently* my death comes towards me and I do my best to be ready.

If I cried out

Ach, wen vermögen wir denn zu brauchen?...Es bliebt uns
vielleicht irgend ein Baum an dem Abhang, daß wir ihn täglich
wiedersähen...die Straße von gestern und das verzogene Treusein
einer Gewohnheit...O und die Nacht, wenn der Wind voller
Weltraum uns am Angesicht zehrt...

Wirf aus den Armen die Leere zu den Raumen hinzu, die wir
atmen; vielleicht das die Vogel die erweiterte Luft fuhlen mit
innigerm Flug.

Who or what is there for us when we don't know what to do with
ourselves?...Maybe the sight of that everyday tree on its slope
sinks in at last...maybe our streetwise habits come back...Oh and
there's night, and the space-wind that blows us away...

Heave the emptiness out of your arms and let it turn to
breathing-room – maybe the birds will feel it and fly deeper.

Rainer Maria Rilke,
Duino Elegies: The First Elegy[81]

A full moon pushes up from behind the range to the east – an ending, a beginning – and a friend comes to walk the labyrinth to mark this transition, bringing intentions and wishes, for herself, for people she's close to, for children she works with. Rising, the moon is not yet high enough to clear the plantings round the edge of the pattern so we enter by the glow of phones and torches, following the long meander in and out and in towards the central space and a fire, lit earlier in the fifth lobe, space of djinns and angels, where the fireplace is marked with the rune *Kenaz*, for inspiration and skilful use. And the friend brings in an orange given to her by a child in her care, bruised and dinted like tonight's moon, and leaves it, a small self, on top of the copper dome in the fourth lobe. And the moon lifts its battered face and looks in, higher and smaller and paler and so bright that later, my shadow sharp behind me on dry grass, I hang out washing by its light, which fills the sheets like spinnakers.

Next morning at moonset the orange still sits, balanced where it was put, with the ashes of the fire on one side, and on the other the water pot of the third lobe. All night it has glowed there, undisturbed by possums and wallabies and devils and quolls and bandicoots that come to the water, undisturbed by bats and owls, which also love to drink and bathe, and continues to sit through a day of heat, its skin baking, while robins and wattlebirds and rosellas and thornbills dip and flick blessings its way.

And as the moon wanes, for three days and nights one of the cows calls for her yearling calf, slaughtered at the end of the grass, ahead of the winter. I thought she had weaned him months ago, kicked him off, put her head down and fended him off when he tried to drink. But she was late to the bull and

the calf inside her hadn't begun its final surge of growth, and the yearling – more than a yearling, well into his second year and tall and heavy as his mother – continued, secretly, to suckle. And when the butcher shoots him where he lies chewing cud, alive and then dead, instead of simply moving away with the herd as from a kill made by any predator, his mother feels her milk gather for him and wants him still, wants the warm heft of him against her side, half-kneeling because of his height, with his horned head turned crown-inward to reach down and under. Her bellowing sounds like grief and anger – *Where are you? Where are you!* Finally she stops. The few mouthfuls of comfort-milk she was still making this late in the season dry up and her restless pacing, looking, calling comes to an end. She puts her head down and grazes.

After about a week the butcher comes back with his clever knives to cut the body up, and the animal is *meat* – food for several families for months to come. We try not to waste the life we've taken – almost everything can be used by us, and the unusable parts of the guts are buried under trees to feed the roots. Big ungainly bags of bones are kept for broth; other bones are put out in the paddock where, within minutes, ravens gather in their dozens and then in their hundreds. The enormous cacophony of their parliament brings in the eagles, who pivot sharply down on fingered wings, shawl-feathers lifting as they stare down the ravens and walk stiffly in, feathered chaps extended behind their shins like flags, towards the shining white and red of the bones. A day later every shred of meat is gone, leaving only a fuzz of pale filaments, picked tendon-attachments.

At moon-dark, blasts of radiation stream outward from a newly active region on the Earth-side surface of the sun;

they press in on Earth's magnetic field and for several nights the black sky lights up green and red as the charged flow hits oxygen and nitrogen particles high in the atmosphere. These are flares of moderate strength and so don't cause great disruption to electrical networks and satellite technology, but still, such an influx of energy into the planetary system has its effects at ground level – there are electrical storms and windstorms arising from increased pressure gradients. Usually a gifted sleeper, I lie awake, teeth on edge as the solar wind blows through my flimsy circuits, while above the clouds, wings and waves of light unfurl and shake themselves across the southern sky.

Flocks of starlings whistle their static along the wires. Pears cook down to pink in cinnamon syrup; quinces are ripe. Suddenly the winter coats of the cows are growing in, their summer gloss giving way to soft shag as the warm undercoat comes through on their flanks, on their udders. They're creatures of the ice and every year they prepare for the blizzard that might come, even the delicate, deer-like Jersey with her smattering of North African, heat-tolerant genes. Mornings and evenings darken. First frost.

We take and inflict the hits. Losses, mistakes – ours and others' – wear us down. What is there when we don't know what to do with ourselves? Heave. Heave again. Make room.

Worship

There are these two young fish swimming along, and they happen to meet an older fish swimming the other way, who nods at them and says, 'Morning, boys, how's the water?' And the two young fish swim on for a bit, and then eventually one of them looks over at the other and goes, 'What the hell is water?'

David Foster Wallace, *This is Water*[82]

In the space of a couple of days, currawongs strip all the wine grapes from the two little vine rows on the north-facing slope below the track to the house. The vines have only begun to produce in the last year or three, and it's clear that unless they're netted we'll never get more than a handful of fruit. Currawongs, though they are raven-sized and are called crows by local people, are not corvids but members of the same family as butcherbirds and woodswallows. They're heavy but streamlined, glossy-dark with a white undertail, white flashes on their wings and a white band across the tail-tip. Inquisitive, omnivorous, they have a massive beak to pry and grab with and are happy to eat whatever's in season – eggs and nestlings, fruit, insects, lizards, grain – and were themselves at one time eaten by humans here in the valley. They hunt the pasture slopes and forest in family groups, posting lookouts like the ravens with whom they sometimes feed, turning over cowpats in search of grubs and beetles or flying in to take ripe apples and pears.

I've never seen them eat carrion the way the ravens do. They often spend summers in the mountains and come down into lowland orchards and gardens in autumn, where alarm calls of small birds announce their movements, as do their own loud, metallic cries, somewhere between the sound of a tambourine and a stripped-thread bolt as it tightens, untightens, or the turn of a tap with a worn washer. When they've cleaned up the grapes, they turn their attention to a patch of newly sown barley, planted to feed to the cows over winter and then to be dug in as a green manure crop in spring – *one seed for the mouse, one for the crow, one to rot, one to grow.*

The sky is dark with ash from torched forestry coupes, post-logging; the air is full of the smell of burning eucalypt. It's very

still, and in the mornings smoke hangs heavy around the hills and mixes with fog in layers over the satin drift of the river. Across the obscure distances of the valley, noises – birdcalls, conversations of apple-pickers walking to work along the road – are thrown as if ventriloquised to materialise close by. In late afternoon, the sun burns purple-red through the fire cloud, *flammagenitus*, that colours the world fever-bright. The air is strangely warm, though the days shorten fast and first frosts have come.

Then, overnight, sleet comes gritting and slicing from the south – there's a scramble to find winter clothes packed away since last year. Cattle lean, head-down, into the wind and look for shelter. Through cold days and nights one swan bobs on the dam where it has fed for weeks, pulling up strands of waterweed, surrounded by smaller birds. Where is its flock, its mate? A few kilometres away where the road runs beside the river, a chaos of black and white feathers tosses in the traffic's slipstream where a swan, killed by a truck or car, has been thrown to the gravelled verge.

On the Korean Peninsula and the seas around it, tension builds as a stand-off that's being compared with the Cuban missile crisis of the 1960s ramps up between North Korea and the US, cheered on, as then, by the military-industrial complex. Is the situation better or worse because both leaders are seen as buffoons, mooncalves, not-quite-human, rather than as statesmen, however flawed? In a moment of sunlight I hear the news on the radio and lie facedown in the shade of the flowering *Corymbia*, showered by stamens as bees and wasps and honeyeaters feast in the canopy above. The ground comes to meet me, holds me up and draws me to it.

We live in the water of language, culture, family, place, and are carried within its self-evidence, organised by its flow, until we learn to feel and think otherwise. In an address at Kenyon College, Ohio, the writer David Foster Wallace exhorted students to become aware of what it is that claims their allegiance in this way:

> There is no such thing as not worshipping. Everybody worships. The only choice we get is *what* to worship...If you worship money and things – if they are where you tap real meaning in life – then you will never have enough...Worship power – you will feel weak and afraid, and you will need ever more power over others to keep the fear at bay...Look, the insidious thing about these forms of worship is not that they're evil or sinful; it is that they are unconscious. They are default-settings.[83]

He points to worship on some spiritual path as an alternative – *be it JC or Allah, be it Yahweh or the Wiccan mother-goddess or the Four Noble Truths or some infrangible set of ethical principles*[84] – but evidence is all around us of how, adhered to unconsciously, unexamined, a spiritual practice can also, as Wallace puts it in relation to worship of money and power and sex and intelligence, *eat you alive.*[85] And when it has eaten you it can scorch the ground under your feet and turn not just your life but also your neighbours' lives to a column of ash.

Wallace himself was fatally gripped by his own worship of what he called the mind as *terrible master*[86] when, after a lifetime of work to subvert the default settings he had inherited, he killed himself. Perhaps he was simply worn out. Perhaps he forgot that the way through is not only by effort of will but also by compassion.

Again and again we give away our power, individually, collectively, whether passively drawn along in the current of things or fighting, exhausted. Is there a way to be alive in the flow? Is there a way to call out and unmask the *terrible masters* inside and outside of us?

Wrens agitate over a snake that hunts the long grass behind the house; a tiger moth caterpillar meanders across open ground, safe in its coat of maddening bristles, in search of a place to make its transformation; there it will shed its fur into the silk of its cocoon for protection; there it will metamorphose.

Beste, best, beast

Foweles in the frith
the fisses in the flod
And I mon waxe wod
mulch sorw I walke with
for beste of bon and blod

Song, thirteenth–fourteenth century[87]

I dream a big plane, a bomber perhaps, that turns and returns low over the gridlocked panic of a city at war, cumbersome and deliberate as a blowfly. It's so close I can see the dents in its silver underbelly. I dream ruined boys, so far removed from manhood that they fixate on cruelty, as if the pain and fear they cause or merely witness could give them power. Nightly, my mind catalogues my fears as strife gathers its grievous attendants and soldiers take to the streets. Of course this is my own internal landscape too. How to be with it.

I've stopped milking, to give the cows a rest before they calve in spring. Their pregnancies are just starting to show, bellies expanding, lopsided, as the bulky rumen is pushed outward by the growing calf. They're due within a week of one another – not an ideal arrangement as it means months with no milk at all, and then a superabundance. The usual pattern when there are two house cows is to have one milking while the other is dry. But the day opens up without dairy routines to attend to, and I'm enjoying that.

In preparation for the coming season, T is building a cheese cellar – it's nearly ready. Earth-walled, earth-floored, it's built between the western wall of the house and the bank of clay we piled up on that side to lift the strong prevailing winds. Insulated, windowless, it will be (I hope) a place where cheeses can mature at a steady temperature, cool and somewhat humid, away from draughts, and where potatoes and apples can be stored as well, and maybe wine if we can find a way to outwit the birds. Till now I've had the cheeses in open shelves on the back verandah, screened from insects and shaded from direct sun but exposed to air movement and to high ambient temperatures in the middle of summer, so some have dried and cracked and others have ripened prematurely, with the risk of rancidity.

Experimenting with limewash mix to paint the inside walls of the cellar, I've settled on a lime-water-salt-whey combination that will seal and inoculate the surfaces with the kind of organisms I want in the storage environment. Having never used whitewash before, I'm surprised to find that it's translucent, almost colourless when wet. At first I think I must have the consistency wrong, but then it dries to a startling white that continues to brighten with time. The mix is thin and will need several coats – thick layers I saw on houses and farm buildings in France and Ireland must have accumulated over many years of repainting.

The light is low and cool – only a little while till the solstice. The local black cockatoo flock gathers together the small groups of its summer and autumn dispersal in high forests and alpine scrub, and begins its winter circum-aviation of the valley. Early in the month, forty birds spend their days moving between stands of dead eucalypts (grubs in the rotting wood), the garden around the house (banksia seeds and curiosity), and the radiata pine windbreak (seeds in the ripening cones), crying back and forth through morning fog and the bright sun that follows. Now there are nearly seventy – they fly in a marvellous clamour that can be heard from far off, their flight an animated script that flows, branching, overhead and into the pines.

Brown falcons that nest in the windbreak seem to be on good terms with the cockatoos but have begun to hunt kookaburras – big kingfishers nearly their own size, which have established themselves in the district in the last twenty years or so, having made their way down from the north of the island where they were brought from the mainland early in the twentieth century. They eat pretty much the same things as the falcons – lizards and snakes, insects, small birds and mammals – so perhaps the falcons' harrying is as much about seeing off competitors as hunting a meal. I can't say I'm sorry the kookaburras have met their match – a whole family has begun to haunt the garden, and this year I didn't see any of the large and beautifully patterned she-oak skinks that usually make an appearance.

This month a research vessel has sailed from Tasmania, north along the edge of the continental shelf to the mainland, dropping bag nets and taking sediment cores in abyssal depths of 2,000, 3,000, 4,000, 5,000 metres.[88] They're making acoustic maps of the deep seabed, about which much less is known than about the planets of the solar system, where currently the entire surface of Jupiter is being mapped to a resolution of a few kilometres.

The vessel's nets bring up creatures from a world whose pressures and necessities create lifeways and shapes that can seem nightmarish when hauled into the light – blind, fanged, irregular, slimed, and banded with sensors that detect movements or electrical currents in darkness beyond the reach of the sun. Many animals produce their own light as lure or decoy; some are camouflaged in the brilliant reds and oranges that become invisible in depths where all but blue light is filtered out.

Those that live in the intermediate depths often move towards the surface at night to feed, then retreat to relative safety in the sparsely populated deeps during the day. Animals that live on the abyssal seabed are almost entirely dependent on food from above – bodies that drift down from the sunlit world at death, whales and sprats alike. They live in a rain of billions of plankton whose calcium carbonate skeletons accrete on the seabed, forming limestones that come around again with tectonic or volcanic uplift, to be built into our houses and our bones, to dress our pastures, whitewash our walls.

When I was in Ireland, in the part of the south-west from which my mother's people emigrated in the nineteenth century, I dreamed an ancient creature, human but imprisoned, by powers afraid of her life and also afraid to kill her, within a hardened carapace of lime. Only her face was visible, her outline simplified, limbs elided to stumps, but her eyes were alive, sane, and she returned my gaze without bitterness despite long abuse, trapped in that white shell. Eventually she was freed, the mortar around her softened by water so that it fell away. Her unbound body was a collection of sacs and pouches, soft and shirred grey-brown like the skin of an orangutan, without a structure that could hold it upright. What was to become of her? She seemed untroubled, though seeing her, held or free, I felt horror.

In a miscellany of medieval documents collected in the seventeenth century, mainly comprising the statutes of various towns, clerical correspondence and records of gifts of land, a few pages of music were gathered up, including the words and notation of the song included in the epigraph to this chapter. In it the anonymous singer sums up in five phrases the predicament of human consciousness – how, while other creatures are at home in their worlds, we watch and worry over the *best*, the *beast* of our living, dying bodysoul. And each night, in reply, it *waxes wod*, grows wild, sends up visions of life from the deeps of our bones and blood, our inheritance and its shuddering rhythms. Through the careful layers of daylight mind a cloud of witnesses erupts; we see them and they look back at us, sometimes benign, sometimes terrifying. But no matter how afraid we are, to turn away is to turn from our best teachers, those ones who can show us where we're lost, bound, what needs growing up out of its cruelty, what needs holding into its strength.

Sun return

*[Then] the individual...must become a bridge over which
something ancient and undifferentiated and outcast may walk to
find a welcome in consciousness.*

Liz Greene, *The Astrology of Fate*[89]

Despite the cold, mushrooms sprout here and there, though
mostly not the edible kind, pushing up fruiting bodies from
their vast invisible networks. Shaggy inkcaps appear in their
usual place where damp soil heaps at a junction in the road,
but the rings and rows of edible field mushrooms, white and
brown, don't show in the pastures; nothing there to add to
the last tomatoes and the dried beans that are coming in for
shelling – beautiful little green-white flageolets, and haricots
and canarios and scarlet runners.

I've been using the outdoor oven to cook fast flatbread
and big slow pots of stew. Darkness looms at my back as I
lean to the warmth – the shadow that accompanies all those
who have lit and tended fires or let them go out by chance
or carelessness or necessity. More and more as I get older, I'm
aware of how those who came before are still here, not just as
stories but as continuing presences. How my life is entwined
with theirs – all those who stayed in one place and those who
walked away; those who sold what they had for a handful of
beans to climb in search of the giant's gold; and all those who

fell to earth and dissolved in rain. Their experiences pass to me as traits expressed or suppressed, genes switched on or off by biochemical wildfires that burned through them, lit by their own joys and sorrows and by those they inherited. And they come to me in the lives of those around me too, and in the absences and silences where lives were cut short.

The generations overlap. I was there as my mother formed in the womb a hundred years ago. Her complement of eggs already complete at five months' gestation, I was among them, with my siblings, little sparks in the noisy darkness. We lived in her there, then, she and all of us blown through by what was dissolved in the water and air and food my grandmother took in for us, and by her terrors and pleasures, her laughter, her fears – of violence in a new country, of madness, destitution, of falling into hell. And we were there through the years of my mother's childhood and adolescence with its own griefs and delights, coming one by one into the light when she joined with our father.

Full moon, new moon, the sun small and pale in its winter hut as the days pace down. The longest night arrives. Last year we didn't light a solstice fire – the ground was saturated by months of rain; green grass grew through the heap of sticks and prunings, and a potato vine sprouted, flowering, from the top. Now it's drier and the moment has come – a struck match and the pyre kindles, first a tall yellow stripe through twigs on the outside of the stack and then orange flags and billows as bigger sticks deeper in begin to catch. Haloes blossom around carbonised branches in the heart of the fire as hundreds of combustion products combine in dozens of reactions in the complex, mutable chemistry of flame.

It will be weeks before the light begins to lengthen properly. Wind and rain follow the solstice in a strange alternation of mild

and cold that repeats – warm wind then frost a day later; warm rain then snow on the mountains. The water tank fills and the first buds burst high in the shrubby wintersweet, sending wafts of cold perfume along the air; belladonna lilies put up their leaves beside the seat in the labyrinth.

Birds bathe all day in the water pot at the labyrinth's heart, keeping their feathers clean and voluminous against the cold, but already there's a turn towards the warmth to come – scarlet robins appear in nesting colours; blackbirds and plovers begin to pair up; bronzewing pigeons, two by two, search the ground under the trees for wattle and lucerne seeds.

And ravens chase each other up and down the wind; their sound is everywhere – their calls and the creaking rustle of their wings. In the week before the solstice, in my dream, a group of seven or eight fly together and apart, together and apart, stately, bodies upright in the air, beaks pointing skyward; I see them at first from far off, and then as through a telescope they spring into focus, huge, dusty green like the bloom that grows on things left in the shade.

From Neolithic times, ravens have been depicted by humans as sun-birds and images of transformation and guidance, three-legged for their role as mediators between sky, earth and the underworld. They watch for the moment of death and, in charge of the changes that follow, dismember and carry off the body for sky burial. In Chinese mythology, sun-crows are often red – bright afterimages of the darkness behind closed eyes – like the red *sanzuwu* who inhabit ten suns held aloft by the branches of a mulberry tree in the eastern underworld, the Valley of the Sun; these ten suns take turns to rise day by day, to travel across the sky in the carriage of the Sun Mother, *Xihe*.[90] Sometimes, though, the stories depict birds that are

305

green – afterimage of an afterimage – like the *qingniao* who serve *Xi Wangmu*, Queen of the West.

The ravens here are my guides too, towards the light inside the dark as I carry the shadowing dead, nourishment and poison, in my bones and blood. They accompany me now through cold that will deepen before it eases, as the ancestors gather at the lock-gates of my veins, jostle upstream, seeking *a welcome in consciousness*. I want to give them what I have to give – a home in my thoughts; prayers for those who are still in pain; heart's open water where they can slip away, free.

Stones ring

Each mortal thing does one thing and the same:
Deals out that being indoors each one dwells;
Selves — goes itself; myself it speaks and spells,
Crying Whát I dó is me: for that I came.

Gerard Manley Hopkins,
'As Kingfishers Catch Fire'[91]

At the start of winter, upwellings of warm air continue to fling far outwards from the equator; they land as spiralling high-pressure systems over the southern mainland of Australia, blocking storms that usually bring rain and snow north from the cold seas. I cross the Tasman as the pattern shifts — snow comes to the high country, and sleet and flooding rain washes over the islands of Aotearoa New Zealand.

Here with my sisters for the first time since our mother died, I feel the strangeness of her absence, and also the luxury of a stay that's not overshadowed by crisis. I fly and touch down, fly and touch down, first in Christchurch, with its disorienting new skylines and streetscapes. Rebuilding of the quake-shattered city is well under way, though some empty spaces remain and roads are still cordoned off in places. Even in the cold and dark of the year, people are about; work and play goes on. With my sister I wrap up warmly to walk in the park; at her house, we sit by the fire and talk, tossing the worn shapes of our lives back and forth between us.

The day I leave to travel north, cloud lifts and the little plane follows the line of the Alps under a huge sky, row on row of ranges covered almost to sea level in a fresh dump of snow, the whole island a jawbone, saw-toothed. Beneath me, mountains grind and spit rock into rivers that pour milky greygreenblue, and in them roll pale boulders of nephrite, *pounamu*, hiding their green hearts, and veined greywacke, and mica schist glitters in the cold, and gold dust gathers where eddies take heavy flakes and specks out of the flow.

The strait between the islands is so calm that shorelines and rocky islets are mirrored in the sea, and the only disturbance I see is a single wavering line of white that marks the ferocious rip where two oceans meet. To the north-west, a swathe of cloud, pierced by the bright peak of Taranaki, then north and east the peaks of Ruapehu, Ngauruhoe, Tongariro. And I circle down, giddy with light and air, into the town where I was born, and sleep in another sister-house over a harbour that's mirror-still within, while at the entrance breakers roll and smash on congealed lava. But even here where oranges grow, it's cold in the breath of snow from further south, and again we put on layer after layer to walk in the sea wind and turn over, one and the other, pieces of the patterns we're part of; we tap them against one another to hear them sound.

Between us, the remaining sisters, we sort through our mother's things: each garment, the rings and earrings she loved to wear, her household ornaments and renovated junk-shop furniture still vivid with her life. She made something of unpromising materials, made them her own, just as we too work with what's available, shaped by the places that name us as we roll in their currents.

I lift away again and return to Australia, to days of warmth in northern New South Wales with a friend I first met at school, where we laughed ourselves slippery out of the grip of the mean girls, shaking loose; we've stayed connected ever since. Now she's a healer and gardener in a rainforest valley she's regenerated from lantana-choked, abandoned farmland over the course of thirty years – a place of restoration.

Back in Tasmania it's snowing. Pine pollen blows from the hedges, yellow in the white wind, and brightly rims the water troughs and puddled footprints around them. And there are other storms about too. One morning in the first week of spring, from the surface of the sun an X9 flare spits a blizzard of rays towards Earth. For the most part they're deflected by the Earth's magnetosphere, but their interaction with the upper atmosphere produces a cascade of secondary particles detectable at ground level. Along with X-rays and gamma rays, there's a spike in neutrinos, chargeless particles that blow through the spaces of things, far out of range of my senses but disturbing still, turning my solid world ghostly, permeable in the solar wind. Telco transmissions are disrupted as the massive jolt of energy reaches us.

Storms intensify in the southern oceans, and into the snow, a few days after the flare, Elsie's calf is born. We worry because her calf died last year, and intervene to hold the baby's hooves as they appear, and pull as she pushes – and this time we feel the calf kick and see his tongue flick – and soon he slithers out, lax and lanky, and shakes his head, and we put his mouth to the teat and he drinks straight away, and is on his feet in minutes.

Within the hour he is practising little four-footed hops and she licks him clean and warm in the cold air. She speaks to him unceasingly – *mm hm mmm mur? hmmmm* – during his first days, even in the dark, even while she's eating.

But it's the other cow, Maggie, sturdy and imperturbable, who's in trouble. She calves a week early, a few days after Elsie, and towards evening of the next day I notice that she's swaying on her feet. It's milk fever – all the calcium in her body has drained into her milk before her hormonal system has had a chance to kick in and regulate, mobilise and replace minerals from her bones. We inject an infusion of calcium, magnesium, glucose under the skin of her neck and shoulder; without it she will collapse within hours and almost certainly die within a day or so. The effect of the injection is miraculous – she walks away and begins to graze.

Then mild air floats in; the cherry plum hedge lifts its white cloud and wattle blossom brightens lemon-yellow before it dulls, ochre then umber. Until daylight saving begins, the sun is risen already at milking time, faintly warm at my back as I return to the house with full buckets, a dew-halo silver in the grass around my long shadow, to make cheese on the stove. This surprising, improvised life.

Turning, turning, my heart is a fist of moss-coloured jasper speckled dark and light, cracked and polished, studded like a temple bell. Its hardness is immaterial now as the breath of life, breath of the ancestors rings it through; I'm home to a gong that shakes me, and, struck, my rumbled history is waking within the sound.

Winter

Roots wait, count the slow sun slower,
then quicken, draw green into yellow, red.

I'm irritable, reactive, heart shut and sad – a hollow space where fragments float, anchorless. When I fall, I fall into nothing, motherless, fatherless, everything fluid, like the ground after a quake when all seems wasted, the years lost as if in the heavy grammar of a foreign tongue, sentences still in their itchy velvet, bloody language that builds in points and ramparts like the antlers of the little fat stag that appeared one morning outside my window and disappeared again, who knows where.

Waiting, waiting, feet hurting, legs heavy, itching to go, twitching all through myself to leap away; hauling back, leaping and hauling. A Saturnian life – bad-tempered, collapsible, unskilled, melancholy. My pack of worries bounding and snapping.

The stove vent is open; points of light walk inside the fire – a city that wakes or the past that shines from every star-field. The fire iron warm beside the stove. Moondark, black as a charcoal stick, burnt willow silky in my hand. Where are the cracks, the fissures through which change can come? Moments of silence when language reaches an end; transformation like a flash from the angled wings of a flock. Movement, something in shadow just out of sight and reach on the edge of sleep; it gleams like fur in the wind, not snow, not rain. I come to a place where nothing is, only a buzzing, itching buzzing, life leaving or entering.

Images slip through, overflow, seep – the feared and welcome other. Something is dying; something has reached an end and wants to be gone. This dried knot of stories near my heart, how to cough up these things for which I have no names? And then this – I dream I'm looking out to sea, watching seabirds gather over something in the water. It looks like a dead animal – brown fur – then I see that it's alive, a creature swimming towards shore, followed by others, a caravan carrying goods to this place. Small and far-off but sharp – the white and grey and black of the birds, the calm blue of the sea, the golden pelts of the animals. Ha! A caravanserai – those ships of the desert, coming in. But they're still far off. Here, now, wattlebirds curse and the bees are angry.

Days flash in the long night like beacons, signalling rock or harbour, harbour and rock. I am adrift again in my winter boat, hung between wave and wave, dragged down the icy beach each year to stare at the polar stars creeping towards midheaven; each year to wait again for a clue, a wink from the wolf overhead – a thylacine holed up beside the centaur – watching me watch for bearings that mark a passage to fresh ground.

A new moon and all things hidden, invisible under smoke like the fires in my dream; I looked across the valley at burning slopes – a mirrored self on fire down to the water, and I put out my hand to quench the flames before they disappeared into black. Each dream a snapshot. Dread – heavy hot dark. Breathe it in, and breathe out – what? Pale moth underbelly against the window in the light of the lamp. *You will die and all you will take with you is your state of mind.* There's work and there's luck or fate – to be free enough of pain or poison or madness to die conscious. J looked awake as she died. Heart failing, the last thing she said: *It's okay. It's all right. It's okay.*

High squally sky with ravens blown, black scraps. A currawong strops its beak on a post and blades its way through bushes looking for insects and lizards slow with cold, and early nests. A young butcherbird carols sweetness and small birds set up the alarm. And the dog scratches up a nest of rabbits under the blackberry – I hear the squeal and the crunch of bone. I know what her expression will be – eyes half-closed in rapture. A death-day then. There's a time when all the old injuries wake – hip, shoulder, knee, silence, shame, betrayal, rebuke – I'd better find a way to talk to them, a way to move them and let them speak.

Parrots call across the garden – three chimed notes thrown back and forth. Hard frost in the night – a bubble of high pressure squeezes down, everything cold and still. Birdsong is ice on silver falling through trees; freezing fog breathes ice to their tops, a side-blur of crystals drawn along the draught from the river; pine hedge needles tipped with frozen drops. In the whiteness of fog and ice a hawk lands, russet and gold, on the frosty lawn. Air so cold I step out of myself.

A fantail comes through the frost to the empty rock hollow of the birdbath and looks at me, hops in, hops out, hops in – *where's the water?* A trickle from the hose and the bird begins to bathe and then a blackbird shivers and dances in the shine of it and later a female robin, chocolate brown and ruddy, white forehead spot. Does it quiet the rough stinging to tell like this, to record this truth, that I was present and grateful?

Yes – just to have the habit of saying, to see what moves towards me from the world. *Go to the end of your sorrow* has been all the advice my soul has given me for years. A life sentence.

And it comes to me that I too, even in my unease, can simply be part of this morning, like the wallaby carcass by the road with its furious cloud; many creatures feasting there – flies and carrion beetles, ravens, the brown falcon that nests in the windbreak, quolls and devils, a feral cat. After four days, just scraps of fur, bones, a greasy stain on flattened grass. All that's required is to be present and to look both ways – in towards the warm light that lets me do my work in the world, and also out towards the dark and its stars. So (sometimes, for a little while) I can unhook the lame knee or the cramped gut, put the words in order because that's what is given to me to do – love like the rasp of a cat's tongue.

Along the shore, something skeins like fog – black snowstorm of a young flock rising. Winter in the leashes of water that burn through my hands; winter in this feast – my animal self running into the lights among pocked stump-holes, the ghost of an orchard. Where I am going, summer billows in saltmarshes. Round eye out of feather and fur, creatures are moving – they leave their tracks all over me, map and compass bearings, my belly the night sky. Voice is a supple body. It walks in the valley of shadow; it is eaten and it lives. I read these echoes blindfold, tell the world like beads smoothed by pleasure and use in a circle or loop, back and forth; dark sound of healing, and all ways the singing direction.

How I tell the hill

From the start the whole place talked.

To travel here was to move through waves of sensation that seemed to come out of the ground, friendly or hostile like patches of warmth and cold. That got my attention. I came here flying, insubstantial, a ghost, and the place gave me its staying power, gave me names and images for sensations that pass through me. Great luck to learn this landscape, this ridge of clay, sandstone, mudstone and what grows from it, to live inside its weather. I can breathe watching a storm pass over, leaving its litter of wreckage but also its aftermath of quiet rain. This and myself and everything around unfolding in Earth's memory and imagination.

People walked to this island over the land bridge during the ice; then – now – whalers came, and sealers, convicts and militiamen, jump-ship sailors and settlers on the run from famine and war and fathers who didn't want them – a smash-up of cultures in which languages were lost, life was ground to a nub and something new began. I know them now, these families sprouted from wreckage – watchful, hardy, mistrustful of distinction except by epithet, sardonic humorists with a taste for salt and bitter.

In this hilly land, left over after the carve-up of richer, leveller ground, here are the traces I find – knapped stones on the riverbank; old pathways; rocks heaped on north-facing slopes cleared for wheat; tracks paved by ticket-of-leave men in the road trusts with their horses and drays. Gone houses – first the slab hut, its only sign a small level place with a view out over the river. Then foundation stones, a rose, a square of hawthorn for the house pushed down by cattle fifty years ago, built for the nearby spring. The pine tree house taken by fire – cobblestones, damsons, pheasant's eye, gallica rose, barberry. Cherry laurel house – broken crockery in a stump-hole, pale pompon roses. Holly tree house – late narcissus sweet on a south slope.

Overwintering silvereyes, small bodies shaded russet to cream to green, feed on insects in a thicket of flowering quince.

Wattlebirds, sleek as young dogs, hang to drink from grevillea blossoms. Bush cherry, stringybark, hawthorn and elder; these are the roots that will scatter my bones.

The bull howls one note like a missile again and again into the dark, each roar a streak of falling sky. *So bos. Woa petty.* Cow in the night paddock, her bulk under the stars warm against warm, black against the dark. Milk music in the side of the morning bucket, forehead in the hollow of a flank, silky furnace. The calf stirring against the fence.

Tiny new skinks hunt flies in the chickweed and fumitory forest that edges the garden and a blue-tongue lizard, long as my forearm, lounges in the returning sun. Big, soft sky-blue tongue, golden eyes, five-toed feet – we share that symmetry. Eagles ride the wind and call, plaintive as kelp gulls, as the whole valley fills with purple rain. Rivulets wash gravel across the road. Two sharp cracks of thunder then strong sunshine and high streaks in blue sky. The river's full. Purple-brown, it brims as the tide lifts, a clear spill onto the edge of the road. I go there.

Out where it's full salt, walking the edge after dark, every movement is phosphor-lit – frilled tidewash, footprints sunk in wet sand, the leap of a fish. Far out to sea, lightning bolts of a great storm jag halfway across the sky, silent – miles high those cloud-towers must be. From south and west a sea wind comes in under warm air from the north. Layers in friction. All night, the flickering.

Next morning clear sky lifts and the air is full of itself, spacious as outbreath. A pademelon and her child graze outside the window, the little one now forbidden the pouch; a week ago it leaned out, browsing as its mother fed. Now it follows her and experiments with this and that – a rose petal held in

319

both hands like a lettuce leaf; a dabble of paws in the water dish – it jumps away, shuddering.

In the dark before speech, I am alive in the gift of breath, harsh and sweet. Life waits to enter. Here, plants and creatures survived the changes of millions of years. Humans resilient too, community formed in collision and fallout in this place crisscrossed by tracks and starred with shell middens, gridded with land-grant farms – a threshold of story.

In the breath-room something turns –
sounds come out of us, singsong,
feeling ourselves moved like that.
Line and stipple and tone
we make a song and dance and picture ourselves.

Here, then – a story.
Shallow sea and in it, pebbles dropped from the ice, fans of life, shells –
laid down in rock plates, stacked leaves in a stony book,
all lifted, falling and rising a long way into wet dark.
Ice again – its reach and retreat;
scrub, tundra and creatures that push the edge southwards.
Syllables in the stone book – liverwort, fern,
velvet worm in the leaf mould,
gum moth, mole cricket,
wattlebird fattening in yellow shade,
goshawk, robin, ringtail, tiger-cat.

And then we arrive, wave on wave.

Cold sharp breath, cold sharp wind off the sea.
Wheel of the weather rolling.

So we're part of it, turning, calling. Old tracks on the ridges;
roads that follow.
Forest burned and grown, cut and burned and grown again.
Trees and the itch of stumps,
stones heaped, a prickle of wheat, raspberries in the shade.
And when I lie down, go back in,
close voices grow up through me, grass to stitch me in;
I hear a song from the mouth of the earth –
a line of sky and hills, a sentence.

After no-breath, no-space,
all of us thrown away and falling scrambled –
these blessed stripes, land running down to the river.
Listen here now we work
talking a seam of water out of the hill
in all its folds and shoulders.
Loose the spring that makes everything possible.

Breathe, tell, go on.
Breathe, tell, go on.

OCTOBER

All souls

This moment of grace between snow and fire.

Early in the month, the first day of warmth comes with an exhalation of dew from grasses grown long and soft wherever they're not cropped back by cattle or pademelons; paddocks and roadsides are startlingly green. Drifts of perfume stray in from fruit trees whose buds were shaken open by days of wind – the sweetness of apple, the fishy scent of pear, wafts of almond from the last of the greengage flowers now giving way to tiny plums. After weeks of mud and cold it's disconcerting to go outside without having to brace against a rainy gale. Under a clear sky, on the peaks across the river, the few remaining pockets of snow gleam against black scree. Next morning, fog-light turns the air grainy and luminous; parrots launch themselves into it and, closing their wings, torpedo through its interstices. Little wattlebirds throw back their heads and send their voices into its depths. Later the fog lifts on bright sunlight.

Reptiles are fully awake now. In the space of ten minutes I see a shining black tiger snake on the track and elsewhere a tiny newborn of the grey colour phase; a beautiful green-grey she-oak skink whisks away into the grass, and a hugely pregnant blue-tongue lizard, thick as a child's arm, blinks at me from a patch of sun. From every side come outraged calls of nesting birds, warning *trouble on the ground*. Then I hear the *trouble from the sky* alarm and think it must be the brown falcon passing over, but T calls me to see a white goshawk crouched in the long grass of the blackwood windbreak behind the house, tearing at the carcass of a ringtail possum it has snatched from its nest of sticks and leaves in the branches. Though it flies up when it sees us, the hawk is unwilling to leave its feast and sits, glaring, on a branch a few metres away, so that we can clearly see its furious red eye and the orange-yellow of its cere and legs, brilliant against white plumage and the polished ebony of its beak and talons.

From the tip of each branch, the fig tree sends up green flame-hands with this summer's fruit swelling among them. Week by week the apricot trees, smashed so badly again by possums over winter I feared they might die this time, cover themselves in healthy leaves, though the flower buds have been eaten. Over the course of the month, lily of the valley flowers in the shadow of tall stalks of Solomon's seal, garden daffodils wither and set seed, and narcissus on the old house site come into flower. Wisteria and roses bud and break; the kowhai's lime-green cloud of flowers darkens to butter-yellow, and the little crimson peony from the L'Arche garden in Hobart opens its sole, bee-haunted flower as always. The first hawthorn blossoms light up hedges and bird-sown thickets; elderflower panicles begin to fluoresce in the shade of leaves; oats and barley, planted as winter cow-fodder and soon to be chopped in as green manure, come into head.

I've transferred last year's hard cheeses to the new cellar and set up a shelf for this year's lot. Every few days when I bring in the newest round of pressed curd, I look over those on the maturing shelf, and turn and wash them in salted whey. Feta sits in its bucket of brine with a plate on top to keep it under the surface; soft cheeses ripen in lidded containers. The room has its own distinct smell – whitewash and salt and cheese, and the gingery, carroty green of sauerkraut maturing in crocks.

The room has vents at floor level and ceiling height to allow for circulation of air – I'm still learning how to use them to regulate temperature and humidity. Some air is needed to keep the space from becoming so damp that mould grows, but when I left the vents partly open on a hot day the temperature went up to 16 degrees Celsius – quite a bit over the ideal 10–12 degrees, so that was a mistake. The best approach in summer is probably to open them wide at night, then close them before sunrise, as we do with the house during days of heat. It works here because, so far, we still have few nights that stay hot, unlike many mainland states, where heatwave conditions are becoming increasingly common.

I walk down the forested slope to the bottom of the farm and back up again with the dog while I wait for curd to set. She trots, wolf-like, and stops from time to time and points into the understorey of bracken and goodenia and prickly coprosma beside the track, and looks back to let me know that she's smelled something we can hunt, and trots on with what looks like a shrug when I don't respond. It's steep ground and I'm hot by the time we get back to the top of the ridge, even with the first of the sea breezes blowing cold off the water. As we come out from under the trees, a raven on lookout coughs a warning and dozens of birds take flight from where they've been digging for bronze beetle grubs in the pasture. The dog ignores them – unlike the old dog before her, who took all incursions over his territory as an affront.

Each day as I sit down to write, quieting the censor and stepping around my fears, I reach a place of anticipation – *what will come to me now?* – as keen as that with which I step into the outer world. Which textures, sounds, images will present themselves for languaging, and how can I meet them to shape my human artefact of words, with all their freight, from the store within me?

Now at the end of the month in the days of the dead near my father's birthday, I think about how he asked the world to enact and carry his inner life; how he pointed to places, creatures, people, though without acknowledging, perhaps most of all to himself, how they corresponded with aspects of his soul. It has left me with a longing to make these connections and to continue to learn from them about hunger and desire and fury and affection. And to speak about them while I can – to ask, how are we to live?

Both

ⲁⲛⲟⲕ ⲡⲉ ⲡⲕⲁⲣⲱϥ ⲉⲧⲉ ⲙⲁⲩϣⲧⲁ ϩⲟϥ·
ⲁⲩⲱ ⲧⲉⲡⲓⲛⲟⲓⲁ ⲉⲧⲉ ⲛⲁϣⲉ ⲡⲉⲥⲣⲡⲙⲉⲉⲩⲉ·|
ⲁⲛⲟⲕ ⲧⲉ ⲧⲉⲥⲙⲏ ⲉⲧⲉ ⲛⲁϣⲉ ⲡⲉⲥ|ϩⲣⲟⲟⲩ·
ⲁⲩⲱ ⲡⲗⲟⲅⲟⲕ ⲉⲧⲉ ⲡⲁϣⲉ | ⲡⲉϥⲉⲓⲛⲉ·
ⲁⲛⲟⲕ ⲡⲉ ⲡⲕⲁϫⲉⲙ̄|ⲡⲁⲣⲁⲛ·

> Nag Hammadi Codex VI,
> 2: *The Thunder: Perfect Mind*[92]

I am the slick silence
*   and the thought that branches there*
I am sounds that speak
*   and words that hide themselves as noise*
I am what my name says

November opens on days of heat and ends in deluge. The green wave breaks and deciduous trees leaf out – even the linden in the labyrinth, always last, shakes its bright flags and makes flower buds. Red chestnut and white chestnut blossoms open and fall. Paddocks ripple; first silage is cut and stored and the rows of wrapped bales begin to give off their tobacco smell as they ferment.

Heat builds day after day; rose petals wither and standing hay starts to look thin. I struggle to keep the cheese cellar cool – we pile more dirt against the western wall and spray it with water; I sit blocks of ice inside to bring the temperature down. Nesting birds are clamorous from first light while the air is soft, then quieten as heat grows, though a bronzewing pigeon calls all day from its nest in the hedge, a murmured, repetitive *hoom* like a storybook owl. At dusk, New Holland honeyeaters make vertical hawking flights for insects from the topmost twigs of the macrocarpas while bats crisscross around them.

The top-bar hive built for us by a friend is set up on the slope behind the house – a kind of sympathetic magic in anticipation of a swarm – build it and they will come! Or rather, build it and I will find a swarm to bring there. But the hot days are followed by prickly humidity as thunder begins to growl from out in the mountains – bees don't like it and generally don't swarm when lightning is on the way.

The dog stares me into a walk and in sticky heat we go down into the forest, where she stays pressed to my side as thunder bawls nearer and nearer. In booming intervals, birds call and I begin to count their different kinds, touching thumb to fingertip – black cockatoo, yellow-throated honeyeater, spotted pardalote, green rosella, strong-billed honeyeater, yellow wattlebird...forest raven, black-faced cuckoo-shrike, olive whistler, shining cuckoo, fan-tailed cuckoo...pallid cuckoo, blue wren, leaden flycatcher, fantail...shrike-thrush, green-finch, thornbill...bronzewing, blackbird...silvereye. The dog sits patiently as I stare into the trees.

Back at the house, a single close *crump* of lightning blasts a channel from ground to cloud and the bellow of shocked air hits me in the chest. Only a few drops fall, though, and the sun is out again, burning, intense – the storm is over. This pattern repeats until a huge rain-bearing weather system on the mainland trails its edge south over the island. Thunderheads lift their columns high, higher, then release a waterfall mixed with hail that overflows gutters and storm drains; afterwards, heavy rain blows from the south-east for three days and nights, with snow in the high country. Everything softens, relaxes. Cattle stand with their backs to the water that sheets in, chewing cud as they wait it out. Hawthorns by the road cast a petal-shade of white and pink to windward across wet brown gravel; the floor of the milking stall is sprinkled with a lacework of elder florets. Winter creeks begin to flow.

Looking for indoor work, I clean a corner of the shed where bottles from long-ago winemaking line the wall in a jumbled mess. Many are empty – collected and never used or filled and emptied – but some have wine in them. When I first arrived, I used to make fruit wines each year in season – cherry plum, damson-and-elderberry, blackberry, pear, quince, hawthorn. Petal wine from roses that grew wild on the old house sites around the farm. There were some successes, especially the combination of ripe, sugary-tart damson plums and astringent, tannin-rich elderberries – very good with a year or two in the bottle. After a while, though, something went wrong – maybe I got overconfident or perhaps I was simply absent, working away from home as I did then. Whatever the reason, the ferments clouded and their taste became acid or too sweet or watery, unbalanced. Still I kept the full bottles and flagons, knowing that fruit and vegetable wines are famously slow to mature. Every year or three I'd open and try some. Nope. Nope. They sat on their racks, thick with dust, knocked sideways by possums and rats, the ends of the corks chewed, labelling gone.

Now, once more I choose a bottle at random and run with it through curtains of rain to the house. I decant it and let it sit overnight, then try it next day. Something has changed. The wine is clear amber, fragrant. Blackberry? It sparkles with secondary fermentation – after thirty years! Delicious, heady

but refreshing; no hangover. A few days later, another bottle the same. Encouraged, I look again at brown-glass flagons pushed to the back wall under a table in the laundry – not thirty years ago, but maybe twenty. I remember the taste – a big batch of cherry plum made from a mixture of ripe and unripe fruit, whose fermentation stopped early and left a sickly syrup that was also acid – worst of both worlds. But now, though still clouded by a pectin haze from the unripe fruit, the taste is rich and complex, its sweetness no longer overpowering, its acidity softened.

On a day of burning brightness before the weather breaks, we go sailing with friends on the bay and I realise, when the engine is switched off, that I've never been on a boat under sail before: motorboats, yes, and sailboats motoring, but not this real thing – the yacht running ahead of a wind that breathes in the canvas and whistles in rigging. A sailing dinghy tacks back and forth around us, the sailor one with her boat as she shifts her weight and moves the tiller to catch the air.

And on a night of thunder I dream that radiance unfurls from me, bright shadow like a sail, and in it, torn by the shock of breath, a track or rent where dark light spills, a path down which my death can come. And the storm-voice says, *read the wind – feel the web of soul around you with its living wound – your guardian and messenger and executioner was always you.* So for that moment I understand that I am in the weave of things and in the force that breaks the weave; sour and sweet conspire together on my tongue.

Field

Hay's cut, shining ridges
like ritual scars in moonlight.
I stretch out on heaps that sweat lightly;
ground I'm on could turn in its sleep.

The world of grasses, standing, fallen, and the plants that grow among them. When the cows come in for milking, stamens of cocksfoot and Yorkshire fog cling to their shining faces from where they've grazed, huge pollinators with the wind among flowering clumps under the cherry plum hedge. In the wallaby-lawns and short-cropped turf of pastures, centaury holds up its small, pink, bitter star-clusters, untouched. Along the roadsides prunella glows purple, and in rich ground where cattle have bedded, nettles are lush. Thistles spread their spiky rosettes to make way for flowers and the downy seed heads loved by finches.

Haying begins late – new year is in before the mowers lay down their swathe-labyrinths in the shut-up paddocks and rush to make their escape, jouncing outwards across the courses of the pattern as soon as the last turn is complete, like beasts breaking free by the shortest path. Stalks all fallen one way, the rows of cut grass form raised glyphs, burnished, until the tedders come to scatter and later the rakes ready the dried grass that the balers swallow and spit.

It's a good year for insect-eaters, and for their predators. Relative cool and damp means pastures are still green and full of plants, among whose roots and leaves butterflies and moths and beetles continue to lay their eggs, which hatch to feed and pupate and scatter skyward in flight after flight, providing rich food at every stage. For the first time in many years, a pair of flame robins rears chicks in the dense shelter of the windbreak along the ridgeline, and scrubwrens – ground-nesters that were among the first to colonise the garden but vanished when quolls moved into the roof-space a few years ago – have reappeared to fossick under shrubs and perennials around the house. They coevolved with quolls so they must have some strategies.

The quolls are very active – they gallop out across the roof at dusk and return at first light to bicker over sleeping spots in the ceiling, stirring now and then throughout the day to groom, and to hiss at one another. They leave their little tarry shits around the garden, glittering with insect husks and flecked with bone. Bats are feasting too. On the floor in a corner of the shed below a favoured rafter, a drift of moth wings gathers where a flittermouse has hung to eat its captures. Over several weeks, a chocolate wattled bat, soft-furred, mouse-sized like all the species found here, repeatedly finds its way inside the house (and out again), who knows how. In search of insects or a roosting place, after the lights go out it emerges from a fold of curtain to elaborate the darkened volumes of the room with purring flight.

Days of heat alternate with squally rain. Froglet mating choruses go up, harsh, rattling, and later the insect-trilling of tree frogs. In cattle troughs and along the reedy margins of the dam, clouds of spawn float in their water-heavens. A lone banjo frog plucks its slack string among the rushes as it has done for

the last six or seven summers. Frogs can live for fifteen years or more; it waits and calls, calls and waits for its answer.

On a dry day of little gusts that lift and fall away, downhill and upwind from us – in our danger zone, that is – machinery strikes a spark, metal on stone, in roadside vegetation. Flame spatters outwards like spilt fuel and runs along a fence line, climbs a tree, jumps the road and splashes through the stubble of a hayfield, where it catches hold of bales not yet brought to the shed. There are people right there – workers in a nearby cherry orchard who rush to stamp it out, and neighbours who call the fire truck. But next morning the tree, a eucalypt, smoulders again. Fire can find its way into punky heartwood or go underground along a root-run and reappear weeks later – this is flame country, this is how death and renewal happens here. We watch and check and check again. Next day comes a relief of rain.

Brown falcons call to one another as they gyre the updrafts or hunt from powerline perches, shadowing and shadowed by a *murmuration* of young starlings in their dark-silver plumage, practising formation flights over the mowed ground. I don't hear the falcons come and go at their usual nest in the pine hedge. Black cockatoos are there in numbers most of the time now – perhaps the falcons have been unsettled by them. And this season only a single swamp harrier quarters the hillsides – I hope, as ever, that a pair didn't choose a hay paddock somewhere in this territory as a nesting site.

In blustery wind, heavy crops of hard little fruit thrash around on the pears and apples; plums and figs begin to colour, hidden then revealed among the leaves and spotlit by intermittent sun.

First blackberries ripen. As gusts buffet from all directions, the huge old pine at the corner of the road, last of a row that led to the stables of a house long gone, leans heavily on elbowing limbs it has laid along the ground as prop and ballast. Thornbills and wrens flit among the crooked complexities of its twigs and niched bark; woodswallows sally out from its tiers after insects; the eagle pair rest a moment in the canopy with this year's fledgling before all three step out onto the wind to play once more when mobbing ravens appear.

After a hot day I go out in last light with the dog who trots, happy to be on the move, circling forward and back to urge me on. We sink into the dusk. Orange-brown butterflies lift from the field of me, small trails cross and recross. Flickering presences hunt the smoke-blue spaces of breath, claws print and crackle my skin, hawk drops to its kill, time lifts and what's left of the little body dissolves to a cloud of flies, resolves to a handful of clean bones in my dirt. The dog's feet throw up dust; I am taken, all in, deep.

Notes

Unless otherwise attributed, epigraphs and images are mine.

Riddle

1 Kathleen Stewart, *Ordinary Affects*, Duke University Press, Durham, North Carolina, 2007, p. 44.

2 Rainer Maria Rilke, 'As once the wingèd energy of delight', *Selected Poetry*, ed. & trans. Stephen Mitchell, Picador, London, 1987, p. 261.

3 Anne Carson, *Autobiography of Red*, Random House, New York, 1999, pp. 3–5.

4 Gilles Deleuze & Félix Guattari, *What Is Philosophy?*, trans. Hugh Tomlinson & Graham Burchell, Columbia University Press, New York, 1994, p. 176.

5 Stewart, *Ordinary Affects*, p. 44.

Year 1

6 Aidan Meehan, *Celtic Design: Maze Patterns*, Thames & Hudson, London, 1993, p. 79.

7 A. H. Leahy (trans. & ed.), 'Táin Bó Fráich', *Heroic Romances of Ireland*, vol. II, David Nutt, London, 1906, maryjones.us/ctexts/fraech.html.

8 The phrase 'cliffs of fall' is a quote from the second stanza of 'No worst, there is none', in Gerard Manley Hopkins, *A Selection of His Poems and Prose*, ed. W. H. Gardner, Penguin, Harmondsworth, 1954, p. 61: *O the mind, mind has mountains; cliffs of fall / Frightful, sheer, no-man-fathomed. Hold them cheap / May who ne'er hung there.*

9 Paul D. MacLean, *The Triune Brain in Evolution: Role in Paleocerebral Functions*, Plenum Press, New York, 1990.

10 See for example Andre M. Goffinet, 'The evolution of cortical development: the synapsid-diapsid divergence', *Development,* vol. 144, 2017, pp. 4061–77.

11 R. S. Bottrill, 'A summary of mineral exploration in the Cygnet–
    Kettering area', *Tasmanian Geological Survey Record 1995/09*, Tasmania
    Development and Resources.

12 John T. Fasullo, Carmen Boening, Felix W. Landerer & R. Steven
    Nerem, 'Australia's unique influence on global sea level in 2010–2011',
    Geophysical Research Letters, vol. 40, 2013, pp. 4368–73.

13 Patrick Hickey, *Famine in West Cork: The Mizen Pensinsula – Land
    and People 1800–1852*, Mercier Press, Douglas Village, Cork, 2002,
    chapters 2, 7, 8.

14 Joseph Banks, 'The Endeavour Journal', State Library of New South
    Wales, gutenberg.net.au/ebooks05/0501141h.html.

15 Jill Rutherford, *Environmental Systems and Societies Course Book:
    Oxford Ib Diploma Programme*, Oxford University Press, Oxford, 2012,
    pp. 288–93.

Year 2

16 Antonio Machado, 'Anoche cuando dormía', *Times Alone: Selected
    Poems*, trans. Robert Bly, Wesleyan University Press, Hanover, New
    Hampshire, 1983, p. 42–3. My translation from the original in this
    dual-language edition.

17 Erik Stokstad, 'Breeders toughen up bees to resist deadly
    mites', *American Association for the Advancement of Science*,
    25 July 2019, https://www.sciencemag.org/news/2019/07/
    breeders-toughen-bees-resist-deadly-mites.

18 Tamika J. Lunn, Melissa Gerwin, Jessie C. Buettel & Barry W. Brook,
    'Impact of intense disturbance on the structure and composition of
    wet-eucalypt forests: a case study from the Tasmanian 2016 wildfires',
    PLoS One, vol. 13, no. 7, 2018.

19 Richard Rhodes, *The Making of the Atomic Bomb*, Simon & Schuster,
    New York, 1986, p. 664.

20 P. J. Canfield, W. J. Hartley & J. P. Dubey, 'Lesions of toxoplasmosis
    in Australian marsupials', *Journal of Comparative Pathology*, vol. 103,
    no. 2, 1990, pp. 159–67.

21 Jaroslav Flegr, 'Influence of latent *Toxoplasma* infection on human
    personality, physiology and morphology: pros and cons of the
    Toxoplasma–human model in studying the manipulation hypothesis',

Journal of Experimental Biology, vol. 216, no. 1, 2013, pp. 127–33, https://jeb.biologists.org/content/216/1/127; Kathleen McCauliffe, 'How your cat is making you crazy', *The Atlantic*, March 2012.

22 C. X. Chan & D. Bhattacharya, 'The origin of plastids', *Nature Education*, vol. 3, no. 9, 2010, p. 84.

23 John M. Archibald, 'Endosymbiosis and eukaryotic cell evolution', *Current Biology*, vol. 25, no. 19, 2015, pp. 911–21.

24 Michel de Certeau, *Heterologies*, trans. Brian Massumi, University of Minnesota Press, Minneapolis, 1986, p. 80.

25 ibid., p. 43.

26 Jess Cockerill, 'In the wake of a Leviathan: the Eastern Australian Current and the future of our oceans', *Overland*, 13 February 2019, https://overland.org.au/2019/02/in-the-wake-of-a-leviathan-the-eastern-australian-current-and-the-of-our-oceans/.

27 G. F. Rockel, *Our Family Story*, privately published, 1997, p. 141.

28 Gaston Bachelard, *The Poetics of Space*, trans. Maria Jolas, Beacon Press, Boston, 1969, p. xi.

29 Diane Colombelli-Négrel, Mark E. Hauber, Jeremy Robertson, Frank J. Sulloway, Herbert Hoi, Matteo Griggio & Sonia Kleindorfer, 'Embryonic learning of vocal passwords in superb fairy-wrens reveals intruder cuckoo nestlings', *Current Biology*, vol. 22, no. 22, 2012, pp. 2155–60.

30 Alexander Carmichael, *Carmina Gadelica: Hymns and Incantations*, vol. 1, Oliver and Boyd, Edinburgh, 1928, p. 258.

31 Ruth Bollongino Joachim Burger, Adam Powell, Marjan Mashkour, Jean-Denis Vigne & Mark G. Thomas, 'Modern taurine cattle descended from small number of near-eastern founders', *Molecular Biology and Evolution*, vol. 29, no. 9, 2012, pp. 2101–04.

32 Carmichael, *Carmina Gadelica*, vol. 1, p. 271.

33 ibid., vol. 4, p. 65.

34 Henry Vaughan, 'The night', *The Metaphysical Poets*, ed. Helen Gardner, Penguin, Harmondsworth, 1957, p. 279.

35 John Cage, *Diary: How to Improve the World (You Will Only Make Matters Worse)*, eds Richard Kraft & Joel Biel, Siglio, Los Angeles, 2015, p. 32.

36 In 'The Tale of Ceix and Alccone', line 51 ff, John Gower describes Iris, the goddess of the rainbow, putting on 'her rainy cloak': *Yris…*

Hire reyny cope dede upon, / *The which was wonderli begon* / *With colours of diverse hewe...* / *The hevene lich unto a bowe* / *Sche bende, and so she cam doun lowe.* Gower, *Confessio Amantis,* vol. 2, book 4, ed. Russell A. Peck, trans. Andrew Galloway, Medieval Institute Publications, Kalamazoo, Michigan, 2013.

Year 3

37 T. K. Hubbard, *The Pindaric Mind: A Study of Logical Structure in Early Greek Poetry,* Mnemosyne Supplements, vol. 85, Brill, Leiden, 1985, p. 42, n. 89.

38 Germaine Guillaume-Coirier, 'Chiron Phillyride', *Kernos,* 1995, vol. 8, pp. 113–22.

39 J. Scott Turner, *The Extended Organism: The Physiology of Animal-Built Structures,* Harvard University Press, Boston, 2000, pp. 182–90.

40 Michel de Certeau, *The Practice of Everyday Life,* trans. Steven Rendall, University of California Press, Berkeley, 1984, p. 92.

41 This epigraph is my paraphrase of the Old Norse from the *Prose Edda,* in which I've chosen to read the feeding of the Earth-god Ymir by the cow Auðumla as a metonymic image for the nourishment of the Earth itself. Snorra Edda, *Völuspá.org,* voluspa.org/gylfaginning1-10.htm.

42 Apollonius Rhodius, *Argonautica* III, 1179–87, trans. R. C. Seaton, Theoi project, theoi.com/Text/ApolloniusRhodius3.html.

43 Christopher McFadden, 'John Loudon McAdam: the father of the modern road', *Interesting Engineering,* 26 October 2017.

44 Patrick Hickey, *Famine in West Cork: The Mizen Pensinsula – Land and People 1800–1852,* Mercier Press, Douglas Village, Cork, 2002, pp. 45 ff, 151 ff.

45 Marguerite Scott, 'Local Government', *Companion to Tasmanian History,* https://www.utas.edu.au/library/companion_to_tasmanian_history/L/Local%20government.htm.

46 Bruce Pascoe, *Dark Emu,* Magabala Books, Broome, 2014, p. 30.

47 Bill Gammage, *The Biggest Estate on Earth: How Aborigines Made Australia,* Allen & Unwin, Sydney, 2011.

48 John Keats, 'Letter XXIV – to George and Thomas Keats', 22 December 1817, *Letters of John Keats to his Family and Friends,* ed. Sidney Colvin, Macmillan, London, 1825, p. 48.

49 Tony Merritt, Kathryn Taylor, Keren Cox-Witton, Hume Field, Kate Wingett, Diana Mendez, Michelle Power & David Durrheim, 'Australian bat lyssavirus', *Australian Journal of General Practice*, vol. 47, no. 3, 2018, pp. 93–6.

50 My paraphrase from the Greek, in *Aeschylus, Vol. 2, Agamemnon*, trans. Herbert Weir Smyth, William Heinemann, London, 1926, lines 100–150 http://www.perseus.tufts.edu/hopper/text?doc=Perseus%3Atext%3A1999.01.0003%3Acard%3D122. For a wonderful translation see Anne Carson, *An Oresteia*, Faber & Faber, New York, 2009.

51 Iñigo Zuberogoitia, Jabi Zabala & José Enrique Martínez, 'Moult in birds of prey: a review of current knowledge and future challenges for research', *Ardeola*, vol. 65, no. 2, 2018, pp. 183–207.

52 Rilke, 'As once the wingèd energy of delight', *Selected Poetry*, p. 261. My paraphrase of the final stanza: *Deine ausgeübten Kräfte spanne, / bis sie reichen, zwischen zwein / Widersprüchen…Denn im Manne / will der Gott beraten sein.*

53 Craig Hardin (ed.), 'Coventry Carol', *The Shearmen and Taylor's Pageant: Two Coventry Corpus Christi Plays*, vol. 87, Early English Text Society, Kegan Paul, Trench, Trübner & Co., London, 1902, p. 32.

54 Alejandra Borunda, 'We know west Antarctica is melting. is the east in danger, too?', *National Geographic*, 10 August 2018, https://www.nationalgeographic.com.au/nature/we-know-west-antarctica-is-melting-is-the-east-in-danger-too.aspx.

55 'Climate change indicators: ocean heat', United States Environmental Protection Agency, https://www.epa.gov/climate-indicators/climate-change-indicators-ocean-heat.

56 Argo Project, http://www.argo.ucsd.edu/.

57 'The great ocean currents – the climate engine', *World Ocean Review*, https://worldoceanreview.com/en/wor-1/climate-system/great-ocean-currents/.

58 Ross Gibson, *Seven Versions of an Australian Badland*, University of Queensland Press, Brisbane, 2002, p. 92.

59 ibid.

Year 4

60 Ursula Le Guin, *The Other Wind*, London, Orion, 2002, p. 231.

61 Alessandro Naso, 'Amber for Artemis', *Jahreshefte des Österreichischen Archäologischen Institutes in Wien*, vol. 82, 2013, pp. 259–78.

62 de Certeau, *Heterologies*, p. 41.

63 Samuel Beckett, *Three Novels: Molloy, Malone Dies, The Unnamable*, Grove Press, New York, 1995, p. 476.

64 Ludwig Wittgenstein, *Remarks on Frazer's 'Golden Bough'* / *Bemerkungen über Frazers 'Golden Bough'*, ed. Rush Rhees, trans. A. C. Miles, rev. Rush Rhees, Brynmill/Edgeways, Retford, Nottinghamshire, 2010, p. 11e.

65 Michael Pollan, *The Botany of Desire*, Bloomsbury, London, 2002, p. 60.

66 Wittgenstein, *Remarks on Frazer's 'Golden Bough'*, pp. 10e, 11e.

67 Michael Taussig, 'The corn-wolf: writing apotropaic texts', *Critical Inquiry*, vol. 37, no. 1, 2010, pp. 26–33, p. 28.

68 'Taliesin', *The Mabinogion*, compiled by Charlotte Guest, 1849, Project Gutenberg, onlinebooks.library.upenn.edu/webbin/gutbook/look up? num=5160.

69 My paraphrase of *Kat Godeu / Llyfr Taliesin VIII*, Peniarth MS 2, f 11 r / p. 23, National Library of Wales, digidol.llgc.org.uk/ METS/ LLT00001/frames? div=29 &subdiv= 0&locale=en&mode=reference..

70 Joseph Jacobs, 'Jack and the beanstalk', *English Fairy Tales*, David Nutt, London, 1890..

71 Linji Yixuan, trans. John Tarrant, 'Why play with koans?', *tarrantworks*, 27 May 2016, tarrantworks.com/2016/05/27/ why-play-with-koans.

72 Simón Díaz, 'Tonada de luna llena', *Criollo y Sabroso* (LP), Palacio, Caracas, 1965.

73 Hopkins, 'God's grandeur', *A Selection of His Poems and Prose*, p. 27.

74 Mylene M. Mariette & Katherine L. Buchanan, 'Prenatal acoustic communication programs offspring for high posthatching temperatures in a songbird', *Science,* vol. 353, no. 6301, 2016, pp. 812–14.

75 John Tarrant, 'How to welcome the end of the world', *tarrantworks*, 9 November 2017.

76 J. D. Salinger, *Franny and Zooey*, Penguin, Harmondsworth, 1983,
    p. 112.
77 Laura Wallace, 'Slow-slip event off the east coast has now finished',
    GeoNet New Zealand, https://www.geonet.org.nz/news/
    FSuvpimDibBoIFRbPaJHQ

Year 5

78 Ella Young (ed.), 'The children of Lir', *Celtic Wonder-Tales*, Dover
    Publications, Mineola, New York, 2014, pp. 146–47.
79 Sue Grand, 'God at an impasse: devotion, social justice, and the
    psychoanalytic subject', *Psychoanalytic Dialogues,* vol. 23, no. 4, 2013,
    pp. 449–63.
80 Russell Hoban, *Pilgermann*, Picador, London, 1984, pp. 88, 102.
81 My paraphrase of Rilke, 'Duino elegies: The first elegy', *Selected
    Poetry*, p. 261.
82 David Foster Wallace, *This is Water: Some Thoughts, Delivered on a
    Significant Occasion, about Living a Compassionate Life*, Little, Brown and
    Company, New York, 2009.
83 ibid., pp. 99–113.
84 ibid., p. 102.
85 ibid.
86 ibid., p. 56.
87 'Foweles in the Frith', Gb-Ob MS, Douce 139, Folio 5, Bodleian
    Library, Oxford, Digital Imaging Archive of Medieval Music, diamm.
    ac.uk/sources/511/#/
88 Matt Marrison, 'Naming faceless fish from the abyss', CSIRO, 21
    February 2018, https://www.csiro.au/en/News/News-releases/2018/
    Naming-faceless-fish-from-the-abyss
89 Liz Greene, *The Astrology of Fate*, Samuel Weiser, York Beach, Maine,
    1984, p. 59.
90 Sarah Allan, *The Shape of the Turtle: Myth, Art, and Cosmos in Early
    China*, SUNY Press, Albany, 1991, p. 72.
91 Hopkins, 'As kingfishers catch fire', *A Selection of His Poems and Prose*,
    p. 51.
92 My paraphrase from the Coptic, in Hal Taussig, Jared Calaway, Maia
    Kotrosits, Celene Lillie & Justin Lasser, *The Thunder: Perfect Mind*,
    Palgrave Macmillan, London, 2010, p. 110.

Acknowledgements

My thanks to the authors and publishers of the following works for their permission to quote their words. Every effort has been made to obtain permission for quotation from the relevant copyright holders.

From *The Practice of Everyday Life* by Michel de Certeau, trans. Steven Rendall, Published by the University of California Press, © 1984 by the Regents of the University of California.

From *Heterologies* by Michel de Certeau, trans. Brian Massumi, University of Minnesota Press, 1986.

From *What Is Philosophy?* by Gilles Deleuze & Félix Guattari, trans. Hugh Tomlinson & Graham Burchell, Columbia University Press, New York, 1994.

From Sue Grand, 'God at an impasse: devotion, social justice, and the psychoanalytic subject', *Psychoanalytic Dialogues*, 2013, vol. 23, no. 4, pp. 449–63.

From *The Astrology of Fate* by Liz Greene, © 1984. Used with permission from Red Wheel Weiser, LLC, Newburyport, MA, www.redwheelweiser.com.

From *The Other Wind* by Ursula Le Guin, © 2001, Orion Publishing Group, London.

From *Celtic Design: Maze Patterns* by Aidan Meehan, © 1993. Reprinted by kind permission of Thames & Hudson Ltd, London.

From *The Botany of Desire* by Michael Pollan, © 2001, Bloomsbury Publishing Plc. (UK, Europe and the Commonwealth); Penguin Random House (US, PI, Canada & Open Market).

ACKNOWLEDGEMENTS

From *Ordinary Affects* by Kathleen Stewart, © 2007, Duke University Press, Durham & London.

From Michael Taussig 'The corn-wolf: writing apotropaic texts', *Critical Inquiry*, Autumn 2010, vol. 37, no. 1, pp. 26–33, © 2015.

From *This Is Water: Some Thoughts, Delivered on a Significant Occasion, about Living a Compassionate Life* by David Foster Wallace, © 2009. Reprinted by permission of Little, Brown and Company, an imprint of Hachette Book Group, Inc.

From Ludwig Wittgenstein, *Remarks on Frazer's 'Golden Bough' / Bemerkungen über Frazers 'Golden Bough'*, ed. Rush Rhees, trans. A. C. Miles, rev. Rush Rhees, © 2010, The Brynmill Press, Ltd.

From *Seven Versions of an Australian Badland* by Ross Gibson, © 2002, University of Queensland Press, St Lucia.

www.ingramcontent.com/pod-product-compliance
Lightning Source LLC
Chambersburg PA
CBHW032342280326
41935CB00008B/421